Master Planning Indian Cities

Achieving Urban Renaissance

The Edinburgh College of Art, Edinburgh, Scotland;

St. Michael's Cathedral, Coventry, which with stood destruction;

And the People of Sovereign, Socialist, Secular, Democratic

Republic of India

Master Planning Indian Cities

Achieving Urban Renaissance

Vikram Bhat

COPAL PUBLISHING GROUP
Inspiring for a better future through publishing

Published by Copal Publishing Group
E-143, Lajpat Nagar, Sahibabad,
Distt. Ghaziabad, UP – 201005, India

www.copalpublishing.com

First Published 2020
© Copal Publishing Group, 2019

This book contains information obtained from authentic and highly regarded sources. Reprinted material is quoted with permission. Reasonable efforts have been made to publish reliable data and information, but the authors and the publishers cannot assume responsibility for the validity of all materials. Neither the authors nor the publishers, nor anyone else associated with this publication, shall be liable for any loss, damage or liability directly or indirectly caused or alleged to be caused by this book.

Neither this book nor any part may be reproduced or transmitted in any form or by any means, electronic or mechanical, including photocopying, microfilming and recording, or by any information storage or retrieval system, without permission in writing from Copal Publishing Group. The consent of Copal Publishing Group does not extend to copying for general distribution, for promotion, for creating new works, or for resale. Specific permission must be obtained in writing from Copal Publishing Group for such copying.

The Author hereby warrants that the Work is original work, that it does not infringe any other copyright. The Publisher is not in anyway responsible for any legal proceedings and expense whatsoever in consequence of the publication or alleged publication in the Work of any pirated, libellous, seditious, scandalous, obscene or other unlawful matter.

Trademark notice: Product or corporate names may be trademarks or registered trademarks, and are used only for identification and explanation, without intent to infringe.

ISBN: 978-93-83419-85-2 (print)
ISBN: 978-93-83419-91-3 (e-book)

Typeset by Bhumi Graphics, New Delhi
Printed and bound by Bhavish Graphics, Chennai

Contents

Preface ix
Acknowledgements x

1. **Introduction** 1
   1.1 Why Analyse Chandigarh and Gandhinagar? 2
   1.2 Objectives of the Study 3
   1.3 Methodology 3
   1.4 Why a Comparison Is Useful 4
   1.5 Importance of City and its Parameters 5
   1.6 Structure of the Book 5
   1.7 Relevance of the Book 7

2. **Town Planning in the Indian Subcontinent** 8
   2.1 Indus Valley Civilization 8
   2.2 Vedic Planning System and Towns 11
   2.3 Moghul Town Planning 14
   2.4 The Princely Town of Jaipur, Natural Setting and Geography 19
   2.5 British Town Planning in India 21
   2.6 Summary 25

3. **Description of Chandigarh** 27
   3.1 Introduction 27
   3.2 Political Background 27
   3.3 Finance 27
   3.4 Site Selection 28
   3.5 Climate 30

	3.6	The Design Team	30
	3.7	Chandigarh Master Plan	30
	3.8	Zoning	35
	3.9	Morphology of the Sector	39
	3.10	Movement	44
	3.11	Built Form	44
	3.12	Plots in Chandigarh	46
	3.13	Open Spaces	47
	3.14	Summary	47
4.	**Description of Gandhinagar**		**49**
	4.1	Introduction	49
	4.2	Political Background	49
	4.3	Finance	49
	4.4	Site Selection	50
	4.5	Climate	51
	4.6	Design Team	51
	4.7	Gandhinagar Master Plan	52
	4.8	Zoning	53
	4.9	Morphology of the Sector	55
	4.10	Movement	58
	4.11	Built Form	60
	4.12	Plots in Gandhinagar	61
	4.13	Open Spaces	61
	4.14	Summary	62
5.	**Analysing Chandigarh and Gandhinagar**		**63**
	5.1	The Site	63
	5.2	The Master Plan	64
	5.3	Finance Planning	64
	5.5	Morphology of the City	67
	5.6	Morphology of the Sector	69

	5.7	Various Arrangements of the Chandigarh Sectors	71
	5.8	Movement Pattern	77
	5.9	Built Form	79
	5.10	Streets and the Built Form	80
	5.11	Availability of Plots	83
	5.12	Open Spaces	84
	5.13	Summary	84

6. The Urban Synthesis — 86

7. Achieving Urban Renaissance: Indian History and Culture — 90

	7.1	Indus Valley Civilization: The Beginning	90
	7.2	The Moghul Era (16–18th Century)	90
	7.3	The British Rule (1858–1947)	90
	7.4	The Age of Democracies (1947–2000)	92
	7.5	City Building and Place-Making Principles: Evolution of Indian Cities	93
	7.6	Indian Cities: Population, Tradition and Culture	99
	7.7	Classification of Indian Cities Based on Geography	100
	7.8	The Urban Morphology	101
	7.9	Movement and Connections: Walking	105
	7.10	Walkability Radius	105
	7.11	The Urban Girth Effect	108
	7.12	Relationship Between the Density and Blocks	116
	7.13	Sustainability and Climate Change	123
	7.14	Relationship Between Landmarks and Frontages	128
	7.15	Mixed-Use Development	130
	7.16	Failure of Tall Buildings and Tower Blocks	134
	7.17	Aftermath of World War II: Post-war Period	135
	7.18	Single Point/Tower Block	135
	7.19	Terrace Development	137
	7.20	Perimeter Development	138
	7.21	Tall Buildings: The Way Forward	138

7.22	Analysis of the Location	139
7.23	Tall Building as Landmark and Its Relationship with Routes	139
7.24	The Wider Context	141
7.25	The Local Environment	141
7.26	Architectural Quality	142
7.28	Views and Viewing Corridors	142
7.29	Tall Buildings: Impact on Street, Height Mass and Transitions Criteria	143
7.30	Design Criteria of Tall Buildings in an Urban Context	145
7.31	Role of Art in Cities	147
7.32	Urban Design: Is It a Cosmetic Product in the Name of City Beautification?	147
7.33	Master Planning: What Is It?	149
7.34	The Master Planning Process: Stages	153

8. Urban Design Principles — 154

8.1	Ecopolis and Sustainability	154
8.2	Legibility	154
8.3	Self-Sustained Localities	154
8.4	Ease of Movement	154
8.5	Heritage Conservation	155
8.6	Human Scale	155
8.7	Architectural Character	155
8.8	Public Spaces for Indian Culture, Traditions and Customs	155
8.9	Quality of Life	155
8.10	Regional Integration	156
8.11	Adaptable Design	156
8.12	Art Expression	156

Glossary — 157

Index — 162

Preface

The book is a collection of experience, travel, living and working in the cities of Mumbai, Bangalore, Mangalore, Cochin, Panaji, New Delhi, Jaipur, Surat, London, Birmingham, Stroke on Trent, Cambridge, Edinburgh, Glasgow, Dundee, Perth, Amsterdam, Rotterdam, San Francisco, Denver, Dublin and Cork.

The book explores few fundamental questions "What is a city?", "How do we live?", "What brings citizens together: Is it the culture, commerce or its edict?", "Is city a living embodiment of many subcultures, or a group of people having something in common?", "Does a city have an anatomy?", "How does a city grow?", "What does nature has to offer with the rise of cities?", and most importantly "How a democratic city should be master planned in the 21st Century?".

Vikram Bhat

Acknowledgements

I would like to acknowledge my Late father Shri K.P. Bhat for introducing me to the world of books and library; my mother Bharathi Bhat for going after my dreams and creative journey; Aarathi, my wife, for giving me the much-needed creative space and being there at all times in the journey of life; my daughter Akvira, nephew Advait, the yet to be born child who have brought joy and laughter in our lives.

My teachers who imparted knowledge Late Shri M.N. Mulay, Principal at Kendriya Vidyalaya, Surat; Shri G.K. Choudhary, former Head of the Department of BMS Engineering College, Bangalore; and SIT Tumkur, Mr. Lesley Forsyth, former Head Department of Urban Design, Edinburgh College of Art, Edinburgh, Scotland.

I am grateful to the countries – the United Kingdom, the United States of America and the European Union in my pursuit of knowledge and inspiration.

1
Introduction

Chandigarh and Gandhinagar were planned Indian cities which were a result of political necessity. Chandigarh was designed on modern planning principles whereas the planning of Gandhinagar shows the relevance of traditional planning.

The book begins by reviewing key Indian cities of historical significance, in a chronological order to form a contextual appraisal, followed by descriptions of the two cities – Chandigarh and Gandhinagar. The descriptions of the two cities are sourced from various architectural books and magazines. The planned cities of Chandigarh and Gandhinagar are further evaluated by comparison highlighting the issues of urban design approaches.

The findings contribute towards the application of urban design approaches in an Indian context.

Chandigarh made its mark on post-independent India as the first planned capital city of India. It was the then first Prime Minister of India, Pandit Nehru, who conceived Chandigarh as *"A new city of free India, totally fresh and wholly responsive to the aspirations of the future generations of this great country"*.[1] The French Architect Le Corbusier designed the Master plan for the city in 1951. Chandigarh was designed as the modern capital of Punjab and Haryana. The capital city has got a distinct identity in terms of its planning and development control, not often found in many Indian cities. Chandigarh gave an emerging nation a new identity in terms of city planning and design. Le Corbusier was part of the CIAM (*Congrès internationaux d'architecture moderne*) and Chandigarh reflected some of CIAM'S doctrine. "CIAM's early attitudes towards town planning were stark: "Urbanization cannot be conditioned by the claims of a pre-existent aestheticism; its essence is of a functional order… the chaotic division of land, resulting from sales, speculations, inheritances, must be abolished by a collective and methodical land policy."[2]

At this early stage the desire to re-shape cities and towns is clear. Out is the "chaotic" jumble of streets, shops, and houses which existed in European cities at the time; in is a zoned city, comprising of standardized dwellings and different areas for work, home, and leisure."[3] In some aspects, Indian cities represented the medieval and traditional character found in European cities with meandering lanes characterized by a closed and compact

---

[1] http://www.architectureweek.com/2001/0822/culture 1-2 html

[2] http://www.open2.net/modernity/4_2.html

[3] http://www.open2.net/modernity/4_2.html

nature of built form. The new capital city of Chandigarh reflects some of CIAM's ideologies mainly because of Le Corbusier who was an active member of the group and also the designer of Chandigarh Master Plan.

The most common criticism of Chandigarh was its lack of context. "We live in countries of great cultural heritage, countries that wear their past as easily as a woman drapes her sari," wrote Charles Correa. Although a planned city Chandigarh misses out on the essence of an Indian city which is an amalgamation of different cultures aptly represented by the built form which presents a strong variety in terms of an urban experience.

Gandhinagar came into existence in 1960 when the old Bombay State was partitioned into Maharashtra and Gujarat. The city of Bombay went to Maharashtra and as a result, the newly constituted Government of Gujarat decided to construct a new capital city. Thus, came into being Gandhinagar, the second planned city in India after Chandigarh.

Gandhinagar in some ways is seen to be a reaction against Chandigarh. "Kalia explains that Gandhinagar, the capital of Gujarat in western India, became a battleground for the competing ideals that had surfaced during the building of Chandigarh and Bhubaneshwar. The mill owners of the neighbouring city of Ahmedabad, backed by Indian architect and planner Balkrishna Doshi, wanted the American Louis Kahn to build Gandhinagar as a worthy rival to Le Corbusier's Chandigarh. There was, however, tremendous political pressure to make Gandhinagar a purely Indian enterprise, partly because the state of Gujarat was the birthplace of Mahatma Gandhi."[4] Thus, Gandhinagar was designed by Indian architects and planners and relies on the planning of traditional Gujarati towns. The city of Ahmedabad provided the range of answers. "The city's medieval fortification, the present urban core, is still regarded by historians, architects and urban designers as one of the finest surviving examples of urbanism and domestic architecture in the Indian tradition. The walled city of Ahmedabad epitomizes the amalgamation of Hindu–Islamic traditions in its urban morphology and in the civic architecture of its forts, mosques and tombs.

The traditional Gujarati towns were densely packed and catered to the outdoor and indoor activities of the inhabitants. The traditional pattern allowed the designers of the city, retrospective and a learning which could be aptly termed as cultural borrowing which was applied to a planned city of Gandhinagar.

1.1   Why Analyse Chandigarh and Gandhinagar?

Chandigarh was the first planned city in post-independent India. It was a time when industrialization was gaining its predominance. The birth of Chandigarh and Gandhinagar were of political necessity combined with the vision of the then Prime Minister Pandit Nehru whose aspirations were for a modern city in a modern India and hence the birth of Chandigarh city. The planning of new town was designed by Le Corbusier on the basis of sectors which were laid in grid-iron fashion.

The sector-based planning gained predominance for the inception of other industrial townships such as Bhubaneshwar and appealed to the middle-class workers and to the industry-going people. Gandhinagar proved

---
[4] Introduction, Ravi Kalia's "Building a National Identity in Postcolonial India"

to be a worthy challenge as to how an Indian planned city should be? Chandigarh being the only capital city after the post-independent era became a role model, and thus Indian architects and planners started designing the cities on the basis of sectors. The sectors thus became a prototype which was perfected in an Indian way in Gandhinagar by the application of context.

"Gandhinagar was inspired by the *pols* of Ahmedabad. The urban morphology of medieval Ahmedabad can be aptly described as organic–accretive, similar to many cities in the Middle East (Cairo, Marrakesh) and even medieval Europe. The generic root of its morphology is essentially the *pole*, both in terms of the physical grain of the urban fabric, as well as socio-economic and religious matrix of the populace."[5] The *pole* provided a contextual reference which was morphologically inspired from the medieval times; it was a vital ingredient in terms of urban design approach.

"India had received and absorbed many foreign influences in the past, and it is arguable that the adjustment of modernism to fit Indian ways and mentalities correspond to an old pattern."[6] Chandigarh and Gandhinagar became critically important as state capitals which were trying to create an image of modern India. These two cities reflect modern town planning in India. The sector-based planning of Chandigarh became a model for other cities and industrial towns in India. Gandhinagar on the other hand combined modern planning principles and traditional planning for building its capital city.

Apart from the modern image, the new towns offered a quality of an urban environment not found in any Indian city. It reduced the chaos of traffic congestion, pollution and provided a cleaner urban environment.

By comparing and evaluating these two cities, author would like to examine how one city is successful over another in terms of their planning and their urban design approaches.

1.2 Objectives of the Study

1. To form a contextual appraisal of Indian cities in a chronological order.
2. To study the urban structure and city building process of two planned cities – Chandigarh and Gandhinagar.
3. To discuss issues arising from the evaluation of Chandigarh and Gandhinagar to highlight both positive and negative aspects of their urban design approaches by comparison.
4. To deduce and synthesize theories of master planning principles
5. To formulate urban design principles

1.3 Methodology

The primary methodology of the book is based on a qualitative analysis to achieve the aim of the book which focuses on the urban structure of two cities and brings forward the urban design issues from the evaluation of two cities by comparison.

---

[5] Quote extracted from "Mimar" Ahmedabad – Of continuity and tradition.
[6] Curtis J. R. William, (1996) Modern Architecture Since 1900, London, Phaidon Press Ltd

Due to the familiarity of context and past experience of visiting the state capitals by the author, the cities would be presented in the form of description. The advantage of using a qualitative approach would bring into light the theories applied during the genesis of the two planned cities which would give a useful insight to the urban design issues.

Visual records of the city and relevant information sourced from architectural magazines and publications are used as data collection, supporting arguments and issues of urban design approaches in the two planned cities.

To study the role of urban design in both the cities, the urban structure is most interesting to examine as it provides an understanding of the various components of urban design such as built form, movement and open spaces and their interrelationship. "The term urban structure refers to the pattern or arrangement of development blocks, streets, buildings, open space and landscape which make up urban areas. It is the inter relationship between all these elements, rather than their particular characteristics that bond together to make a place. Urban structure does not imply any particular kind of urbanism: it applies equally to the centre and to the suburb and every thing in between; and of course, it applies equally to the city, the town and the village."[7]

The components of urban structure such as blocks, streets, buildings, open spaces would be used to study the capital cities and not necessarily consider the recommendation as it is suited for a particular context. The cities are further studied under morphology of the sectors and plots which were the characteristics of the planned cities.

Apart from the urban components mentioned above, the city development is triggered by factors such as the political process, finance for the city development, the developers involved and the time scale of the project which highlights the city building process.

1.4 Why a Comparison Is Useful

The comparison would highlight how successful one city is over another in terms of their urban design approaches. The comparison would also highlight the positive and negative aspects of the urban design approaches in both the cities. Apart from evaluating the qualitative characters, the comparison would also bring forth the advantages and disadvantages of the urban design theories which were applied during the shaping of these two Indian state capital cities.

The description of both the cities and their urban components is studied and their relationship is further evaluated. The relationship is analysed in each city with the contextual backdrop which will bring forward issues for discussions. We can thus asses the degree of relationship in each city and their comparison would determine whether the city contributes to good urbanism; and the role of urban design principles and theories in both the cities would also enable us to judge which city is successful over another.

---

[7] http://www.rudi.net/whatson/desguides/udc/udc3.pdf

1.5 Importance of City and its Parameters

Cities are a complex entity to study due to the nature of their size, shape, form, range of activities and the inhabitants living in it. In terms of urban design, built form, movement, the spaces in between and their relationships are of critical importance and reflect the true nature of the city. This degree of relationship contributes to successful urbanism and the resultant is a successful place. For instance, if the density of built form is of high order, it creates an impact on the movement (pedestrians, vehicular and the user of the buildings) and vice versa. Open spaces in conjunction with the built form have a strong relationship which caters to a range of activities when dealt carefully and attracts people. Cities being planned on sectors, the morphology of the sector and the plot subdivision are worth examining, which contribute to the arrangement of built form, movement and open space. Inherent to the parameters mentioned above, the city is also affected by city forefathers, political process and decisions. City building and maintenance is attributed by finance. Also, successful urbanism is triggered by the buying capacity of the inhabitants which is also a resultant of financial implication. Thus, these parameters are the essential ingredients which in turn highlight the city building process and the product; and critically important is the role of urban design.

1.6 Structure of the Book

The book is set out into six chapters (Fig. 1.1).

The first chapter appraises key Indian towns from different eras. It examines the early town planning of Mohenjo-Daro and Harappa. The description will reveal various components of the city such as the street, built form and open spaces and how these elements unify in making the city as a whole. An examination of early town planning attitudes will give an insight into the planning scenario and its imagery.

The Islamic era of town planning brought significant changes and development in terms of city planning. The Moghuls were lovers of art and poetry and during their reign the city saw the contribution of the *garden* in mosques and palaces. The description will highlight the major contributions of Islamic planning. During the Colonial period British town planning principles brought substantial transformation to the design and layout of Indian cities. The description will examine the making of capital city New Delhi. The second and third chapter will consist of descriptions of Chandigarh and Gandhinagar. The descriptions of these two cities will highlight contributory factors to their development such as politics, finance, developers and time scale. The description will also look into the urban structure of Chandigarh and Gandhinagar, focusing on built form, movement and open spaces. The cities will be further described under morphology and plots.

The fourth chapter considers the evolution of the city building process and urban structures such as built form, movement and open spaces in both the cities.

The fifth chapter is the analysis and conclusion of post-independent cities of Chandigarh and Gandhinagar and focuses on the following issues.

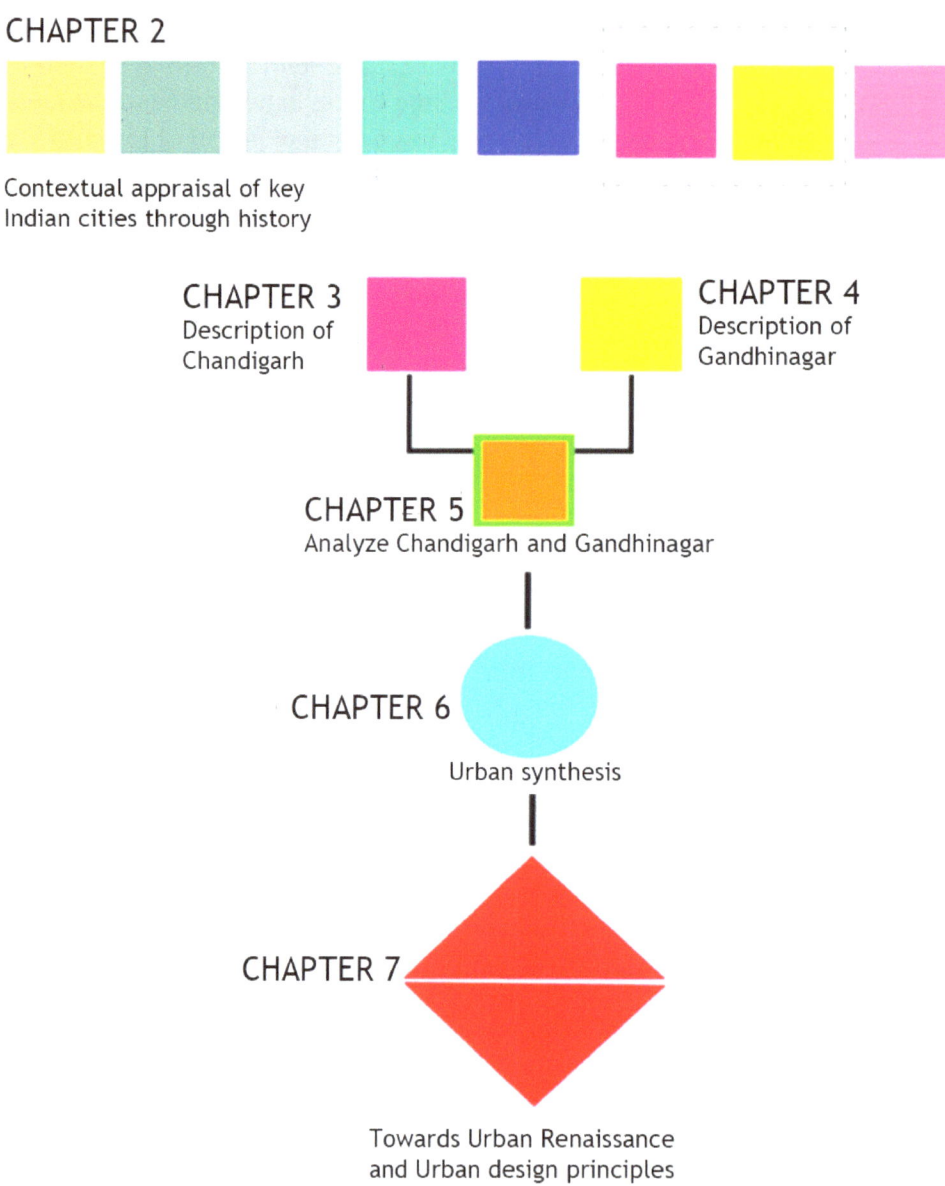

Figure 1.1 Structure of the book [*Source*: Author]

- Were there any lessons learnt from the past, and if so, how were these incorporated in generating the master plans of these new towns?
- A city is a complex organism which is a growing entity whatever shape or form it may take; how do these cities respond to growth?
- How did the new towns respond to the Indian context and, more importantly, the Indian culture?

The sixth and final chapter focuses on the urban renaissance principles of Indian cities.

1.7 Relevance of the Book

The two state capitals, Chandigarh and Gandhinagar, were blueprints for future Indian cities and industrial towns. Recent town planning developments in India highlight certain aspects of traditional settlements and layouts.

The purpose of this book is to create sensitivity towards the *relevance of context* and explore the planning approaches as well as the relevant urban design issues associated with planned cities in India especially in Chandigarh and Gandhinagar.

2

Town Planning in the Indian Subcontinent

2.1 Indus Valley Civilization

Mohenjo-Daro and Harappa date back to the 3rd millennium BC[1], the period of the Indus Valley Civilization. These towns were planned on the grid iron system which applied to the entire urban form[2]. The city had a distinct division and each part segregated from the other in terms of broad street and small gullies (alleyways).

Figure 2.1 Location of Mohenjo-Daro and Harappa along the Indus river

---
[1] Tadgell Christopher (1990), *The History of Architecture in India*, Phaidon Press Ltd., p.1
[2] Kostof Spiro (1990), *The City Shaped*, London, Thames and Hudson Ltd., p.34

Around the Indus river, fertility of the soil encouraged agriculture which resulted in an Agrarian society. Writing was developed and seals were in the form of pictographic inscriptions, not deciphered till date. The population of Mohenjo-Daro was covering 60 Ha (150 acres) with a population of 40,000.

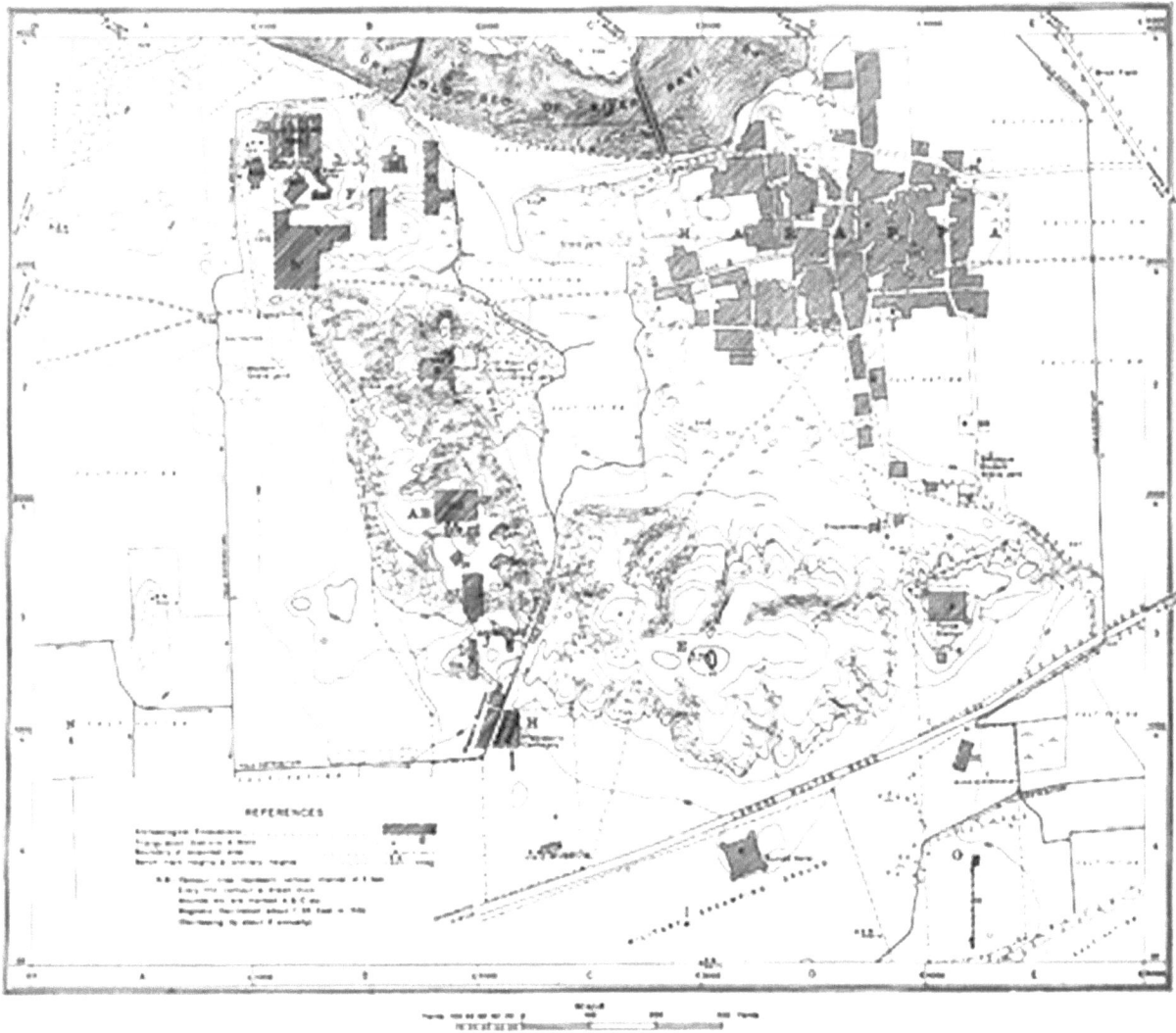

Figure 2.2 Plan of Harappa [*Source*: Vats (1940)]

Archaeological findings suggest that there was a network of clay pipelines beneath the streets. The dwellings were built round a central court, which was essential for the performance of everyday activities such as daily religious rituals, drying of vegetables and recreational activities. Thus, the court became the central feature of the houses. Mohenjo-Daro and Harappa towns were compact horizontal cities. Absence of any landmarks suggests all built form had an equal status and no hierarchy in its forms.

The dwelling was constructed from locally available materials: sun dried bricks and wood for roofs. The facade facing the street had very few windows, maintaining privacy for the inhabitants. According to the research carried by Dr. J. M. Kenoyer[3], "The latest phase of construction also included a large east–west-oriented doorway leading through the eastern edge of the gateway. This doorway appears to have constructed with wooden beams with a threshold embedded in the baked brick structure. The rendition of Mohenjo-Daro and Harappa (see Figure 2.3) leads us to believe that the buildings were closely knit together in a compact fashion, flanked by entry gates in various directions."[4]

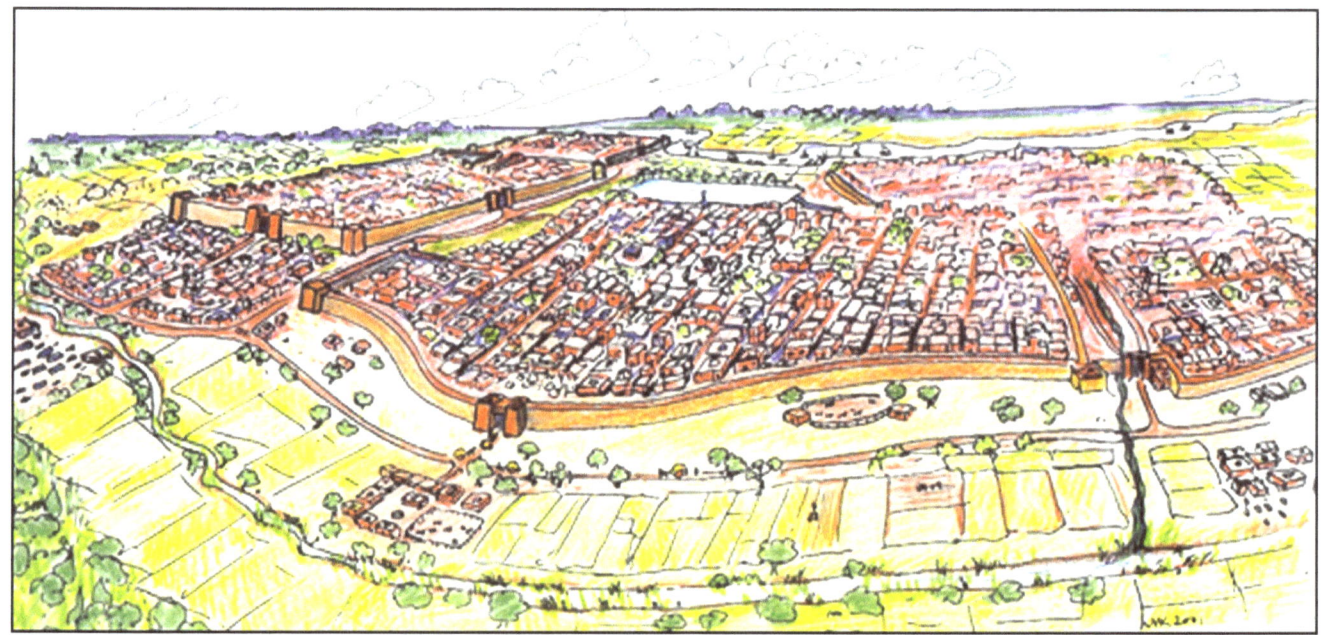

Figure 2.3 Rendition of ancient Harappa panorama as it may have appeared in the late period 3B or early period 3C. The granary and working platforms of Mound F are in the north-western corner of the city (upper left). [© Jonathan Mark Kenoyer]

---

[3] Dr. Kenoyer J.M. *Harappa*, harrapa.com, http://www.harappa.com/indus3/kenoyer.html, 8 July 2004
[4] Dr. Kenoyer J.M. *Harappa*, harrapa.com, http://www.harappa.com/3D/9.html, 8 July 2004

On the evidence of Mohenjo-Daro and Harappa, it can be deduced that the Indus Valley Civilization had functional towns and reflected the cultural and the social aspiration of its inhabitants. According to a study, the Indus Valley Civilization was wiped out 4350 years ago because of 900 years long draught. It was found that rains played truant in the northwest of Himalayas for 900 long years drying up the source of water that fed rivers along which the Indus Valley Civilization thrived.

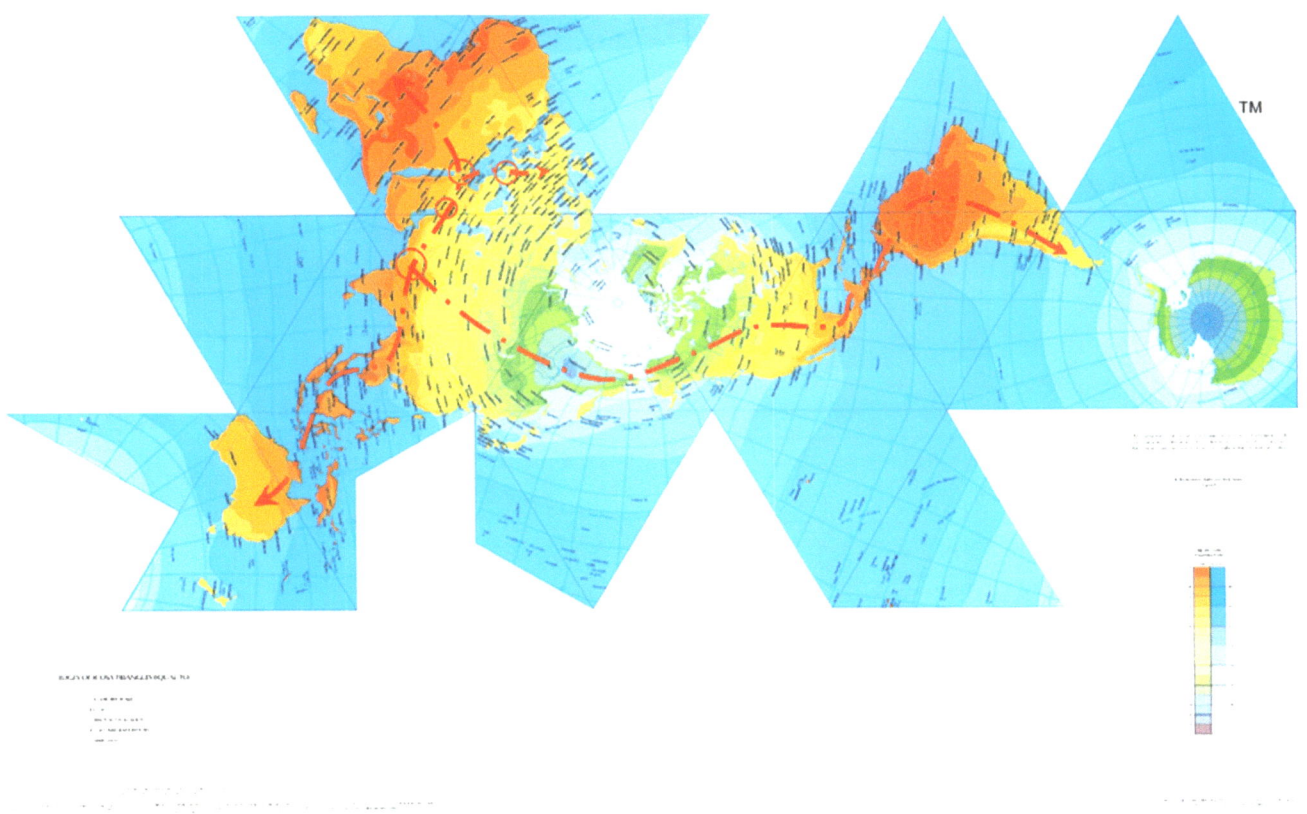

Figure 2.4 Location of Indus valley and human migration on the DYMAXIAN Map

2.2 Vedic Planning System and Towns

After the Indus Valley Civilization, the inhabitants moved eastwards towards the Gangetic Plains. The planning of towns and villages dates back to Vedic times. The Vedic towns were planned in a scientific manner with specific areas for different trades and uses. A glance at the ancient treatises on town administration and architecture like

Vastu Shastra, Manasara-Silpasastra and Kautilya-Arthashastra revealed the scientific study of town planning during 5th millennium BC[5].

The Vedic towns were designed on the basis of diagrams called Mandalas, representing the eternal religious beliefs and taking analogies based on the Nature. "The different Mandalas available were the Urban Mandala called the Swastika, the Cruciform Mandala or Dandaka and the lotus leaf or Padmaka."[6] In Vedic times, Indian towns were comprised of temples, market streets, narrow lanes and royal palaces with squares and gardens.

Figure 2.5 Vedic mandalas such as Dandaka, Swastika, Sarvatobhadra and Padmaka (a clockwise manner)

---

[5] Freedictionaries.com., Farlex Inc., http://encyclopedia.thefreedictionary.com/vedic%20civilization, 20 July 2004
[6] Kostof Spiro (1990), *The City Shaped*, London, Thames and Hudson Ltd, p.182

Town Planning in the Indian Subcontinent   13

For instance, Madurai (South India) is depicted in the 18th century plan as a concentric pattern of walls (Figure 2.6). Madurai is referred to as the temple town because of its layout in a concentric pattern with the temple at its centre. The temple was a major landmark flanked by four gateways pointing towards the cardinal direction. "Open spaces and city blocks were organized around the sacred kernel of its temple precinct, with its own square wall pierced by four tower gates or *gopuras*."[7]

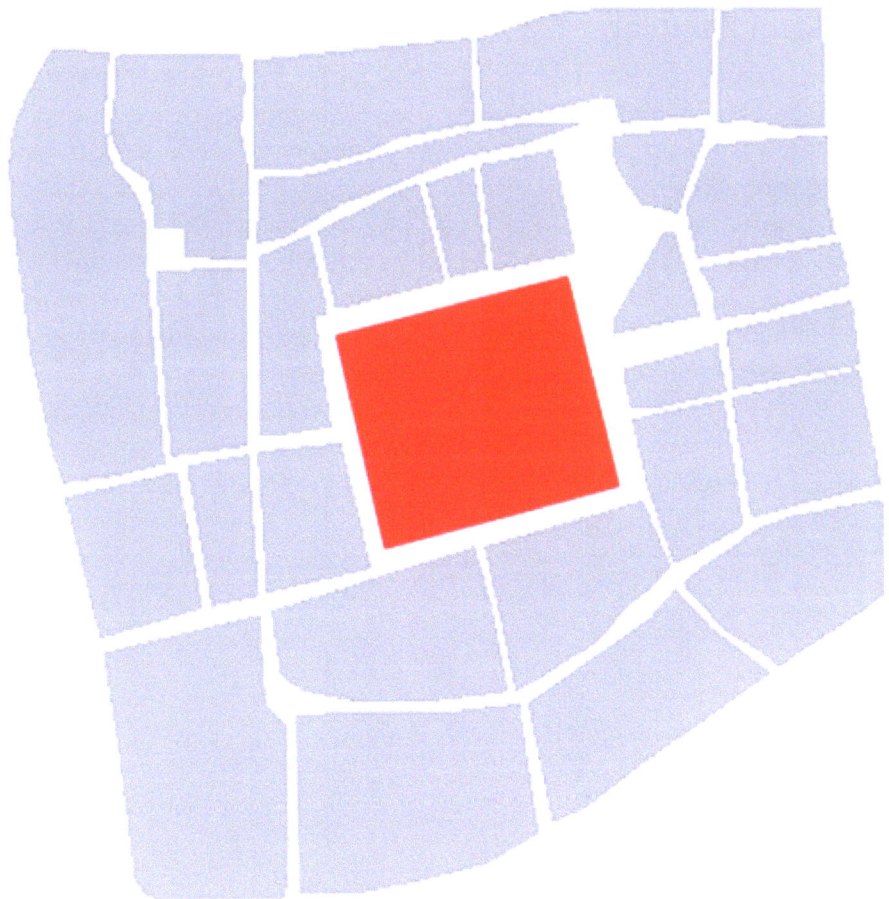

Figure 2.6 18th century urban structure of Madurai

---
[7] Kostof Spiro (1990), *The City Shaped*, London, Thames and Hudson Ltd., p.32

Madurai, the capital of the Pandyas, was a fortified city. In this city there were different streets allocated for different groups of citizens and different uses. Madurai comprised of a royal street, market street, street for goldsmiths and a cloth merchant street. Also, Patliputra (now Patna), as described by Megasthenes, was a grid iron pattern city surrounded by a moat. The city had numerous towers and gates with well-laid parks and fountains.

2.3 Moghul Town Planning

During the Mogul period, the Muslim rulers established several new towns as part of their rapidly growing empire. Most of the early Moghul towns bear the impressions of traditional town planning. As such no special contribution was made towards the art and science of town planning during their reign, except the splendour that highlighted the cities. Mogul towns such as Delhi, Lucknow and Lahore were built in splendor with spacious courts, pleasure gardens, water fountains and richly decorated buildings. The emphasis was given for royal palaces and religious buildings such as Mosques. Garden was the important contribution of the Moghuls. The Moghul approach to gardens is an important contribution to Indian architecture. According to Tillotson G.H.R., "The Persian Charbagh tradition, on which the plan of all such gardens is based, can be traced back at least to eighth century; and it is based on an organic idea: the Koran repeatedly asserts that heaven – the reward of the faithful is a garden, and among the gardens specific detail it mentions is watercourses and fountains."[8] The Mogul gardens were often introverted and symmetrical in design. This was part of sanctuaries and Mosques and segregated in zones which were reserved for the various classes of the society." The Nishat Bagh in Srinagar is a series of terraced gardens lined with fountains opening up towards the lake with a breathtaking view and the ingenious use of natural setting."[9]

---

[8] Tillotson G.H.R. (1990), *Moghul India*, London, Penguin Group, p.128
[9] Tillotson G.H.R. (1990), *Moghul India*, London, Penguin Group, p.130

Town Planning in the Indian Subcontinent   15

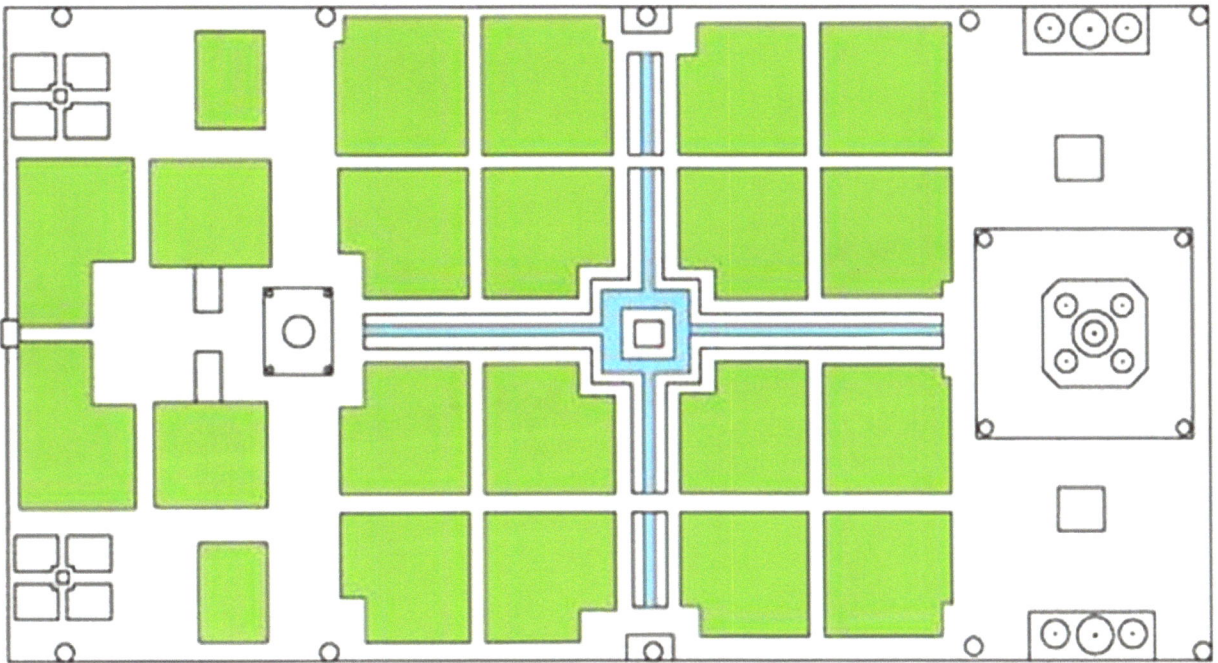

Figure 2.7 Plan showing the gardens of Taj Mahal at Agra

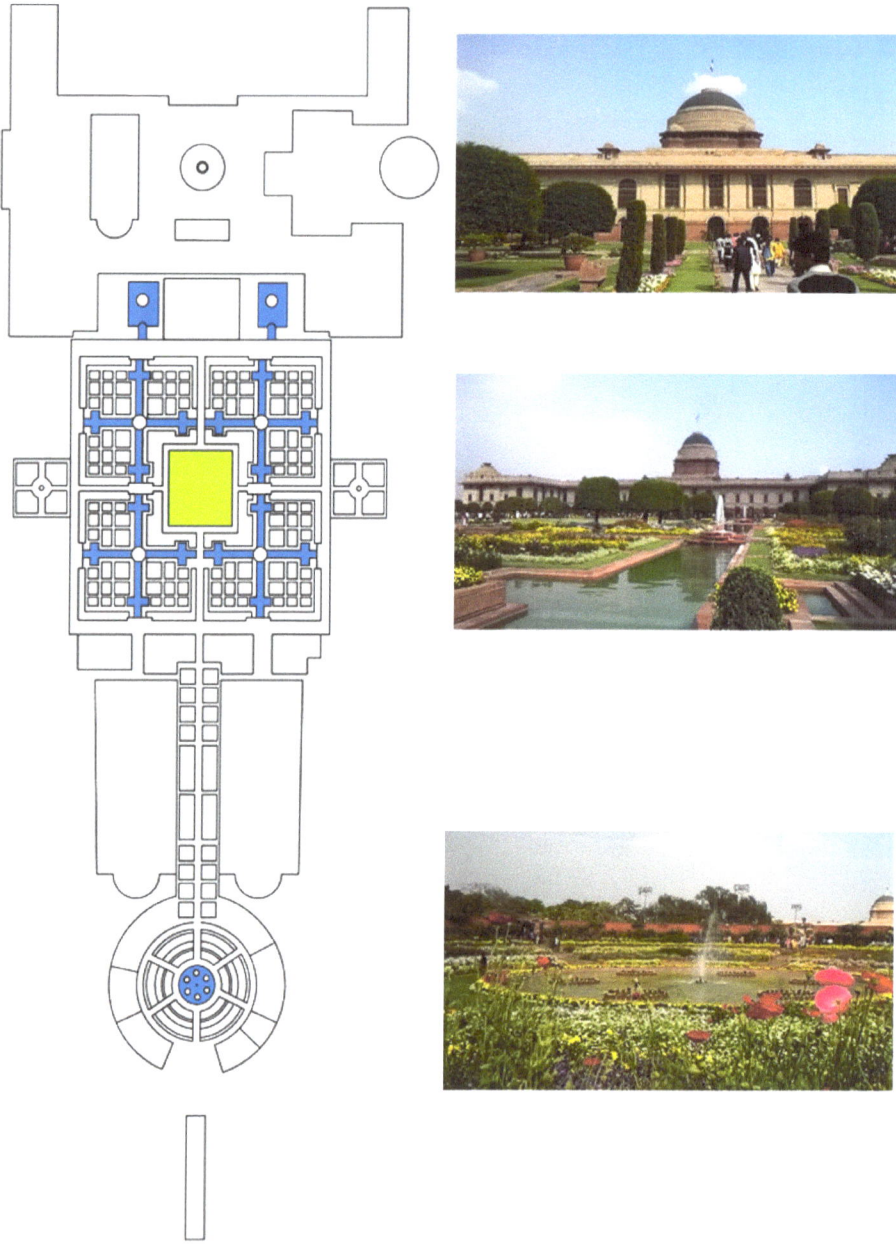

Figure 2.8 Plan and views of Rashtrapati Bhavan, Moghul gardens with water channels, New Delhi

Town Planning in the Indian Subcontinent 17

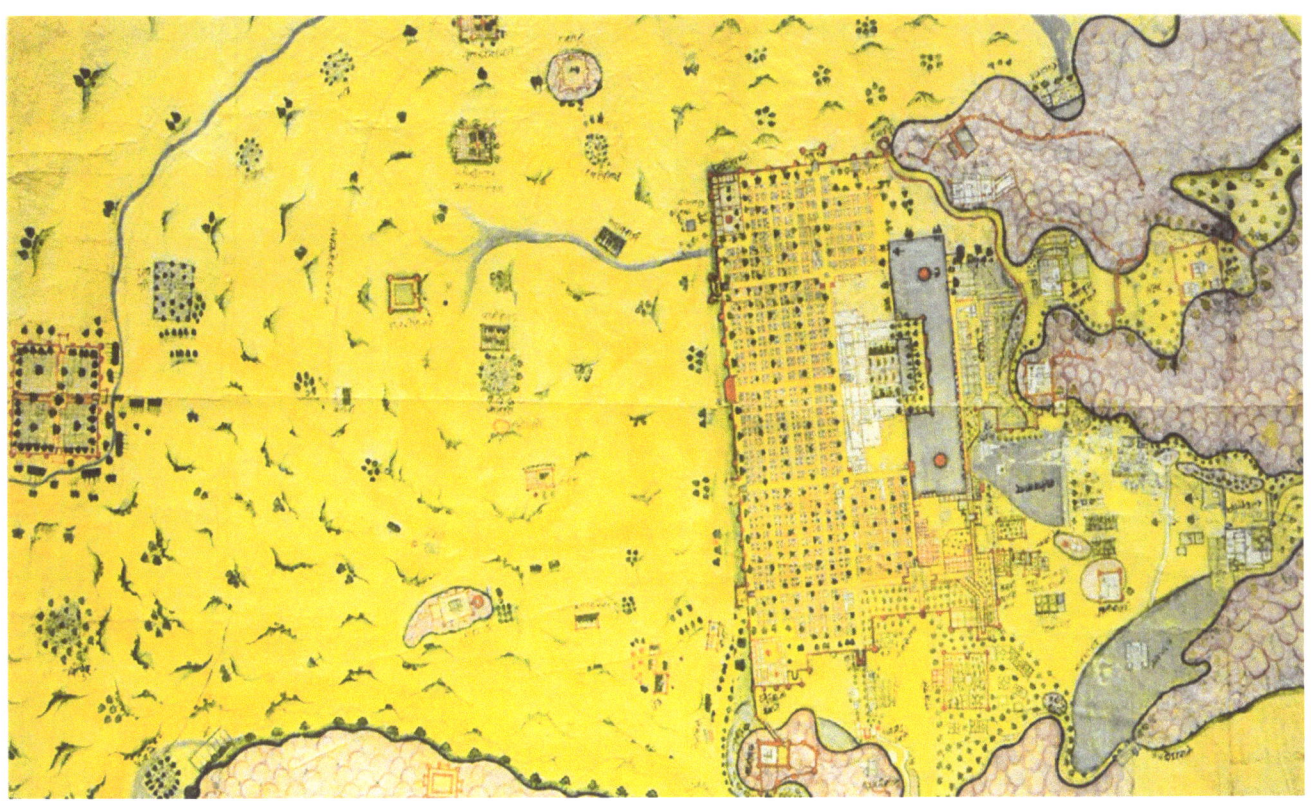

Figure 2.9 Early map of Jaipur [*Courtesy*: Maharaja Sawai Man Singh II Museum Trust, The City Palace Jaipur]

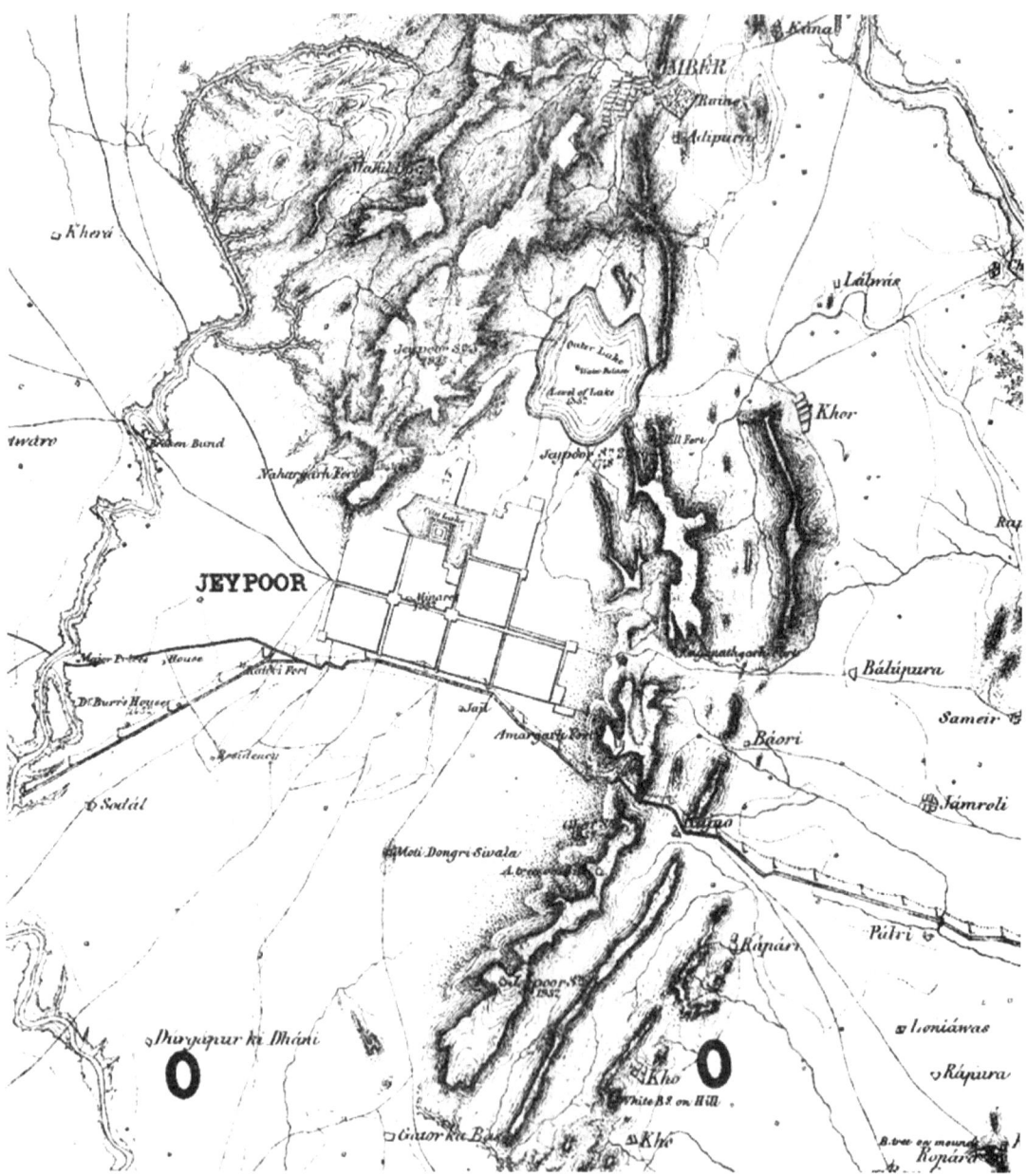

Figure 2.10 Extract from the map of Jaipur and its environs [Reproduced from original map of 1868, Survey of India]

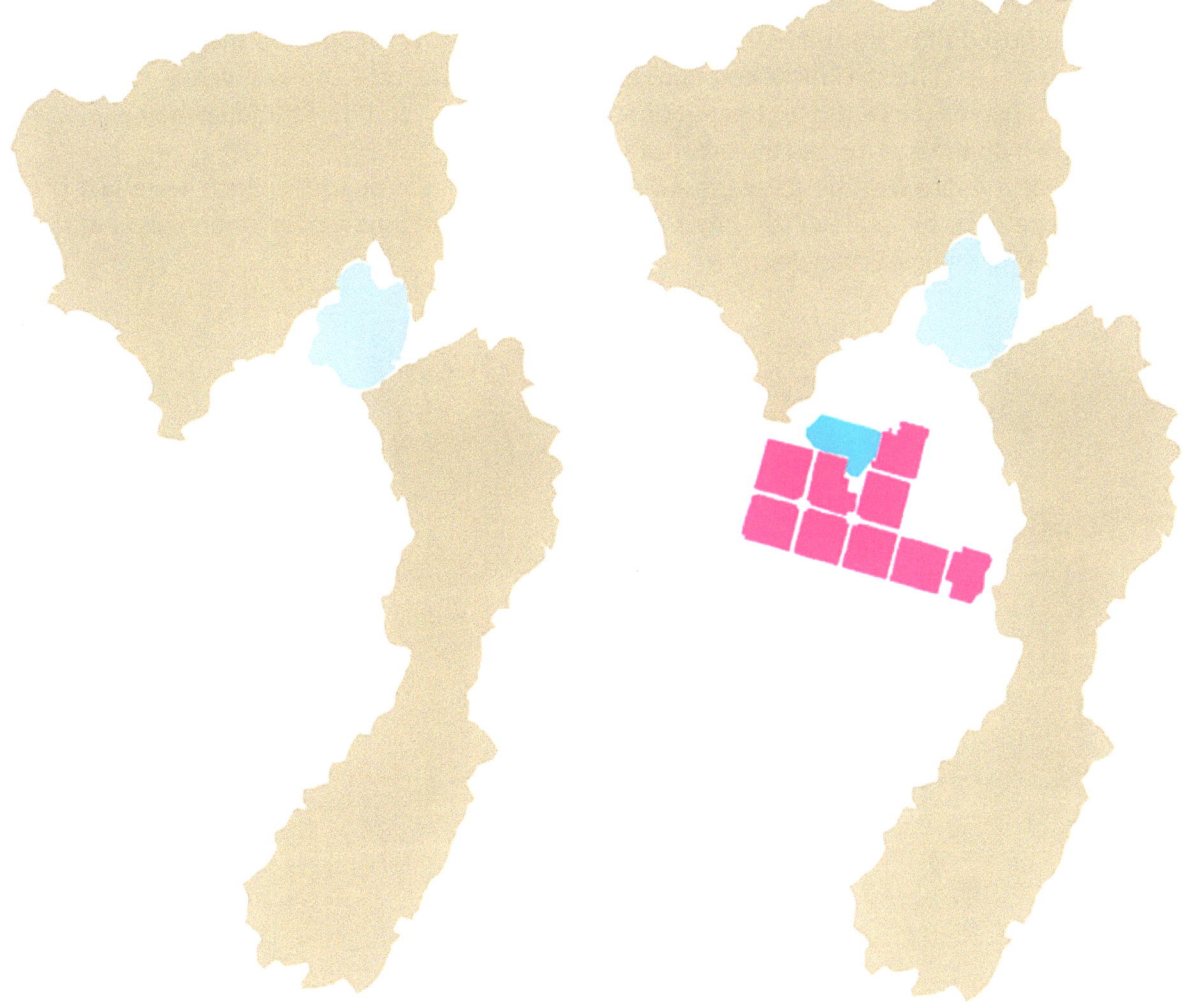

Figure 2.11 Jaipur city and its relationship with the surrounding hills; strategic location of Jaipur at the base of the hills

2.4 The Princely Town of Jaipur, Natural Setting and Geography

Many new towns have been planned and built by the rulers of the various provinces of India: One excellent example of such a city is Jaipur, planned and built by Maharaja Jai Singh II in 1727, a man of advanced ideas and scientific mind. The area among the natural setting of the foot hills founded the basis of Jaipur city. It was strategically placed which shielded the city from the invaders, thus taking the natural element as a defensive wall. The city comprised of nine squares, reflecting the Indian ethos of Paramasiya Mandala. One of the squares was tilted to avoid harsh climatic conditions such as wind. The nine squares were further divided into plots, with temples as the landmark. Intersections of the roads formed the city squares or *chowks*. Nine square blocks based on the grid formed the urban structure of Jaipur.

At the heart of the city was the palace, surrounded by residential quarters which were laid on an orthogonal street pattern. Jai Singh built the city in an integrated harmonious setting around his new palace; the whole constituting a single urban unit.

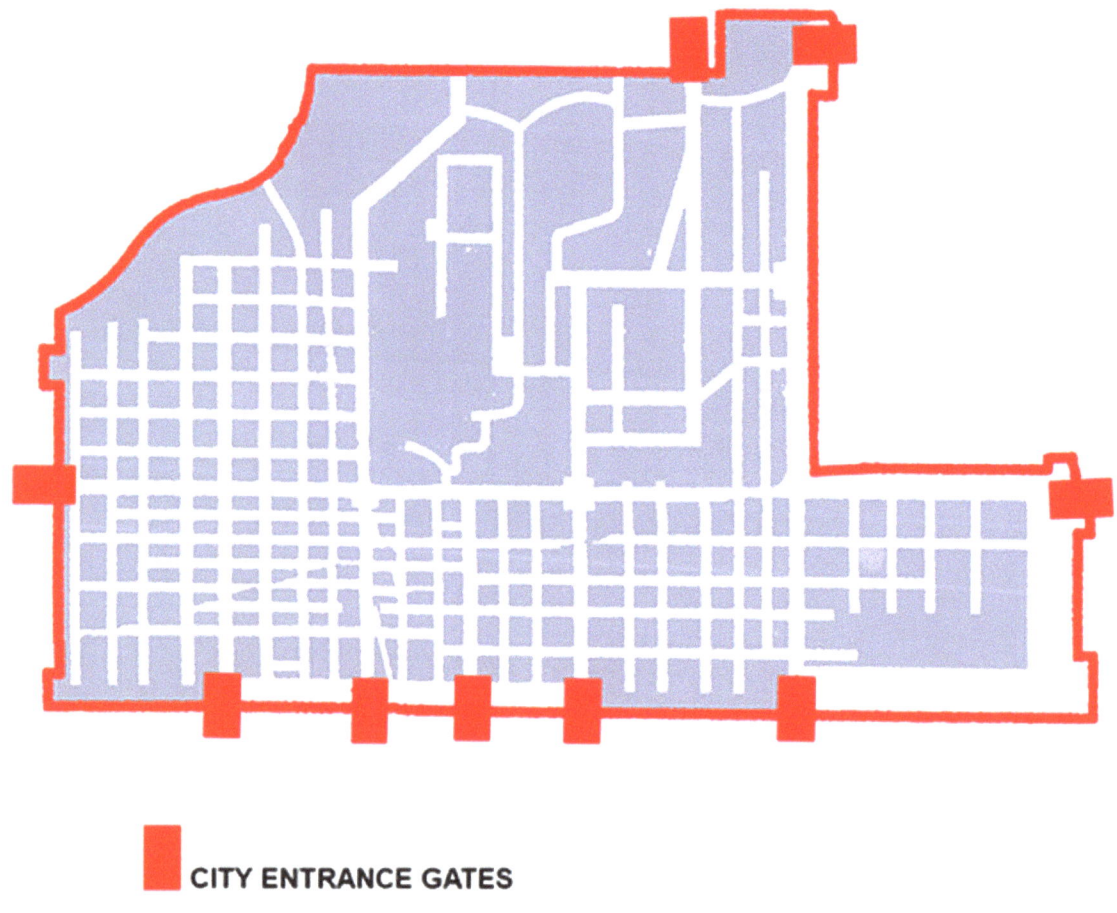

Figure 2.12 Grid iron plan of Jaipur with fortified wall and gates

Jaipur is therefore not only a planned city but also an ensemble palace city which makes it more than a city and also something more than a *collection of palaces.*

2.5   British Town Planning in India

Colonial India saw the emergence of cities as industrial magnets, attracting poor people from nearby towns and villages seeking work. The villages took inspiration from the city planning; thus, one could see a total disintegration in the development of towns and villages which had been so well founded and adopted in the previous centuries. In addition, the Industrial Revolution made the cities bigger, leading to heavy congestion and poor insanitary conditions.

In the early part of the twentieth century, attempts were made by engineers, social administrators and enlightened rulers to improve towns and villages with a view to providing adequate amenities and services. Bangalore and Mysore were the "Garden Cities" of South India, absorbing the theories of Ebenezer Howard.

The contribution of Patrick Geddes is noteworthy among the British town planners. He believed in preserving the urban fabric and advocated the organic growth of the settlement and preserving features such as "the tree-shaded *chowks*, the mid-street openings that harbour the public life in traditional Indian cities."[10]

The renewal project in Balarampur is an example of Geddes Theory of "diagnosis before treatment".[11] This involved conserving the urban fabric and improving hygiene and traffic flow.

New Delhi's existence dates back to 1911 – the coronation of King George V. It was the King who formally announced that the capital would be shifted from Calcutta to Delhi.

Sir Edwin Lutyens was appointed as an architect of the project. His challenge was to design a capital in a heterogeneous culture which would be the iconic capital of the British Empire. Lutyens, however, maintained the view that the capital should withstand the passing of few centuries."[12] Thus, he sought inspiration from Greek temple architecture and modern European planning methodologies. *"Key nodes were emphasized by the hexagons and through which enormous radials sprang out in every direction. All the buildings were at the centre or mid-size of the hexagons. Thus, the formal geometry was the key to planning of the new capital that took sixteen years to complete."*[13]

The core of the buildings is situated on the Raisina Hills which offers a splendid view of wide boulevards, which form the main axis and run through these core buildings down to India Gate. The boulevard, now called the Raj Path, maintains a clear vista towards the Raisina Hills, revealing the buildings partially when approached.

Delhi the new imperial capital successfully ignored the small streets and meandering lanes of old Delhi.

---

[10] Kostof Spiro (1990), *The City Shaped*, London, Thames and Hudson Ltd, p.86
[11] Kostof Spiro (1990), *The City Shaped*, London, Thames and Hudson Ltd, p.86
[12] Kostof Spiro (1990), *The City Shaped*, London, Thames and Hudson Ltd., p.86
[13] Hall Peter (1988), Cities of Tomorrow, Oxford, Basil Blackwell Ltd., p.191

Figure 2.13 Lutyens's plan of Delhi, viewed from a satellite [*Source*: European Space Agency]

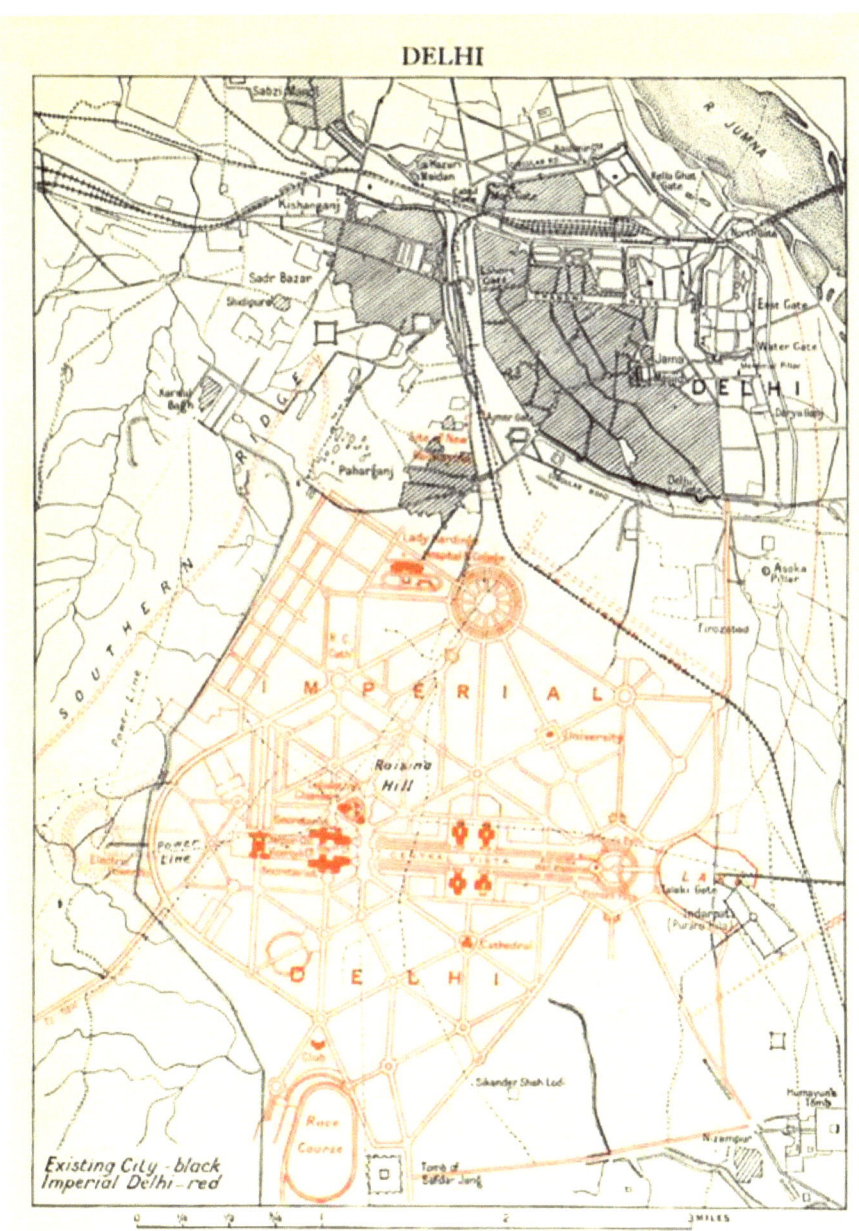

Figure 2.14 Map of Lutyens's plan of Delhi

Figure 2.15 Present-day map of New Delhi [*Source*: Survey of India]

To this day, it feels the city has two distinct parts: Old Delhi, with the meandering streets where the urban grain is closely knit; and New Delhi, where one is stunned by the sheer scale and size of the planning concept. According to Satish Grover, "In the Bungalow Zone the population density is 12–15 people per acre; in the old walled city of Delhi it is 1,500 people per acre."[14]

2.6 Summary

Early towns such as Mohenjo-Daro and Harappa revealed planning based on climatic considerations and the fulfilment of the social and cultural aspirations of their inhabitants. The outdoor spaces served many functions, predominantly promoting interaction and attracting retail activity. The Moghul town planning emphasized the importance of outdoor environment, with gardens, water plants and shaded courts. Moghul cities such as Fatehpur Sikri can be referred as *city within a city*. Colonial town planning saw the emergence of society propelled by industry and the establishment of government buildings. The city saw a major shift in land marks which were often royal palaces. Modern town planning in cities such as Chandigarh and Gandhinagar brought a remarkable change to Indian society and formed precedents for numerous industrial towns in India. Recent town planning developments such as New Bagalkot and Aranya incorporate certain traditional planning approaches and an emphasis on communal feeling, promoting social interaction.

---
[14] https://www.outlookindia.com/website/story/lutyens-delhi/235665

Figure 3.1 *La Main Ouverte* (The Open Hand), 1954 [© FLC/ADAGP]

3
Description of Chandigarh

3.1 Introduction

Chandigarh, the joint capital of Haryana and Punjab, was designed by Le Corbusier in 1960. It is often referred to as the "*City Green*" owing to its generous and spacious landscape design features. The capital city is regarded as a landmark in terms of city planning and architecture in India.

3.2 Political Background

The formation of Chandigarh is linked to India's independence in 1947, which left the state of Punjab devoid of a state capital when Lahore, the former capital of Punjab, was lost to Pakistan. Jawaharlal Lal Nehru, the then first Prime Minister of India, said of Chandigarh, "Let this be a new town, symbolic of the freedom of India unfettered by the traditions of the past... an expression of the nation's faith in the future."[1] The creation of Chandigarh was of historical significance which would reflect the vision of Modern[2] India.

3.3 Finance

The underlying philosophy of Chandigarh's development as a "self-financed" city was spelt out by Le Corbusier in 1959, in his typical style: "*When the following operation has been started in the city; obtaining the money, buying the necessary land, framing of the first by-laws permitting the beginning of construction, selling of the first plot, arriving of the first inhabitant, a phenomenon is born: it is the appreciation in the value of the piece of land. A game, a play, has begun. One can sell cheaply or at high price; it depends on the kind of tactics and the strategy employed in the operation. One phrase must be affirmed: good urbanism makes money; bad urbanism loses money.*"[3]

The principles of good urbanism as suggested by Corbusier are a key to providing good infrastructure and quality of life in a city. Corbusier's inherent belief in the industry as part of society building clearly demonstrates

---

[1] Anklesaria Sarosh, *Chandigarh: Vision and Reality*, Architecture week, http://www.architectureweek.com/2001/0822/culture1-2.html, 2 May 2004
[2] Modern India is referred here as the Industrial Age after 1947 by the author
[3] Sarin Madhu (1982), *Urban Planning in the Third World*, Mansell Publishing Ltd., p.60

the vision as perceived by the then Prime Minister J. L. Nehru. It also demonstrates the ethos of the machine age.

The city could regulate the sale of plots and thus raise revenues for its much-needed civic infrastructure for building an effective sewerage system, water supply, roads, public buildings such as schools, museum and government buildings.

All the costs pertaining to the infrastructure were made, which was then added to the price of land bought by the developers, who then carried out various developments in the city. In consonance with Le Corbusier's doctrine of using rising land values as a means of financing urban development, foreign architects attempted to persuade the Punjab Government to adopt a policy of selling land on a leasehold basis from the very beginning. In spite of their attempts, the Punjab Government opted for the freehold system for two reasons: firstly, to raise the necessary cash (immediately) to carry out the project estimates; and secondly, to provide psychological assurance to the potential settlers, many of whom were insecure and uprooted refugees.

Here the role of the architect as a developer for the city can be clearly seen which was instrumental for developing city's infrastructure. About a quarter of Chandigarh's revenue was obtained from the central government. The government of Chandigarh is now looking to generate sources of income through the information technology market, which is a very lucrative market for all the states in India at the present moment.

"The software development centre will open this month with 60 developers, a number that will increase to 200 by the end of next year, and to 400 by the end of year 2000. The estimated amount of investment is about 10 million US dollars".[4]

Looking at the industrial ownership 93 percent (refer Appendix 1, Table 1) of the industries are privately owned which indicates the potential of a growing industrial segment due to good city infrastructure.

3.4 Site Selection

The new town in 1951 was initially envisaged for a population of 1.5 lakhs[5] with a scope for expansion to 5.0 lakhs. According to Mahendra Raj, "it had been estimated that land of about 9,000 acres or 40 sq. km of land would be required for the new city"[6]. A site was chosen near the foothills of the Shivalik range. The site does not have any steep contours but with a gentle slope – an ideal from the drainage point of view. The seasonal rivers, Sukhmo Cho and Patiali Rao, form the natural boundaries on the east and west respectively, with the Shivalik mountain range forming a dramatic backdrop.

---

[4] Doshi B.V., Kathpalia Rajiv, and Sharma Utpal (2002), In Search of India's Future Cities, *Celebrating Chandigarh*, Ahmedabad, Mapin Publishers Ltd., p.253
[5] 1 lakh = 0.1 million
[6] Mahendra Raj (2002), Other Contributors, Celebrating Chandigarh, Ahmedabad, Mapin Publishers Ltd., p.83

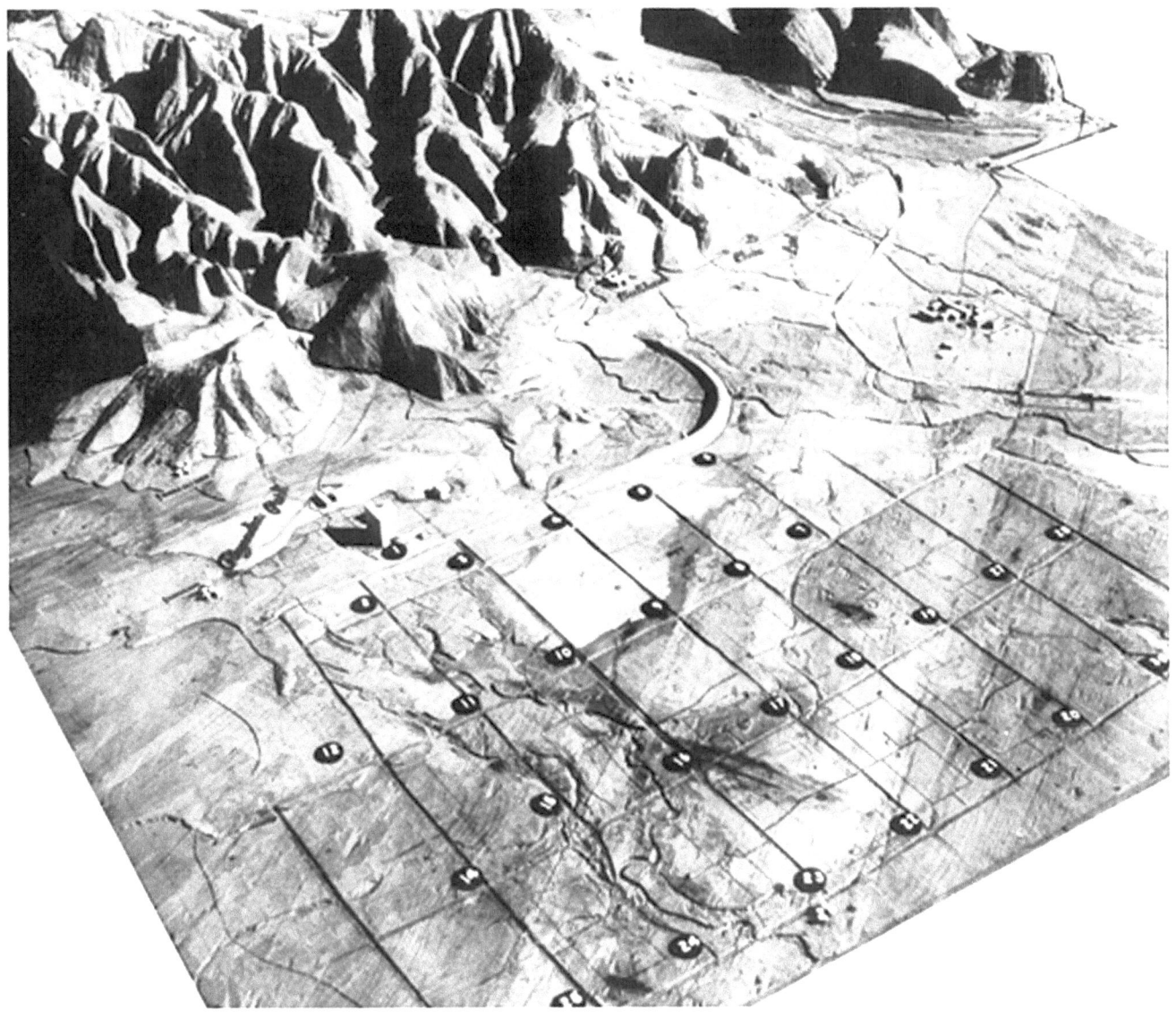

Figure 3.2 Physical model of Chandigarh, site and its surroundings [© FLC/ADAGP]

3.5 Climate

The climate of Chandigarh has a maximum temperature of 43° Celsius in summer and reaches freezing levels in winter. The prevailing winds blow from the southeast during summer and from the northwest during winter.

3.6 The Design Team

The planning of Chandigarh was entrusted to the firm of Albert Mayer in New York. The terms were subsequently changed by a technical organization and the project was offered to Le Corbusier who was appointed the Chief Architect and other architects such as Jane Drew, Maxwell Fry and Pierre Jeanneret were appointed as full time personal for 3 years. The detailed plans would include the master layout of the city and plans of some important buildings.

3.7 Chandigarh Master Plan

At the time of inception, the morphology of Chandigarh, as observed in both the schemes of Mayer and Nowicki, had basic generally accepted principles of civic design (see Fig. 3.2). Mayer sought to combine a clear city framework with elements of the picturesque – traceable to Camillio Sitte's[7] theories but more directly related to the garden city idea – and pedestrian/vehicle separation, the so-called Raybradburn layout. Le Corbusier detested Sitte's idea: *'Man walks in a straight line because he has a goal and knows where he is going'* – and called the winding road *'the donkey's way'*[8]. Le Corbusier abandoned Mayer's plan for superblocks and replaced it with sectors. Had Mayer's plan been incorporated for Chandigarh, it would have related to traditional Indian cities with public places.

Le Corbusier's Master plan changed the morphology of the city and to a certain extent, did alter its density. However, the two plans did not change significantly. "Le Corbusier criticized Mayer's plan for its absence of merchant and artisan life, a social phenomenon indispensable in India and compared Lutyens' Connaught Place unfavourably with the linear Indian bazaar which was what the V4 Central Street in each sector was intended but failed to be." According to architect B. V. Doshi, "although Chandigarh was intended to be a capital city, the designers failed to study capital cities such as Delhi or Jaipur." Also, Chandigarh's planners did not have interdisciplinary team: there were no sociologists, no anthropologists and no economists."[9]

---

[7] Please refer http://www.library.cornell.edu/Reps/DOCS/sitte.htm
[8] Prasad Sunand (1987), *Le Corbusier-Architect of the Century*, Arts council of Great Britain, Mansell UK Limited, p.287
[9] Doshi B.V. (1989), Indian Architect and Builder, January 1999, p.82

Description of Chandigarh 31

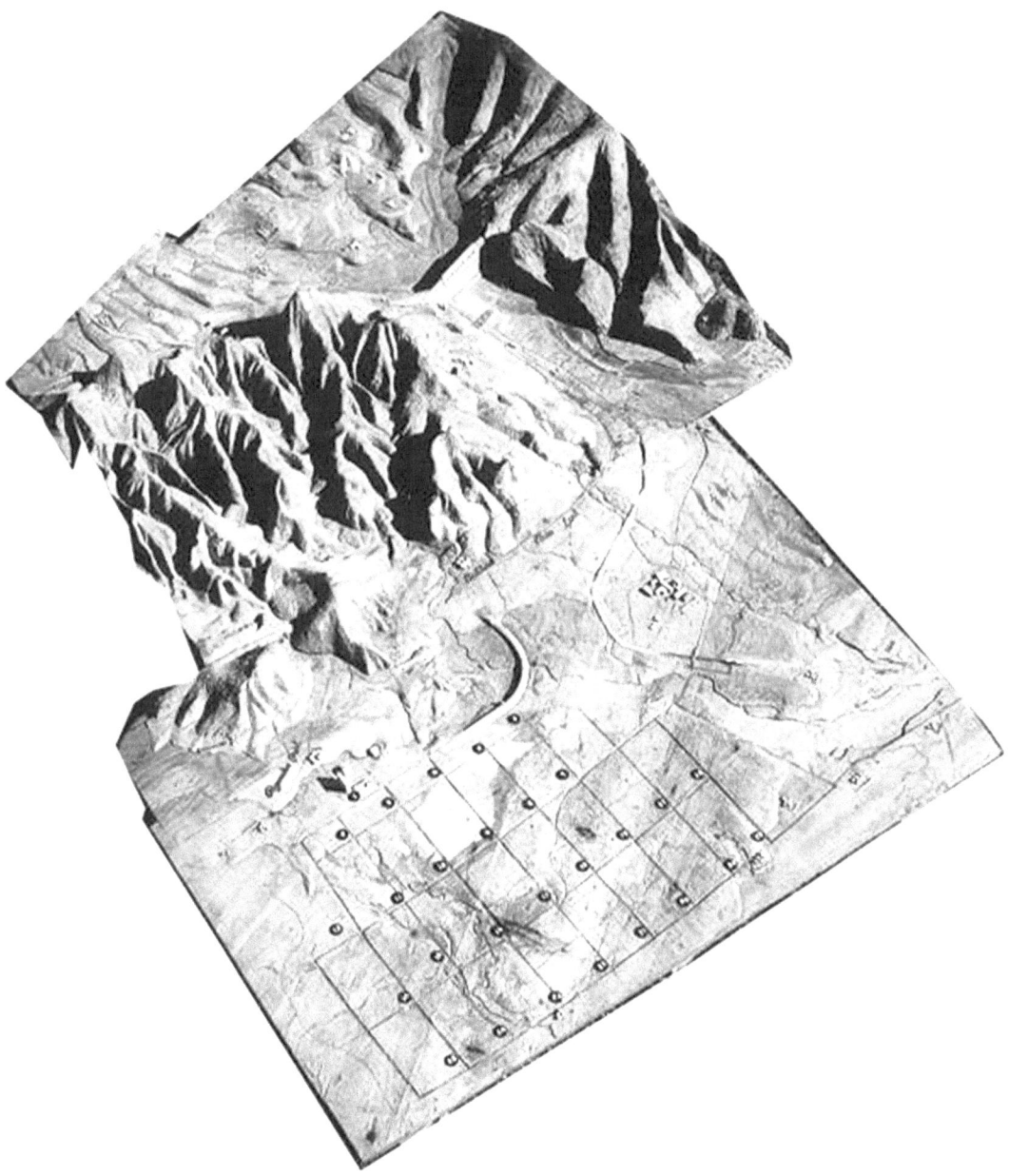

Figure 3.3 Physical model of the terrain profile [© FLC/ADAGP]

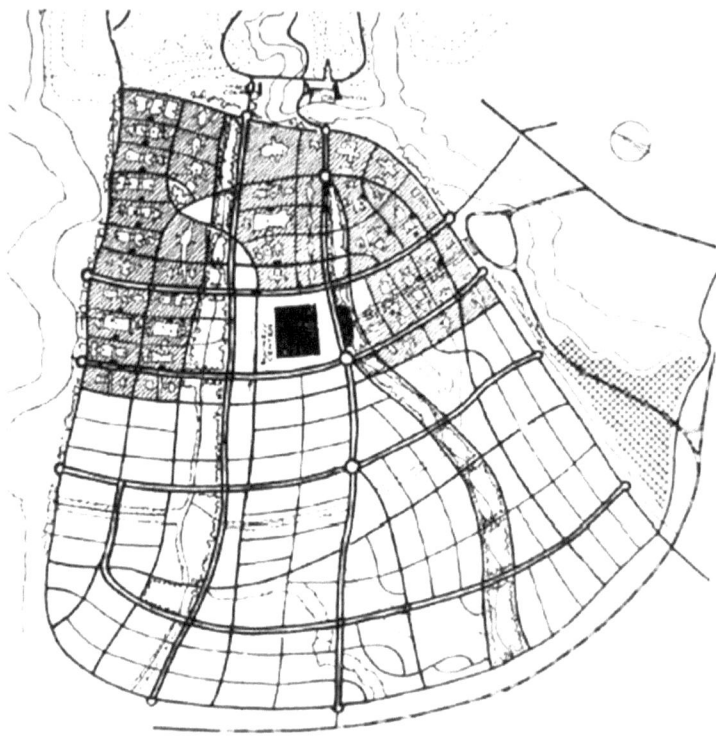

Figure 3.4 Master Plan of Chandigarh as proposed by Albert Mayer, 1949 [*Source*: Le Corbusier, Architect of the Century, Arts Council of Great Britain, Mansell U.K. Limited 1987, p.287]

3.7.1 Plan of the city

The plan of the city is based on one of the oldest formal urban plans – the grid iron pattern. The conception of the city as an organism is found frequently throughout the Le Corbusier urban theories. In explaining his analogy, Le Corbusier stated that "a plan arranges organs in order, thus creating an organism for organisms. The organs possess distinct qualities, specific differences…"[10]

The city was conceived as a square containing a cross axis, with the Capitol Complex culminating on the northeast axis towards the mountains. In Jane Drew's words, "The Master plan was of poetic significance. It is almost biological in its form."[11]

[10,11] Frampton Keneth (2002), Other Contributors, *Celebrating Chandigarh*, Ahmedabad, Mapin Publishers Ltd., p.83

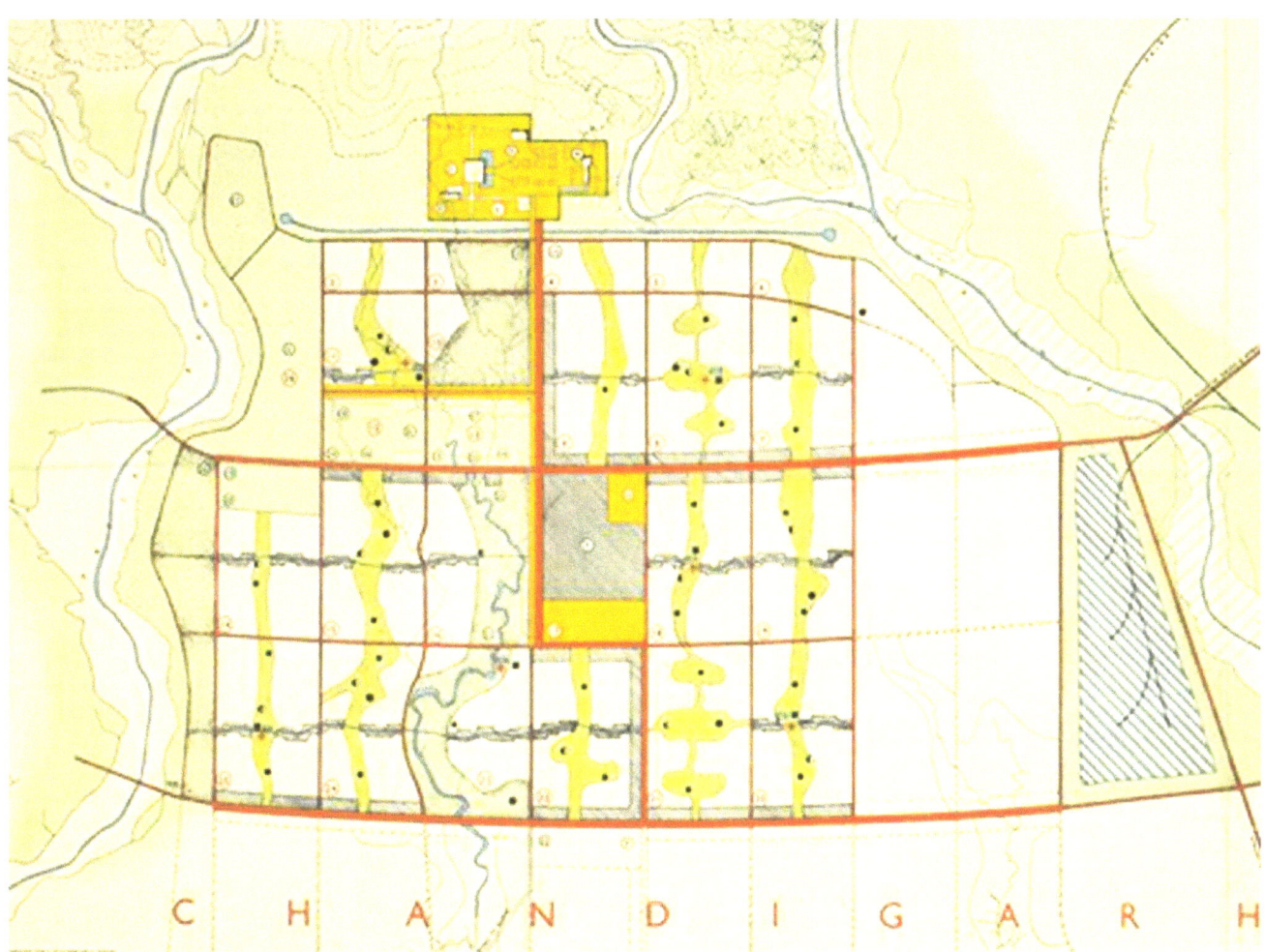

Figure 3.5 Master Plan of Chandigarh as proposed by Le Corbusier in the year 1949 [© FLC/ADAGP]

34 Master Planning Indian Cities: Achieving Urban Renaissance

Figure 3.6 Zoning in Chandigarh

Description of Chandigarh   35

3.8 Zoning

Chandigarh is segregated into four parts: the Capitol Complex, Civic Centre, Education Centre and industries.

3.8.1 Capitol Complex

The focal point of the city, both visually and symbolically, is the Capitol. It is the part of the city where most people work and earn their living.

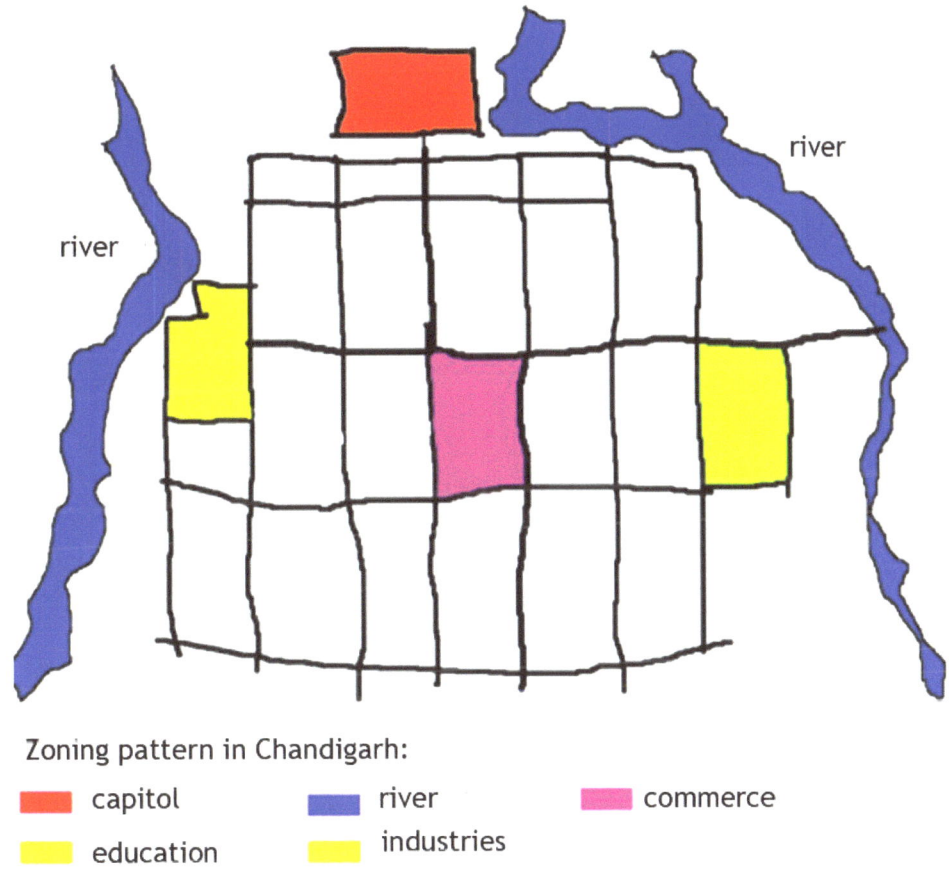

Figure 3.7 Plan of Chandigarh and surrounding areas

The Complex comprises an ensemble of the High Court building, the Secretariat, the Assembly and the Museum of Knowledge. The Capitol as a whole was designed as a great pedestrian plaza with the motor traffic separated into sunken trenches leading to parking areas. The generating motif of the complex, like that of the city itself, is a cross axis; the arrangement of buildings is carefully avoided of the static balance of rigid symmetry.

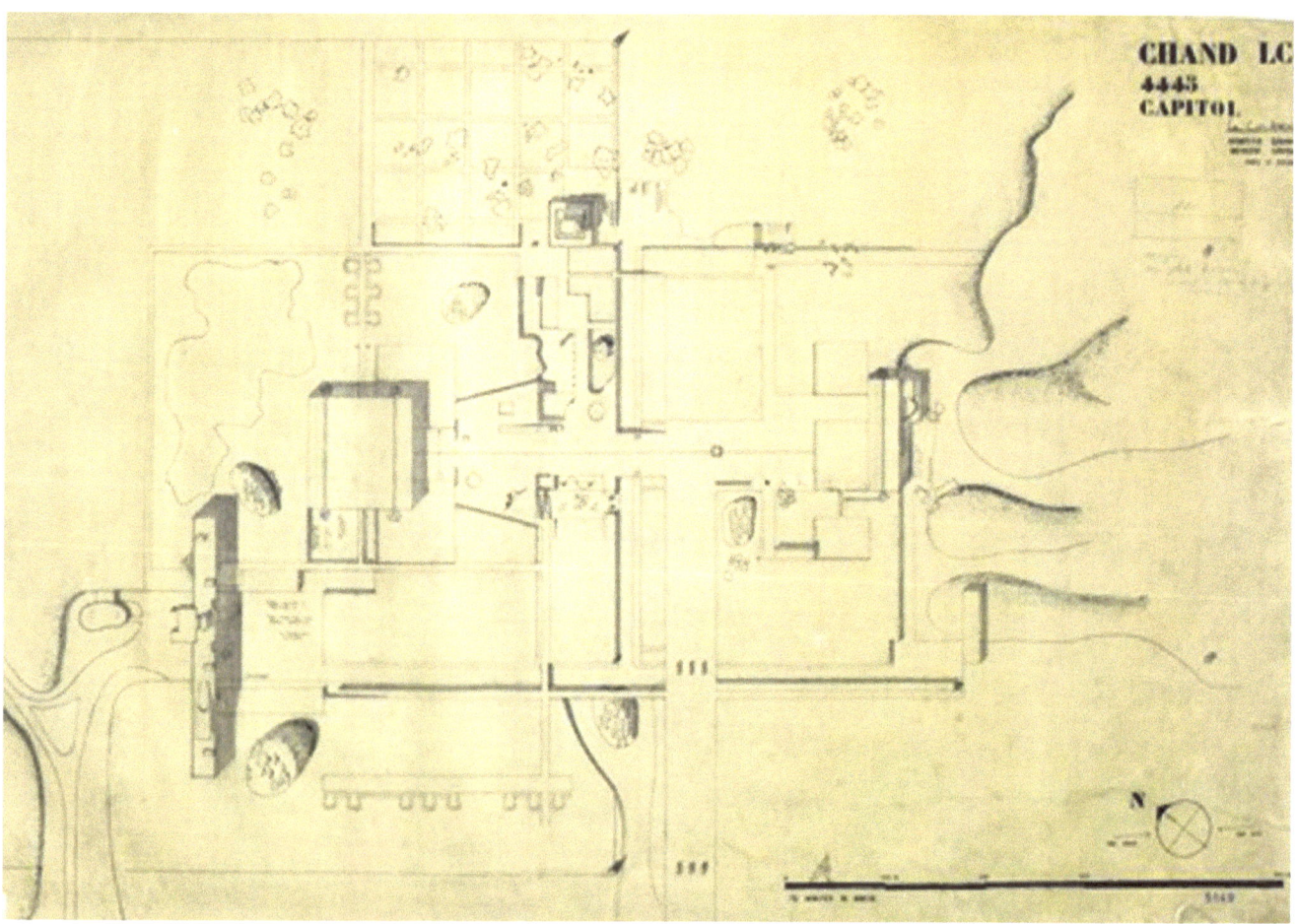

Figure 3.8 Capitol Complex, Chandigarh [© FLC/ADAGP]

3.8.2 The Commercial Centre

Sector 17 is the central business district and houses the Civic Centre. The south of the shopping street V4 divides the sector into two divisions which is the centre of district administration. The other half serves the major commercial and civic functions of the city. The southern part consists of the District Court, Police Headquarters and Central Bus Terminal.

The main business district was designed to repeat the cross-axial motif established in the Capital Complex and the Master plan. Four pedestrian ways were designed to lead into a central *chowk* or square; in the square are the principal buildings of the area: the town hall, the central library, and commercial establishments such as banks.

Figure 3.9 The Assembly building, Chandigarh [© FLC/ADAGP]

Figure 3.10 Governor's Palace, unbuilt [*Source*: © FLC/ADAGP]

3.8.3 Educational centre

Chandigarh is the seat of Punjab University. All the university buildings are located in the west end, i.e. Sector 14 in park land.

3.8.4 Industries

Architectural controls were established for the development of the industrial area. Industries are located at the east end of the city near the railroad terminus, allowing easy transfer of raw materials and finished goods without the need of transporting these through the city. Industries are separated from the residential areas by a buffer area of trees.

Figure 3.11 Open spaces of Sector 17, Chandigarh

3.9 Morphology of the Sector

Chandigarh is made up of sectors measuring 800 × 1200 m. The adaptation of sectors "can be argued to lay in the two sets of plans of the 1920s: the plan called the new towns of America pioneered by Clarence Stein and Henry Wright, and the various theoretical plans of Le Corbusier."[12]

The city was conceived as an organic form right from inception; it was Matthew Nowicki described the plan of Chandigarh as "*a leaf*"[13]. Each sector was designed with basic amenities such as shopping centres, schools and parks.

Each sector is comprised of green strips which run in linear fashion, over which vehicles do not cross. The self-sufficiency of these sectors can be seen as the achievement of Chandigarh's original creator Albert Mayer, who saw the plan as "greenbelt applied to the entire city".[14]

---

[12] Julian Beinart (2002), Chandigarh 1999: Diagrams and Realties, *Celebrating Chandigarh*, Ahmedabad, Mapin Publishers Ltd., p.143
[13] Julian Beinart (2002), Chandigarh 1999: Diagrams and Realties, *Celebrating Chandigarh*, Ahmedabad, Mapin Publishers Ltd., p.144
[14] Julian Beinart (2002), Chandigarh 1999: Diagrams and Realties, *Celebrating Chandigarh*, Ahmedabad, Mapin Publishers Ltd., p.143

According to Julian Beinart, "The organic, anti-technological bias manifested itself in the placing of the child, the most vulnerable of the species, in the centre of the plan. The block size was determined by children's walking distances; hence, the large area, 1200 meters × 1200 metres. Diversity was celebrated through the presence of different income, religious and racial groups – artists as well as social workers. In the biological model, nature, especially trees, would be everywhere and everything would be in its right place."[15]

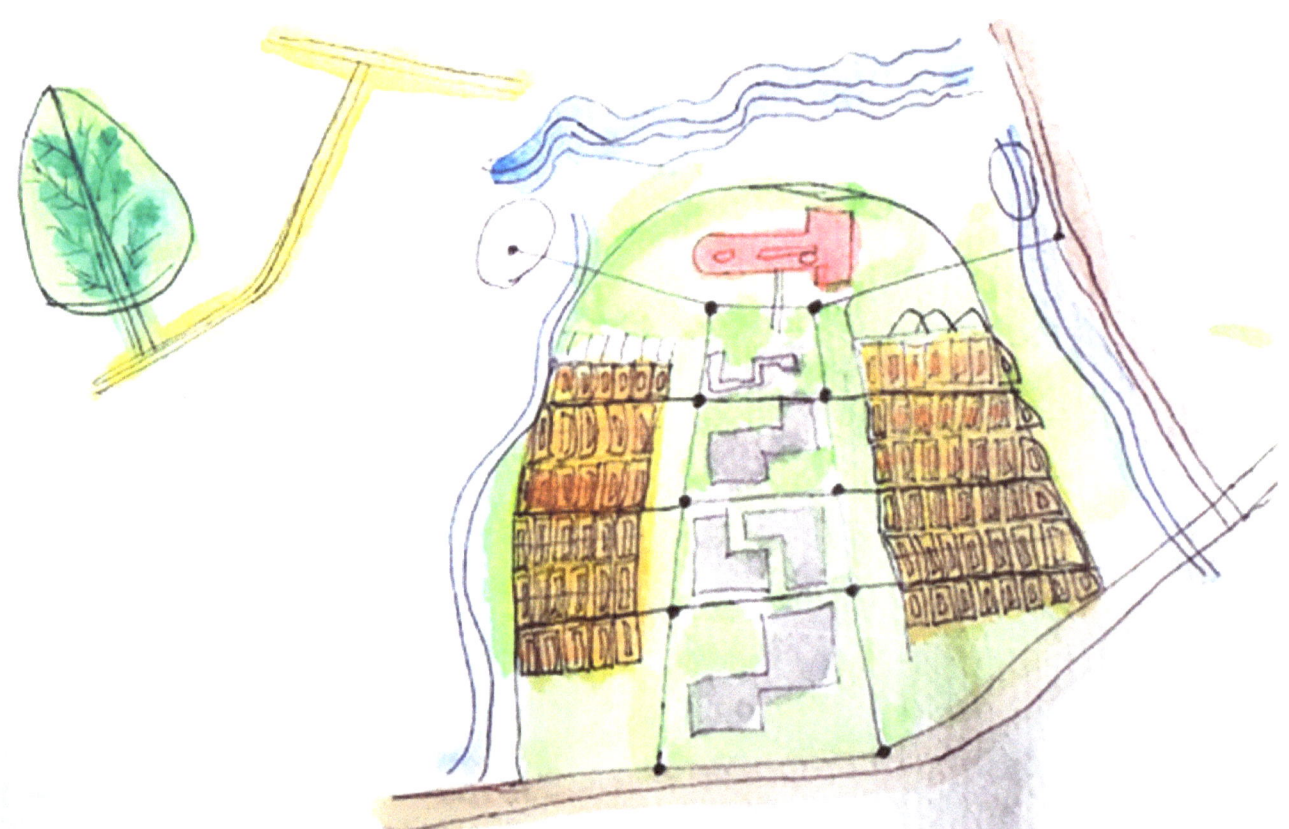

Figure 3.12 Diagram interpreted from Matthew Nowicki's "leaf" plan for Chandigarh, 1950

---

[15] Julian Beinart (2002), Chandigarh 1999: Diagrams and Realties, *Celebrating Chandigarh*, Ahmedabad, Mapin Publishers Ltd., p.146

Figure 3.13 Plumeria "Champa" leaf and its details

Nowicki's plan for Chandigarh was derived from nature, and hence it is organic in layout. The main advantage of the organic layout was its compact form which in some ways relates to the traditional Indian cities, which were sometimes derived from the Nature[16].

---

[16] Refer Chapter 2, Section 2.2 Vedic Planning

3.9.1 Euclidian geometrical systems: "The grid" vs. natural systems

The leaf such as the Plumeria (Native Indian name: *Champa*) displays an organization with parts such as the Blade, the Veins linked to the Midrib. The interconnection and interlinks of veins with the Midrib are nature's response towards an organization which is economical, compact and devoid of any Euclidean geometric principles. Such a natural organization, i.e. arrangement of leaf components, is based on the necessity to gather sunlight and transportation of mineral and water.

If we were to take the very concept of 'money' and its application towards the basic unit of land subdivision which is always rectangular or square is not due to its function other than the quantification, so that an area is achieved which is far higher than any of the other Euclidean geometric forms such as the circle or triangle where we get a volume or space which is based on the dynamics of fiscal.

Whereas, a natural system such as the leaf the primary aim of which is to gather sunlight and facilitate the movement of water and minerals organizes itself in a pattern based on a principle devoid of any ulterior motive or self-centric goals.

Le Corbusier regarded the sector as the "key of modern urbanism, the container of modern life". The population of individual sectors might be as low as 5,000 persons or as high as 25,000 – and even much more now.

The precise size of the sectors, 800 × 1200 m, was no accident. Between 1929 and 1949, Le Corbusier had closely studied the pattern of the traditional Spanish *Cuadra*: this measured 110 × 100 m. He wrote: "*A useful reclassification of them led me to adopt a ratio of harmonious dimensions and productive combinations: 7 to 8 cuadras on one side, 10 to 12 cuadras on the other; that is to say 800 × 1200 meters. And this was the 'Sector', issued from an ancestral and valid geometry established in the past on the stride of a man, an ox, or a horse, but hence to be adapted to mechanical speeds.*"[17]

The sectors are vertically integrated by green space oriented in the direction of the mountains. Le Corbusier envisaged the construction of schools and playing fields in these green belts in Chandigarh; the sector is based on the functional differentiation of the city integrated with the traffic system; the sector as planned contains housing, local shopping and community buildings.

The physical dimensions of the sector are 1200 × 800[18] m which is about three blocks of the Mayer's plan.

The sector is crossed by a street through inside at its half-way point. This street has a line of functions which are necessary for daily life: food supply, artisans, police, fire brigade, cinema and restaurants. Each sector has green spaces which are the green bands. These bands are reserved for schools and playgrounds. Within the irregular pattern of street, blocks or buildings were laid out. Surrounding the residential sectors forming the grid pattern of the city are the V streets reserved for fast-moving motor traffic. Access to the fast-moving traffic is limited and there is no frontage development permitted. Sector 22 and the first sector to be developed, is located

---
[17] *Sampark, An official website of Chandigarh Administration*, http://164.100.147.7/esampark_web/living,12 September 2004
[18] Julian Beinart (2002), Chandigarh 1999: Diagrams and Realties, *Celebrating Chandigarh*, Mapin Publishers Ltd., p.146

right below the business civic centre sectors. The sector is surrounded by V3 avenues intended for rapid traffic and bisected by the V4 bazaar street. The V5 loop road serves as the primary traffic distributor and is reserved for future commercial use. With this type of transportation network of 7 Vs, Le Corbusier also introduced the idea of green spaces running throughout the city. In addition to the major park areas, there are park belts running through the residential areas and furnishing local recreation areas and sites for schools and community buildings

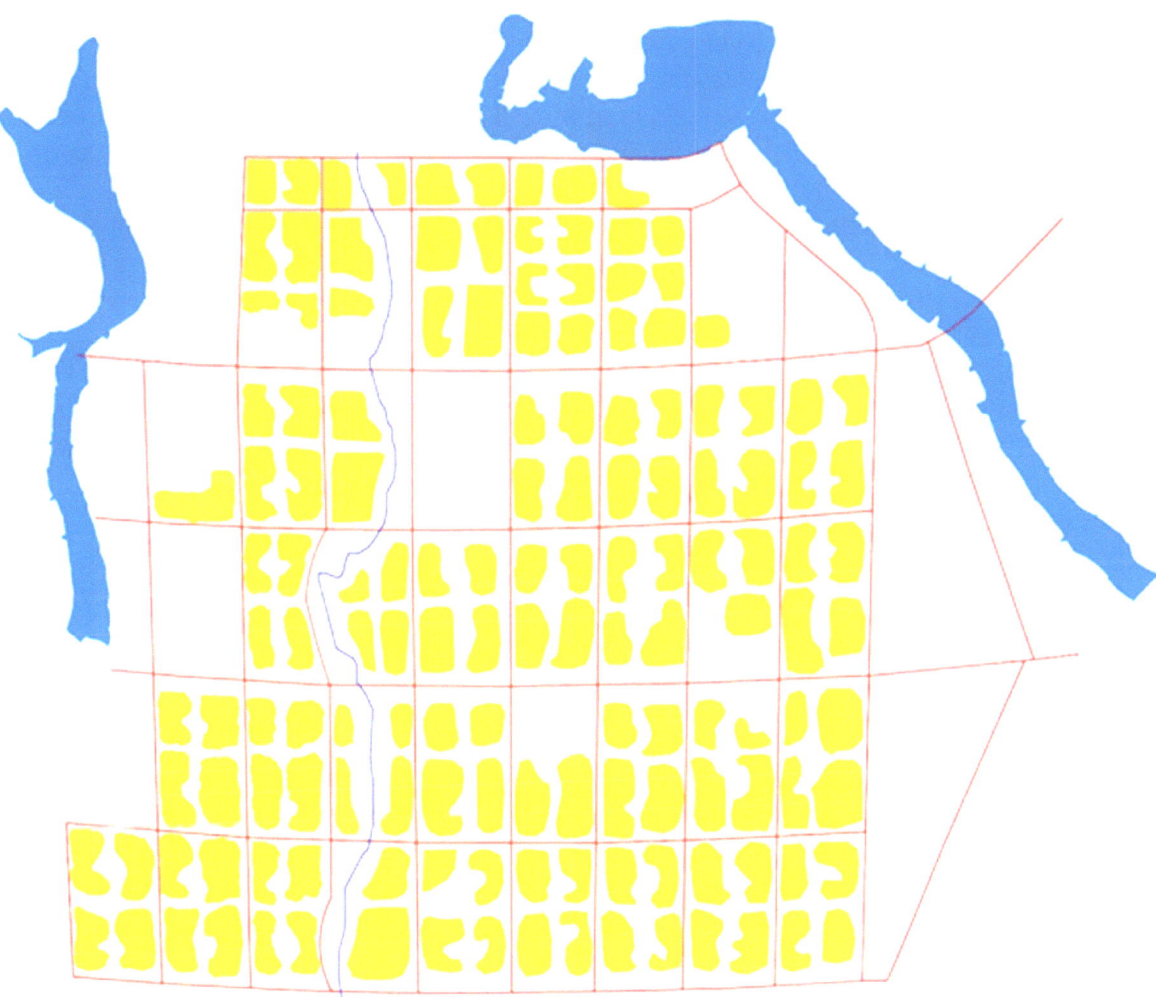

Figure 3.14 Living and housing of Chandigarh in sectors

3.10 Movement

"From his earliest studies in urbanism, Le Corbusier had identified the motor car as a central factor of modern town planning. The 7 Vs act in the town plan as the blood stream, the lymph system and the respiratory system act in the town plan, as the blood-stream, the lymph system and the respiratory system act in biology"[19]. The plan of the city is a system of traffic (see Fig. 3.12) separation based on a scheme of organization which Le Corbusier termed "*les Sept Voics*"[20] (the seven Vs). He used these concepts in his post-war planning schemes. The seven Vs separate traffic into a series of seven categories containing every level of circulation from arterial roads to apartment house corridors. The V1 represents the national trunk road coming from Delhi on one side and from Shimla on the other. The V2 forms the main horizontal axis of the town, intersecting the street leading to the Capitol Complex. This street borders the business centre and intersects at the lower edge of the present city (another projected V2).

The V2 boulevards were designed ultimately to employ a system to separate lanes, which would accommodate all classes of traffic, fast- and slow-moving vehicles, cycles and pedestrians. Surrounding the residential sectors and forming the grid pattern of the city are the V3s. These are the streets reserved for fast-moving motor traffic. Bisecting each street is a V4 or shopping street.

Intersecting the V4 at two points is a V5, a loop distributing slow traffic within the confines of the sector and connecting with the adjoining sector. The extremities of the network are the V6 paths leading to the doors of the houses. The V7 paths are designed to carry pedestrians and cyclists through park belts of the city, which contain the schools and playing fields. These paths also go underneath the V3 roads and link sectors, making it theoretically possible to traverse the entire city on foot via the park.

3.11 Built Form

As per the usage of building types, the built form can be categorized into the following:

3.11.1 Government buildings

The government buildings include the Capitol Complex, which include the Secretariat, place for justice and the assembly hall. According to Jim Antoniou, "His main concept for the Capitol was to tap into the cultural traditions of India, while expressing the values of the mid-twentieth century. To achieve this, he used a variable balance of forms, with columns, terraces, ramps and screens in a range of colours. Yet, in this vast complex of space, he related each building intimately to its own approach, entry, solid and void elements and even texture."[21]

---

[19] Prasad Sunand (1987), Le Corbusier: *Architect of the Century*, Arts council of Great Britain, Mansell U.K. Limited, p.287
[20] *e-Sampark*, *An official website of Chandigarh Administration*, http://164.100.147.7/esampark_web/city_living,12 September 2004
[21] http://www.findarticles.com/p/articles/mi_m3575/is_1273_213/ai_99215199/pg_2

Description of Chandigarh   45

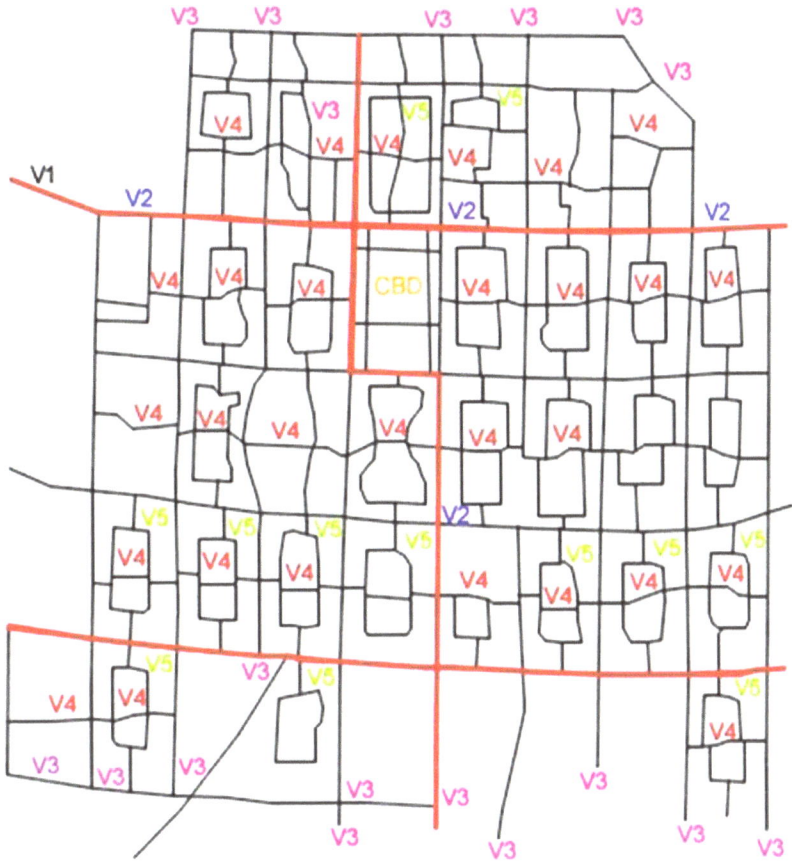

Figure 3.15 Hierarchy of road system in Chandigarh

These buildings were grouped amidst a big plaza intended for public use. It occupies the uppermost part of the grid which is isolated and detached in relation to whole of the city. The Chandigarh government has fenced off most of the individual buildings of the Capitol Complex due to security reasons resulting into an isolated plaza. Further Jim Antoniou points that "Walking through the desolate spaces between the buildings, with their rough and worn surfaces, the Capitol conveys an uncomfortable impression of a living ruin, frozen since its inception."[22]

---

[22] http://www.findarticles.com/p/articles/mi_m3575/is_1273_213/ai_99215199/pg_2

3.11.2 Housing

The primary housing idea in Chandigarh was to establish one- or two-storey block houses. The government housing was the first to be built. The housing is divided into 13 types based on income level. About 80% of housing was in the lower income group (LIG).

Different economic levels had different forms of accommodation. The next range is a two-storey flat. There are also the two-storey row houses falling into the eight and nine types. From the type seven onwards, semi-detached houses were built and all the higher ranks were provided with detached bungalows with front and back gardens.

3.11.3 Commercial buildings

The Commerce Centre is the heart of Chandigarh; the buildings are grouped around a pedestrian precinct which caters to the retail activity. Here, the residents do shop, lounge around or simply relax in the beautiful surroundings. Big showrooms and departmental stores cater to the needs of shoppers. Evenings here are generally found bustling with crowds. The ultimate lightning effects at night are a must-watch."[23]

3.12 **Plots in Chandigarh**

In 1960 the residential plots were sold to the public for a price fixed by the government. The plots fetched a huge price instantly due to the greater demand for housing. Due to the on-going demand for plots, the Chandigarh government decided to release limited number of plots through auction. "The highest average price fetched by each plot category in one auction was used as a basis for fixing the minimum reserve price for a like plot in a subsequent one"[24].

According to Madhu Sarin, "the high demand for sale of plots was attributed to Le Corbusier's views of good urbanism. The land policy was reassessed in 1970 to habilitate people from the low-income group at a price which included the cost for development of land. Finally, the land policy adopted for Chandigarh was to limit the plot size to 500 square yards. The restriction of plot sizes was kept in mind to increase the density. For commercial purpose, the Chandigarh government decided to construct all the buildings and then sell them. The individual plots were also sold to developers who would build commercial buildings according to strict architectural control. Due to the location of the industrial zone, the land was sold below the development price to attract prospective investors.

---

[23] http://www.1upindia.com/states/chandigarh/
[24] Sarin Madhu, *Urban Planning in Third World*, Mansell Publishing Limited, 1982, p.83

3.13 Open Spaces

The most important part of the city was developed on an eroded stream bed running through the city. The area, which is known as the Valley of Leisure, contains a gorge 5–6 metres deep, which varies in width from 100 to 300 metres. The most important recreational area in the city is the artificial lake created by forming a dam on the river Sukhmo Cho in the east of the Capitol Complex. This dam formed an extension of the Capitol Boulevard. Although not a part of the original plan, a park has subsequently been proposed for the area to the northeast of the Capitol Complex. A private club with swimming pool and other sports facilities is provided in this area. The trees in Chandigarh give each sector a different identity as one moves from one sector to another. According to Sunand Prasad, "Like New Delhi, but unlike the traditional city, Chandigarh is full of trees; trees are carefully chosen to blossom at different times, in different colours, in different streets. They make for a strange feeling of never arriving, almost as if they were hiding from the wide main roads; the setback low mass of buildings behind the walls of the sectors."[25]

3.14 Summary

The city of Chandigarh was born out of political necessity as the previous capital of Punjab, Lahore, was lost to Pakistan in 1947. Initially designed by Mayer, later Le Corbusier designed the Master plan for Chandigarh. Le Corbusier incorporated modern planning in the city. Primary emphasis was given to vehicular traffic. The city had the self-contained units called the sectors. The Master plan according to Jane Drew was of poetic significance.

Overall it was a modern living for a modern country. The emergence of Chandigarh as an urban entity highlighted the idea of self-financing, which contributed the funding of city building. The idea of self-financing proved beneficial in a developing country like India. Chandigarh created an impact in India as the first planned city in post-independent India, which saw the emergence of industrial towns like G.S.F.C townships in Baroda and Bhubaneshwar.

---

[25] Prasad Sunand (1987), *Le Corbusier: Architect of the Century*, Arts Council of Great Britain, Mansell U.K. Limited, p.22

4
Description of Gandhinagar

4.1 Introduction

The state of Bombay was divided in 1960, and the state of Gujarat was formed. The need for a capital city was felt, and Gandhinagar came into existence. Gandhinagar was named after Mahatma Gandhi, regarded as Father of the Nation in India.

4.2 Political Background

After the separation of the bilingual Bombay state, a separate state of Gujarat came into existence on the 1st of May 1960. "The chief minister designate Jivraj Mehta had declared on the 19th of March 1960 that the state should have a new capital city to be named Gandhinagar, on a site about 24 km north of Ahmedabad."

4.3 Finance

Bombay state (now Maharashtra state) had agreed to contribute nearly 2 million US dollars[1] to build the new capital. The rest of the finance was provided by the state budget and state revenues.

The estimated cost of the first phase of the project (1965–1971 when the government shifted to Gandhinagar) was 75 million US dollars[2].

As in Chandigarh town planning scheme, mechanism of Gandhinagar was based on self-financing. It is a people-friendly land management tool practiced extensively in Gujarat state. This scheme in turn helps the city with land development funding its infrastructure and road construction. Various other methods have been adopted in implementing the development plan; one example is the Build, Operate and Transfer (BOT) model. The balance amount was met from the state govt. grants, loans and the loans from HUDCO (Housing Development Cooperative).

The Gandhinagar Town Planning Department is also looking at other sources of revenue generation such as:
 1. Development charges, sewerage, road and infrastructure charges

---

[1] 1 USD = Rs. 42.30 Calculated as on 10.08.04, http://www.xe.com/ucc/.
[2] 1 USD = Rs. 42.30 Calculated as on 10.08.04, http://www.xe.com/ucc/

2. Services and amenities fees, incremental contribution by the land owners in town planning schemes for the serviced land provided, advertising fees, parking fees, etc.

4.4　Site Selection

The site chosen for Gandhinagar measures 5738 hectares and is situated on the banks of the Sabarmati river. It comprises of 30 sectors. The city was first planned on the western bank of the river Sabarmati. The site was levelled with a gentle slope from northeast to southwest.

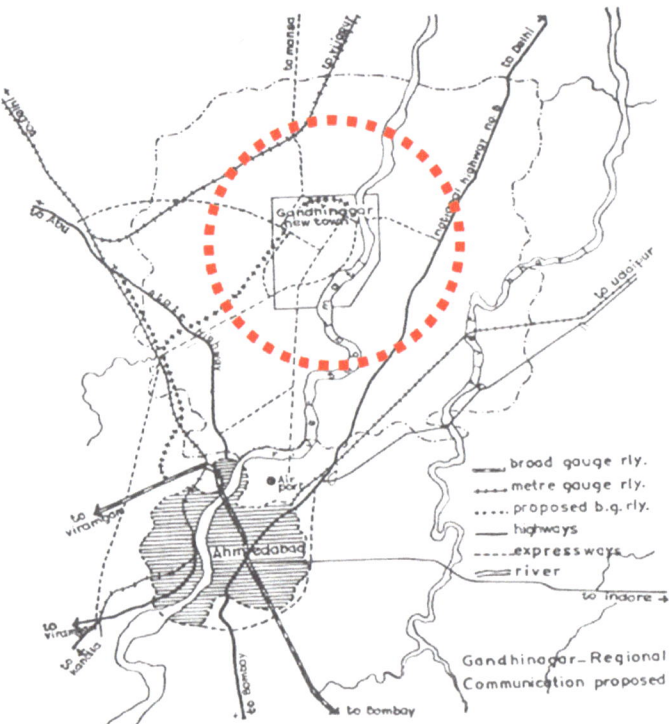

Figure 4.1 Gandhinagar regional communication proposed [*Source*: The Building of Gandhinagar, New Capital of Gujarat, P.M. Apte]

The soil was classified as being mostly sandy loam, which was suitable for building construction work. The site is conveniently located in close proximity to major state highways, and the existing Ahmedabad airport is midway between the sites. The approach roads from Khodiyar railway station and Ahmedabad join towards the south, forming an entrance to the city. The character of the city was influenced by various factors such as its regional setting and site conditions.

4.5 Climate

The climate is similar to that of Ahmedabad, with a maximum average temperature of 40°C [3] in April and a minimum average temperature of 29°C [4] in December.

4.6 Design Team

The design team for Gandhinagar was set up under the Public Works Department (PWD). The project was executed by architects and planners from the state town planning department.

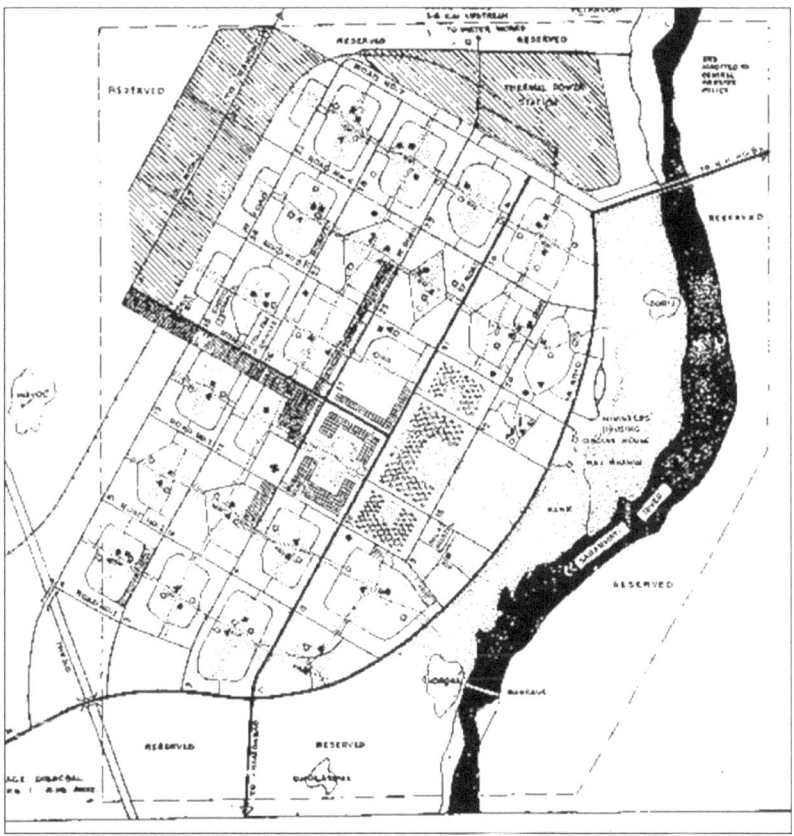

Figure 4.2 Gandhinagar town concept [*Source*: The Building of Gandhinagar, New Capital of Gujarat, P.M. Apte]

---

[3] http://www.weather.com/weather/climatology/daily/INXX0048?climoMonth=4,
[4] http://www.weather.com/weather/climatology/daily/INXX0048?climoMonth=12

4.7 Gandhinagar Master Plan

The central aim of the Gandhinagar master plan (Fig 4.3) was to create a balanced and healthy community socially as well as economically. According to architect and planner P.M. Apte *"the residential communities were planned so that everyone is within six minutes walking distance of the local, social and shopping centre where the cycle pedestrian ways are located."*[5]

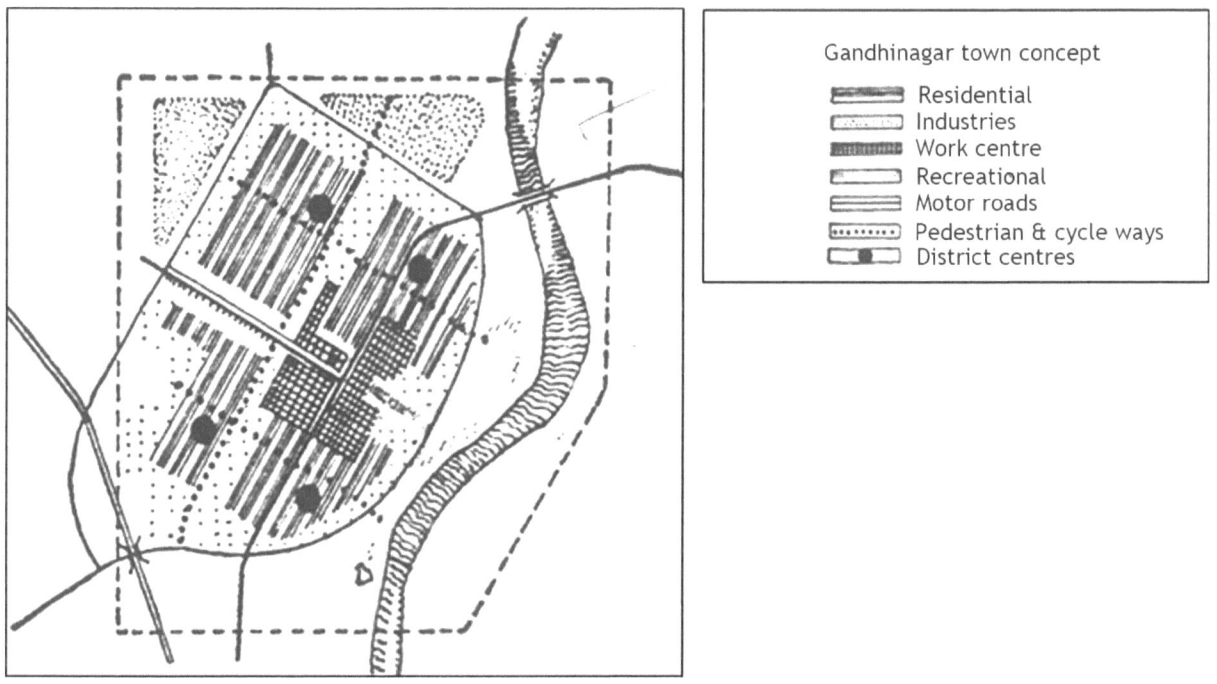

Figure 4.3 Gandhinagar Master Plan [*Source*: The Building of Gandhinagar, New Capital of Gujarat, P.M. Apte]

The principal employer in the city would be the state government and as such, the city would cater largely to the government employees on a site of 135 acres.

"The new town was planned for a population of 1.5 lakh over a period of 25 years, with a further possible expansion to 3 lakh by the end of 50 years."[6]

The living areas, work areas and the recreational areas were interrelated in the town plan. This means that the time spent by the people in journey to work areas and the recreational areas have been minimized.

---

[5] Apte P.M., Gandhinagar: New Capital City of Gujarat, p.46, India, Power Publishers
[6] Apte P.M, Gandhinagar: New Capital City of Gujarat, India, Power Publishers

4.8 Zoning

The zoning in Gandhinagar can be classified as:
1. Capitol Complex and government offices
2. Light industrial area
3. City Centre
4. Public institutional area
5. Shopping, commercial and warehousing areas

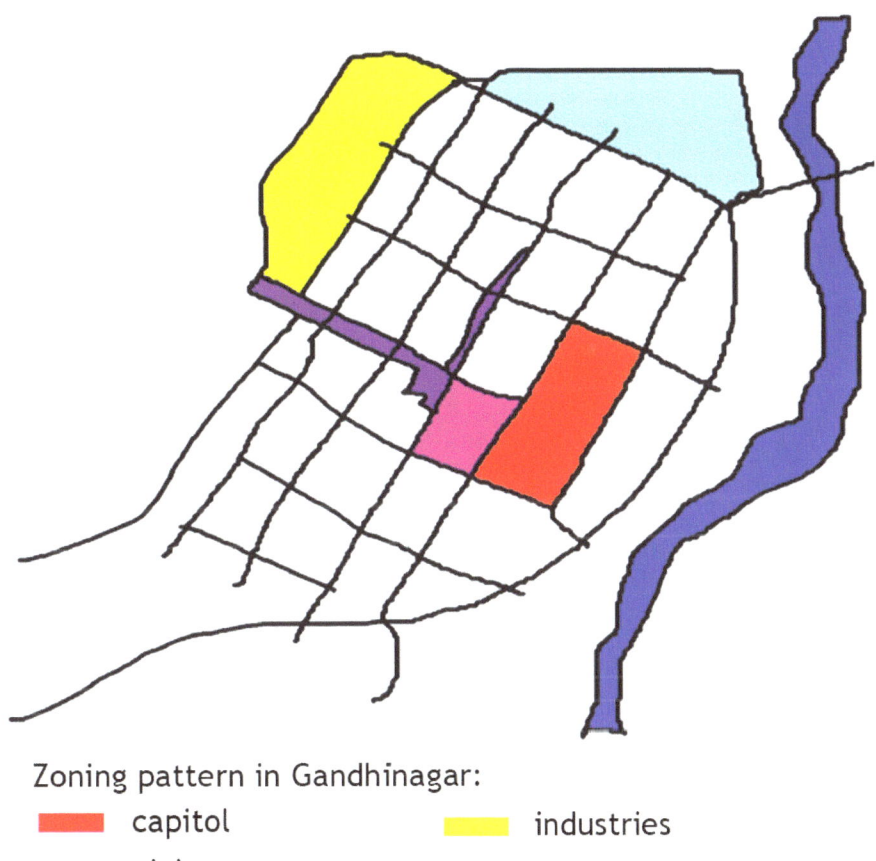

Figure 4.4 Zoning of Gandhinagar

4.8.1 Capitol Complex and government offices

The most important work place in the city is the Capitol Complex and government offices. It is located centrally in Sector 10 which covers an area of 185 acres. It is ideally located in close proximity to the river front in a natural setting. The Capitol Complex (see Figs. 4.5 and 4.6) comprises the Secretariat, the Legislative Assembly, High Court and offices of the heads of the department.

Provision for light industrial areas is provided at the north end of the city. The proposed area chalked for the industrial area is about 297 acres. Light industries are classified as technical workshops which could run in close the image of Gandhinagar as an administrative capital; it also helps in keeping the city's diversified economic base.

Figure 4.5 Model of Sachivalaya [*Source*: The Building of Gandhinagar, New Capital of Gujarat, P.M. Apte]

Figure 4.6 View of Sachivalaya

4.8.2 City Centre

The city centre as proposed in the master plan is about 185 acres, used for major civic, cultural and business facilities of the city. The bus station is in close proximity to the city centre.

4.8.3 Public institution area

The public institutions are situated alongside a crescent road covering approximately 123 acres. Also accommodated are public and residential schools. An educational environment is envisioned close to the waterfront in close proximity with nature.

4.9 Morphology of the Sector

The residential groups in Gandhinagar have a basic fundamental resemblance with the community structure of "pols"[7] (narrow lanes) as obtained in almost all of the cities in Gujarat (see Fig. 4.7).

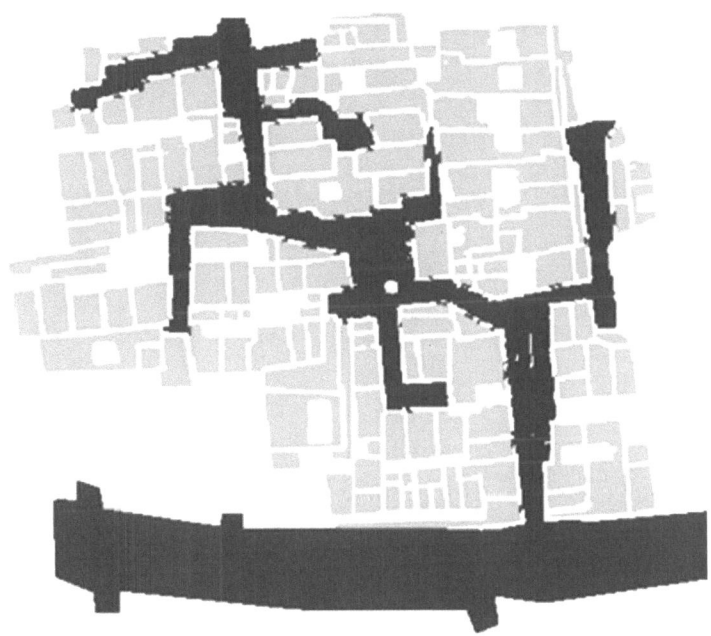

Figure 4.7 Community structure in "pols" found in old cities of Gujarat [*Source*: The Building of Gandhinagar, New Capital of Gujarat, P.M. Apte]

---

[7] Apte P.M., Gandhinagar: New Capital City of Gujarat, p.53, India, Power Publishers

56   Master Planning Indian Cities: Achieving Urban Renaissance

As in these "pols", houses in the residential groups are grouped along a street, which opens out to open places for social interaction between people of all ages and also for acts as play space for children. The street pattern in the residential groups is informal, free of fast-moving traffic and serving only local traffic generated by the residential groups.

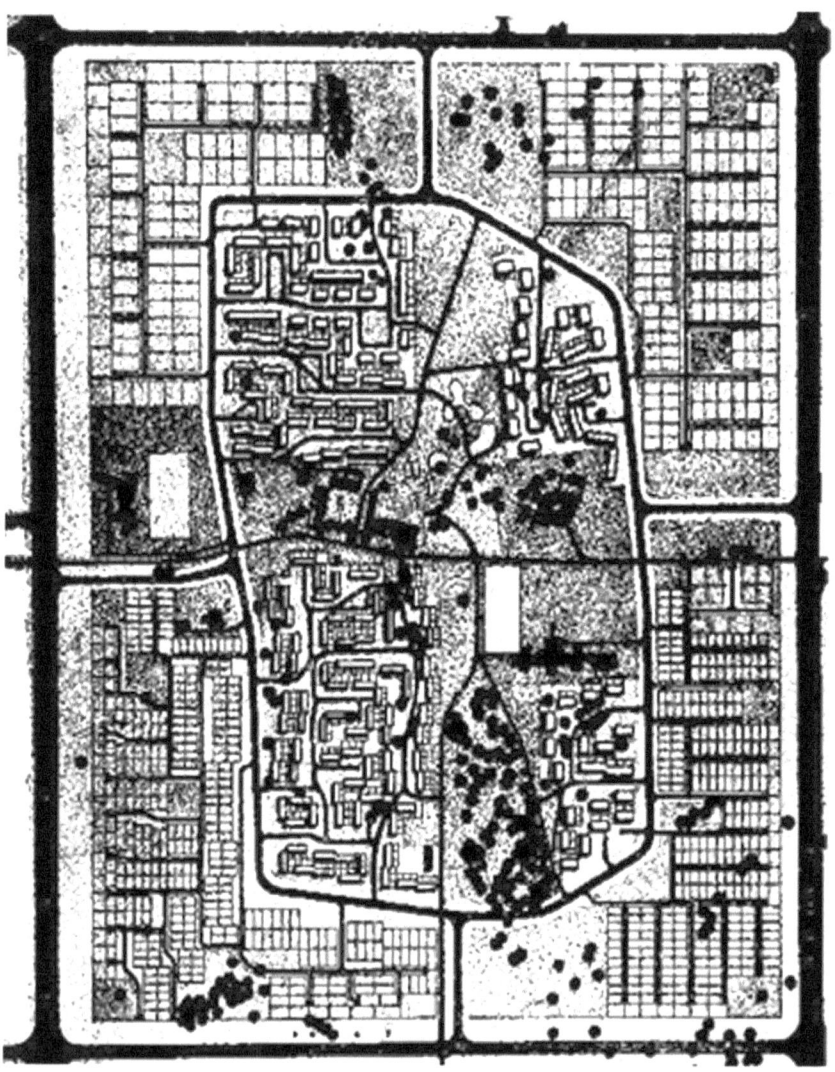

Figure 4.8 Layout of sectors in Gandhinagar [*Source*: The Building of Gandhinagar, New Capital of Gujarat, P.M. Apte]

"The clustering of various communities grouped in the form of 'pols' which is a common feature in the cities of Gujarat also evolved due to the consideration of safety and security. These 'pols' act as the second line of defense in case the city wall gave way.

A typical 'pole' was a narrow street bounded by residential buildings with gates at either end of this street where it joined the main roads of the town. Once these two gates were closed it was difficult to enter the area. Within these pols, we find the community structure grouped on the basis of cast or kinship consideration. The 'pole' had its own small civic square with a place of worship and also a permanent source of water supply which was normally a well."[8]

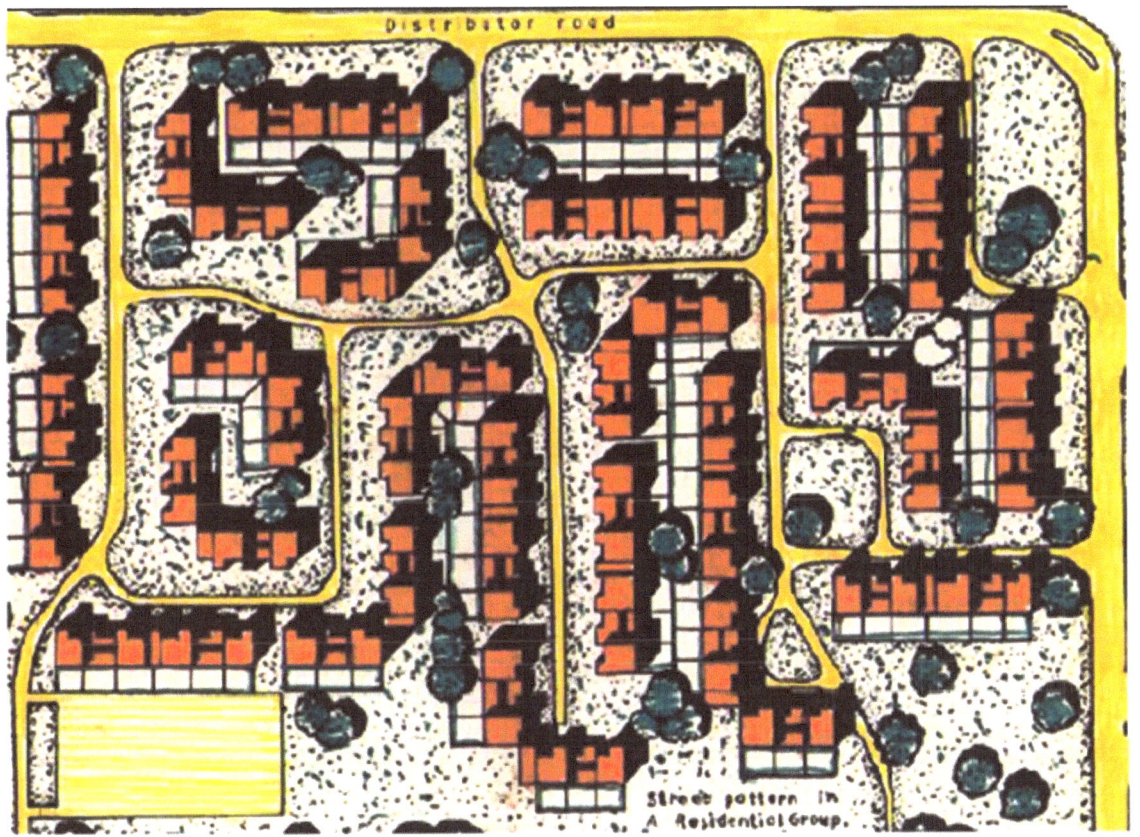

Figure 4.9 Interior layout of sector in Gandhinagar [*Source*: The Building of Gandhinagar, New Capital of Gujarat, P.M. Apte]

---

[8] Apte P.M., Gandhinagar: New Capital City of Gujarat, p.53, India, Power Publishers

As one walks amidst few of the sectors of Gandhinagar, there is a blissful feeling, walking amidst the shady trees and meandering streets which lead to the various clusters of residences. The poles are immensely helpful in reflecting the community structure of the Gujarati community.

In the master plan, shopping facilities have been provided in all residential sectors, district centres and the main town centre. In the residential sectors two or three categories of plots for shops have been provided which were sold to the public. However, in order to act as a catalyst, incentive was given to the shopping centres to start; and for the convenience of the people residing in the sectors, the government has constructed the smallest category of shops in each sector. These shopping booths house all the essential shops and services required for each sector. A dispensary provides the necessary medical aid to the residents of the private sector.

All the community facilities such as primary and secondary schools, shopping centre, community centre, parks and playgrounds, dispensary, police station, rang manch and site for religious purposes are provided along the cycle–pedestrian way which forms continuous green spaces in each sector.

On the basis of anticipated age structure of the population in the new city and based on the age structure as observed in Ahmedabad, there is a provision of a primary school for 3000–4000 population and a secondary school for 10,000–12000 population. Average standard for open space is about 4–5 acres per 1000 population, excluding school play areas and city level parks.

An area of about 500 square metres per 1,000 population is provided for retail shopping. A district centre is provided for a group of four or five residential communities. The population served by each district centre is about 40,000 to 50,000. It has shops of selective nature, restaurant, cinema, dispensary, police station, post office, banks, club and playing fields for organized games.

4.10 Movement

The patterns of main city roads are based on the grid pattern, generally rectangular, measuring 1000 × 750 m. The roads have been oriented to run 30 degrees north and 60 degrees north of east to avoid direct facing sun during journeys to work areas.

This road orientation ensures that buildings are screened from the sun. The river side road follows the natural features and forms a crescent, skirting the recreational area along the river front. The peripheral roads and the access road to the city centre are 65 meters wide. Roads to the government offices from southwest and northwest and the crescent road are 100 m wide: rest of the main roads are 45 m wide.

4.10.1 Classification of roads

"Gandhinagar has 'letter roads' (CH, CHH and JA) and 'number roads' (1, 2 and 3). The letter roads run parallel across the city perpendicular to the number roads. The number and letter roads intersect each other forming a grid; each block or square in the grid is given a sector number. Each intersection is marked by signal names such as CH1, CH2, CH3 or JA1, JA2."[9]

Figure 4.10 View of Crescent Road

The cycle pedestrian ways are part of the traffic system adopted for the new city. The traffic system comprises a grid (1000 × 750 m) of motor roads and another grid approximately (1000 × 750 m) of cycle pedestrian ways for the residents of each sector. The main town roads have been so oriented to suit the climatic needs of the built form. The alignment of the distributor road within the sector for residential quarters has been correctly oriented in accordance to suit the best possible climatic conditions.

---

[9] http://india.asinah.net/en/wikipedia/g/ga/gandhinagar.html

Figure 4.11 Urban structure of Gandhinagar sectors

4.11 Built Form

The built form in Gandhinagar can be categorized into the following:

4.11.1 Government buildings

The groups of buildings are placed near the central edge of the grid. The buildings are fronted on a linear axis. The buildings give a grand appeal and the frontage is lined with ornamental garden. The placement of the buildings on a strong linear axis is in some ways comparable to the arrangement of historical buildings such as the Taj Mahal in Agra. The buildings are a landmark which highlights the governance of the state capital.

4.11.2 Housing

Residential housing in Gandhinagar varies from individual bungalows to three-storey flats. Government housing comprises eight categories of housing which are based on pay scale. Each residential community has a cycle–pedestrian way. Major facilities such as primary and secondary schools, shopping centres, health and community centres are located along the cycle–pedestrian way, making them easily accessible without having to cross main vehicular roads.

The smallest apartments for government employee are in three-storey flats. In the design of housing, care has been taken to see that while a person on ground floor gets about 16 feet of garden in the front and 20 feet of garden in the back, the families on the upper floor gets an attached open terrace in addition to the minimum accommodation provided. In addition, the housing has been designed in the form of row houses so that considerable economy can be achieved with effective land use.

4.11.3 Commercial buildings

The commercial activity in Gandhinagar is catered by the use of vertical mixed use. The buildings are lined on the main road in city centre which provides front parking and encourage commercial activity along the street. The rest of the floor pace is used to utilize as office space.

4.12 Plots in Gandhinagar

There are eight categories of housing plots, ranging from 135 sq. m to 1600 sq. m. Each residential community has four categories of private plots and government quarters to achieve a balanced social and economic structure. Mixing occupation based on residential units prevented the isolation of government colonies and residences.

In order to achieve economy in development costs and facilitate maximum benefit from social integration, the residential units are planned in a compact form; consequently, larger open spaces and playgrounds are available and accessible to the people within walking distance.

4.13 Open Spaces

The central vista in front of the Sachivalaya complex is developed as an ornamental garden in addition to a large town park along the river front. A barrage is proposed along the river, resulting in a long-elongated lake. The lake measures a depth of 5 feet to 15 feet making opportunities for boating and fishing. Thus, a lake surrounded by parks and gardens will be within the reach of all the inhabitants. The residential communities will have access to the town park by continuous greenways accommodating pedestrian way. Gandhinagar has a theme park for children, and a major tourist attraction developed on 25 acres of land attracting visitors from surrounding districts.

4.14 Summary

The capital city of Gujarat, Gandhinagar, came into existence when the states of Maharashtra and Gujarat were formed. It was named after the Father of the Nation Mahatma Gandhi.

The Master plan of Gandhinagar was designed by Indian architects and planners. The urban grain of Gandhinagar is comprised of sectors, and the interior layout of these sectors was based on traditional Gujarati towns. The traditional layout was compact, closely knit and the streets were used for a variety of purposes.

The main objective of Gandhinagar was to achieve a well-balanced and healthy society. The master plan had an important feature which was to reduce time travel to work from residences. The roads were oriented to avoid harsh climatic considerations. The city was funded mainly through self-finance.

The planning of Gandhinagar shows the relevance of context and attempts to incorporate certain traditional Indian planning layouts.

5
Analysing Chandigarh and Gandhinagar

5.1   The Site

The sites for the two capital cities, Gandhinagar and Chandigarh, were located next to the river, and on flat sites. The site area for Gandhinagar is 14,174 acres, situated next to the Sabarmati River. The site next to river provided a pleasant natural environment; in addition, the site was suitable for recreational purposes such as boating.

The site chosen for Chandigarh was between two rivers, Sukhmo Cho and the Patiali Rao, with the Himalayas as a backdrop. It covers an area of 28,158 acres.

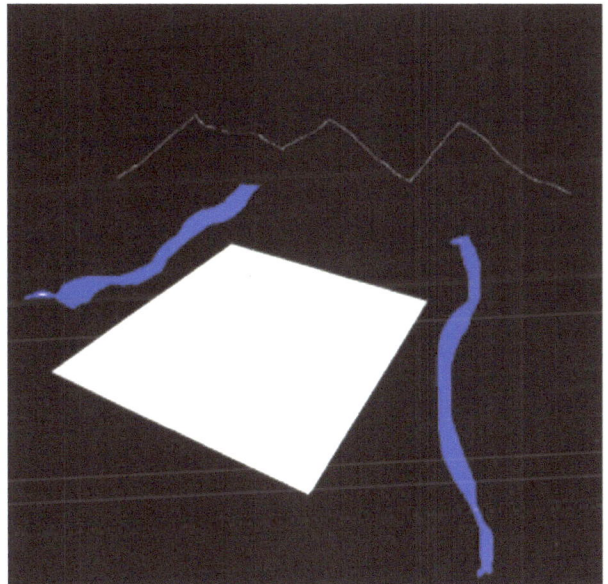
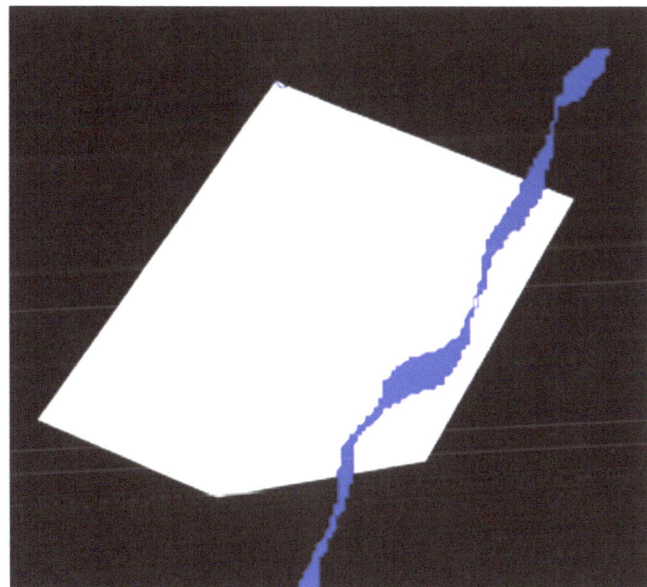

Figure 5.1 Chandigarh – Site and its features   **Figure 5.2** Gandhinagar – Site and its features

The two rivers would form natural boundaries to east and west, allowing the city to expand towards the south. The main criterion for site selection of the Chandigarh was to create a modern town which was devoid of any past, according to J.L. Nehru, the then Prime Minister of India.

The site chosen for Gandhinagar was based on its regional link; one of these being proximity to the city of Ahmedabad, located at a distance of 24 km. Gandhinagar is served by major roads from relatively all directions, and can be termed as "well connected" in terms of road networking.

5.2 The Master Plan

Mathew Nowicki proposed the original master plan of Chandigarh: it can be described as *organic* layout which was in the form of a "*leaf plan*". After the death of Mathew Nowicki, the master plan was entrusted to Albert Mayer. Mayer designed the plan of Chandigarh on the basis of superblocks which were curved at certain places. It had elements of American planning theories: "the neighbourhood unit, superblock and sector had all been used in a number of American projects, of which Baldwin Hills (1941) by Clarence Stein – who was consulted on Chandigarh by Mayer – was the intermediate ancestor for the Mayer plan"[1].

After a short period, the administrators of Chandigarh entrusted the plan of Chandigarh to Le Corbusier. Le Corbusier designed the master plan which did not change significantly from Mayer's but added an orthogonal grid which would support fast-moving vehicular traffic.

The master plan of Gandhinagar was prepared by an Indian architect. The urban grain of Gandhinagar is comprised of 'sectors' which were part of an orthogonal grid. The master plan of Gandhinagar was designed to developed as a socially balanced town, and yet to serve the administrative needs of the state.

5.3 Finance Planning

Gandhinagar was initially funded by the governments of Maharashtra and Gujarat. Later on, the Gandhinagar town planning department adopted the policy of self-financing.

Apart from a self-financing scheme to carry out city development, the town planning development of Gandhinagar adopted the BOT (Build Operate and Transfer) scheme, under which land was given for development as specified by the town planning department. The developers then carry out the building activity and in turn have the right to transfer the building to a third party.

The inspiration for the self-financing scheme came from Le Corbusier, who was responsible for designing the master plan of Chandigarh. According to Corbusier, providing good infrastructure was an essential ingredient for city development. In the case of Chandigarh the high land prices can be attributed to good urbanism, and in many ways seen as a success story for future city development.

---

[1] Prasad Sunand (1987), *Le Corbusier – Architect of the Century* – Arts Council of Great Britain, Mansell U.K. Limited, p.287

5.4 Zoning Pattern

The location of various zones in the city of Chandigarh was based on the analogy of human form: the head being the Capitol Complex and heart, the City Centre; the hands being the industrial area, its veins and nerves the roads.

In Gandhinagar the zoning is based on climatic and geographical considerations. The Capitol Complex and offices are located on the southeast, which is the direction of the prevailing breeze (see Fig. 5.3). The City Centre and the commercial area are situated on the northeast side of the city. The industrial zone lies to the north of the city.

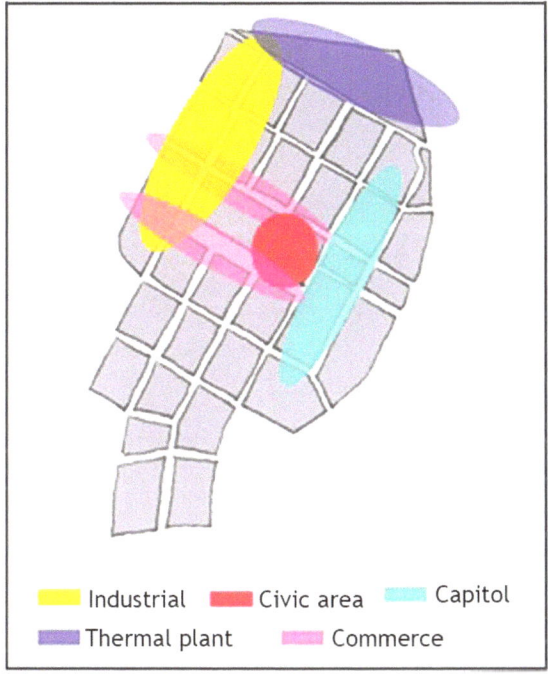

Figure 5.3 Gandhinagar – Zoning pattern

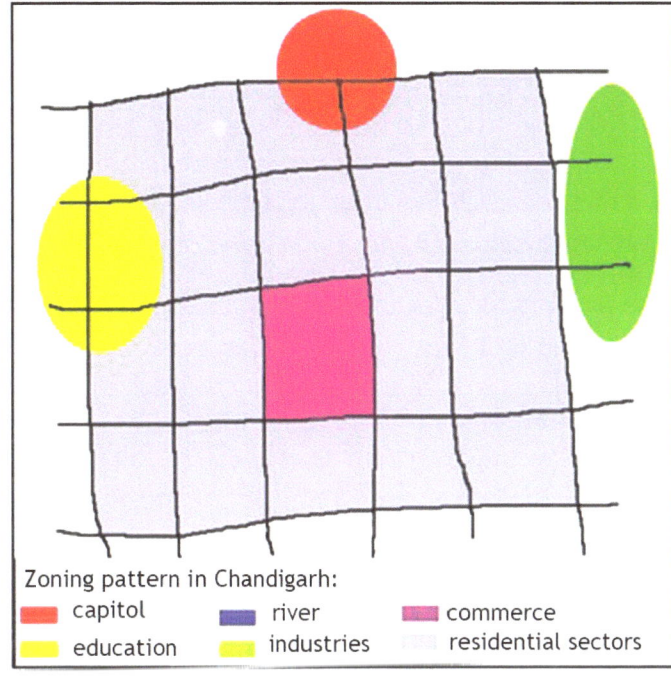

Figure 5.4 Chandigarh – Zoning pattern

The zoning pattern in Chandigarh and Gandhinagar represents distinct functional districts. Functional districts in India were non-existent until the development of Chandigarh and Gandhinagar. A typical Indian city is often compact which promoted social interaction and to some extent also catered to the retail activity.

In Chandigarh, the focal point of the city, located on the upper edge, is an area reserved for government buildings such as the High Court, the Assembly, the Secretariat and the Museum (see Fig. 5.4). The Capitol

Complex is a pedestrian, and all the motor traffic is separated, coming through roads below the plaza, leading to the parking area. According to architect B.V. Doshi, "there is nothing urban about Chandigarh. The only urban design is the Capitol Complex. The city is like a temple without an idol. The only place which caters to civic activity apart from the commercial centre is the Capitol Complex".[2] The Capitol Complex with its big wide plaza was intended to be a civic area. Due to its distance from the main residential enclave, the surrounding buildings being predominantly of government use, the plaza seems to be under-utilized.

In Gandhinagar, located centrally in one sector covering 185 acres is the most important part of the city, comprising the Capitol Complex, the Secretariat, the Legislative Assembly, the High Court and the offices of heads of department.

In Gandhinagar the planners decided to have an economic base and yet maintain the character of the city, which was of an administrative nature. Light industry was proposed to make it lively and to help maintain the diversity of the city; the establishment of technical workshops in conjunction with the technical institute was proposed on the northeast part of the city, an area of 296 acres.

In Chandigarh the industries are located on the eastern end of the city, buffered by an area of trees which formed the green belt. The location of the industries was chosen next to the rail terminus to allow easy access of raw materials. Strict architectural controls were established for the development of the industrial area which provides an economic base for the city.

According to Sunand Prasad, "In addition, zoning precludes the mix of activities essential for rich and complex street life. Chandigarh was in fact given its own vision of Connaught Place in the business sector whose vast empty plaza Le Corbusier disingenuously described as the traditional Indian *chowk*"[3].

The City Centre in Gandhinagar is used for the civic, administrative and cultural functions of the city. The area covered by the City Centre is 75 hectares. The retail area is spread along the intersection of the city's two major central roads. Wholesale and warehousing are located at the north-western part of the city, which keeps heavy traffic vehicles such as mini trucks and trucks at the periphery of the city.

Sector 17 of Chandigarh is the central business district, which is also the Civic Centre; it is located in the centre of the city. The commercial centre offers a variety of shops, banks, library and cinema, thus attracting a lot of visitors; and other aspects also make it the liveliest part of the city.

The public institutions in Gandhinagar, such as public schools and colleges with residential facilities, are located along the Crescent Road. Chandigarh is the seat of Punjab University; all the university buildings are located on the western end in Sector 14, in the parklands, and the horizontal and the vertical roads divide the area into sectors, measuring 1000 × 750 m having an area of 185 acres. These sectors accommodate a residential community of 7000 people, and provide facilities such as schools, shopping, playgrounds and parks. The residential

---

[2] Doshi B.V. (1989), Indian Architect and Builder, January 1999, p.89
[3] Prasad Sunand (1987), *Le Corbusier – Architect of the Century* – Arts Council of Great Britain, Mansell U.K. Limited, p.281

quarters are arranged in sectors. In Chandigarh each sector, measuring 1200 × 800 m, contains a market centre, health centre, school and park.

5.5 Morphology of the City

The morphology of the city as proposed by Albert Mayer (see Fig. 5.5) reflects certain hierarchy of plots subdivision, which are placed closely. In terms of city experience, the morphology of the route becomes interesting and gives a leisurely experience to the inhabitants, which in some ways is a characteristic of temple towns of Southern India. For instance, the routes were circumvented and the urban structure was of compact nature. One often took the route which was lined with market streets and the final destination being the temple, which was the climax in terms of the visual experience and given an important hierarchy (refer Fig. 2.8).

The morphology of Chandigarh as proposed by Le Corbusier shows the city form in terms of sectors which are often rectilinear in nature. In terms of routes, it offers the inhabitants a clear path and one often misses the enrichment along those routes. The sectors are often uniform in nature and identical (Fig. 5.6).

Figure 5.5 Initial plan of the city as proposed by Albert Mayer

Figure 5.6 Plan of the city as proposed by Le Corbusier

Overall the city experience is thus missed out due to the monotony of the street edge and frontage, which is a result of the uniformity in the arrangement of sectors. However, the city gives rise to multiple vistas confronted by big roundabouts which act as nodes.

The city form of Gandhinagar is tilted due to the proximity of the river and allowing natural breeze to benefit the city. The city form is characterized by sectors which are non-uniform in some places. The routes however tend to be monotonous and, in some places, enable the inhabitants the much-needed city experience.

The city on the whole is comprised of sectors which are more uniform and identical. One often gets the feeling of being lost due to the identical subdivision of these sectors. The city form however gives rise to multiple vistas, which is directed towards the river (Fig. 5.7).

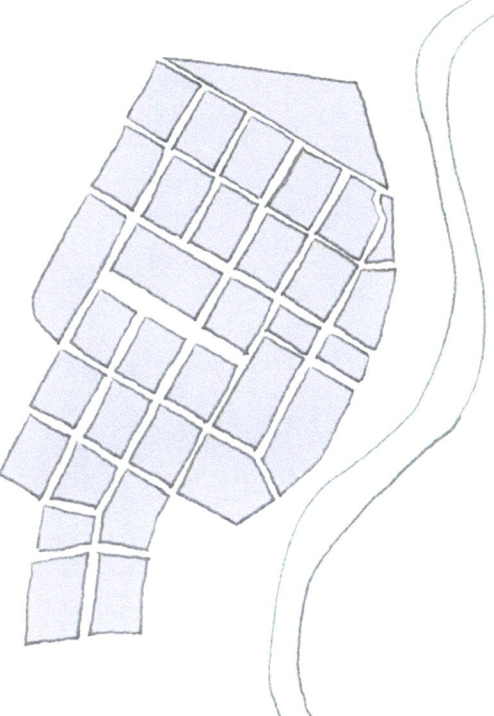

Figure 5.7 Plan of the city as proposed by P. M. Apte

5.6   Morphology of the Sector

The physical structure of Chandigarh is based on an orthogonal grid iron pattern comprising of sectors. These 48 sectors make up the basic form of the city; each sector measures about 1200 × 800 m. "The grid dimensions are derived from the optimum distance between bus stops and/or crossovers into sectors from the main roads, which occur at 400 m, as well as to notions, substantially developed before the new team took over, about the size of population necessary to sustain a degree of self sufficiency In the sectors"[4].

Each sector according to Le Corbusier is a *self-contained unit* (Fig. 5.8) which would provide basic amenities such as school, shopping facilities for residences and parks. These self-contained units were then replicated to the boundaries of the city. The sectors are traversed by roads which distribute traffic inside the sectors. The majority of sectors in Chandigarh are residential areas classified according to the pay scale of government employees.

---

[4] Prasad Sunand (1987), *Le Corbusier – Architect of the Century* – Arts Council of Great Britain, Mansell U.K. Limited, p.281

Figure 5.8 Typical sector as a self-contained unit [*Source*: Chandigarh guide map, Survey of India]

Currently, all the sectors in Chandigarh are of introvert nature. The self-contained unit neglects the use of street frontage which could be used for retail or as an interactive space. As one travels through these sectors the edges become monotonous and one loses the sense of place. The various proposals for possible changes in sectors (Fig. 5.9) reveal the opening up of sectors making it more permeable to the roads, which would enhance the edge developments and create vitality along the street corridors.

There are 30 sectors in Gandhinagar and each sector measures 1000 × 750 m. In Gandhinagar the layout of the city is in form of sectors, as the planning was based on Chandigarh. The interesting feature of the sectors in Gandhinagar is the internal layout, derived from traditional Gujarati towns. The internal layouts of Gujarati towns were compact; layout of traditional towns had *pols* with a civic square.

Each sector in Gandhinagar is self-sufficient, as it provides basic amenities like a shopping complex, a dispensary and an area for recreational purposes (Fig. 4.8). The concept of sectors in Gandhinagar was based on Chandigarh, but the dimensions of the sectors were derived in accordance to time and distance travelled to work. The distances travelled to work resulted in a smaller sector size but created a functional district as observed in Chandigarh which would be commuted through automobile.

5.7 Various Arrangements of the Chandigarh Sectors

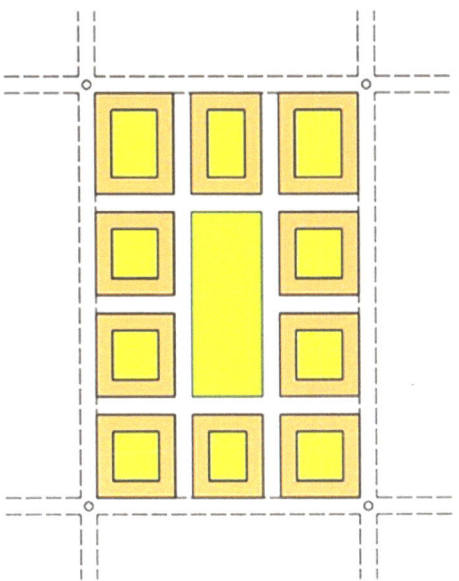

Figure 5.9 Sector re-structuring – Perimeter blocks with central park

Square and rectangular perimeter block - I
The square and rectangular perimeter block typology is placed around a central park or a central garden.
This ensures that the community utilizes the open courtyard as well as the central park/garden for the community interactions.
Greater emphasis is on the central/park as it provides the green lung for the sector.

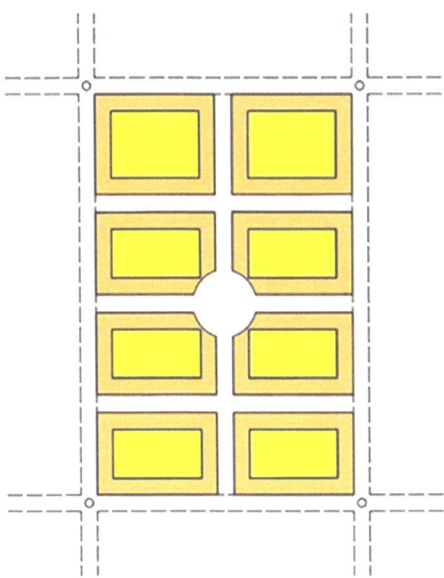

Figure 5.10 Sector re-structuring – Perimeter blocks

Rectangular perimeter block
The rectangular perimeter block, with central open courtyard, offers multiple activities in its open space, which defines the street edge bringing the community together. In terms of urban design, the people interaction is highest in open courtyard perimeter blocks.
Crime and disorder is also very less as compared to other typologies, as there is a community watch on to the entrance and the premises.

72 Master Planning Indian Cities: Achieving Urban Renaissance

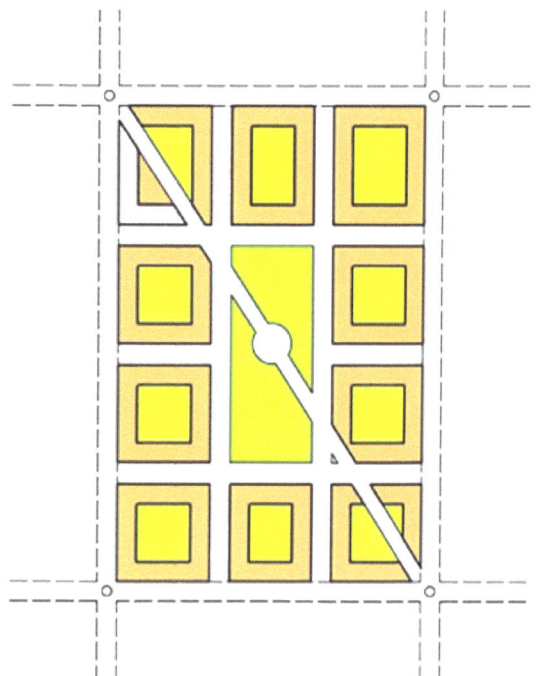

Figure 5.11 Sector re-structuring –Perimeter blocks with diagonal

Square perimeter block with diagonal-II
The square and rectangular block typology has a diagonal pedestrian route running across the sector, the diagonal being the shortest distance in a rectangular sector profile.
The diagonal is the pedestrian route traversing across all sectors of the city.

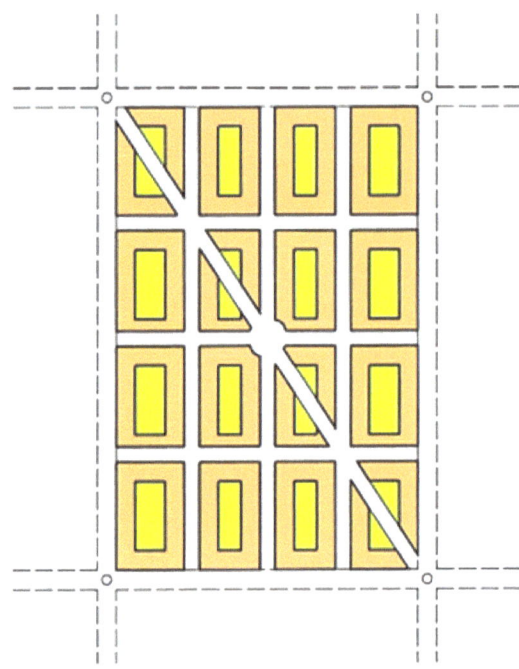

Figure 5.12 Sector re-structuring – Perimeter blocks with high density

Rectangular perimeter block with diagonal-II
The rectangular perimeter block is densely packed together with higher density and connected through a pedestrian diagonal.
More number of blocks can be arranged in the sector; however, there are no communal or central open spaces.

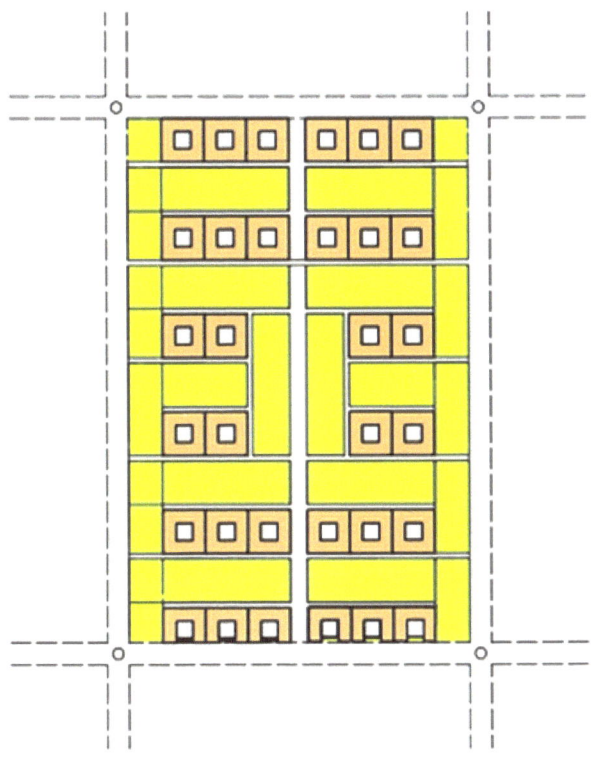

Figure 5.13 Sector re-structuring – Apartments with court and open spaces

Apartment blocks occupy the sector in form of terraces. There are large open spaces with front and back green spaces for community interaction.
The apartments in turn have an atrium space for allowing day lighting and ventilation.

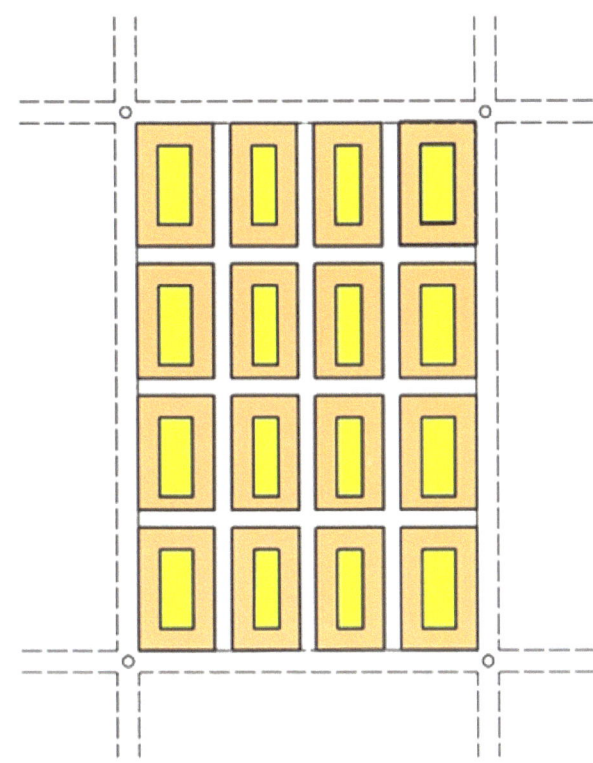

Figure 5.14 Sector re-structuring – Perimeter blocks with high density

Rectangular perimeter block with diagonal-II
The rectangular perimeter block is densely packed together with higher density.
More number of blocks can be arranged in the sector; however, there are no communal or central open spaces.

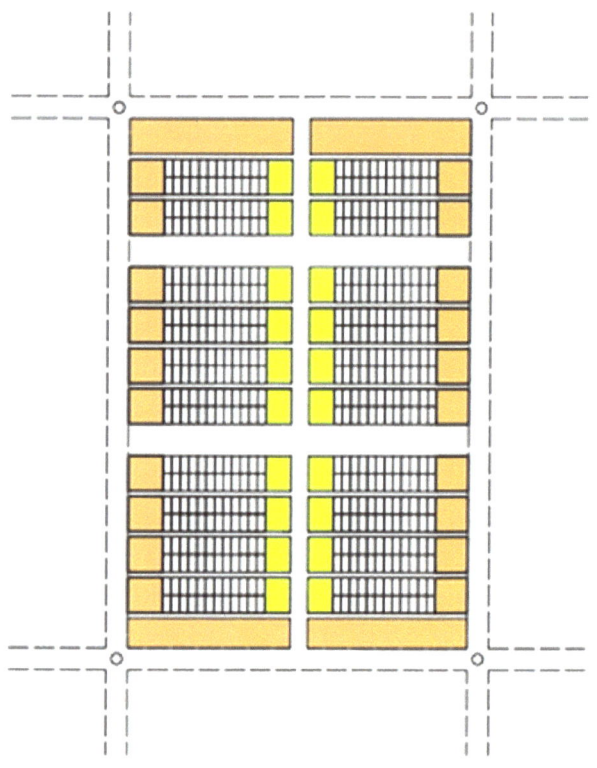

Figure 5.15 Sector re-structuring – Plots with retail perimeter

The sector can be divided further into plots with retail outlets at its periphery. The landowners can design their buildings according to their requirements.
To avoid any clash in the aesthetics of the place, a design code can be used as a central document highlighting the form, colour and the volume of the buildings.

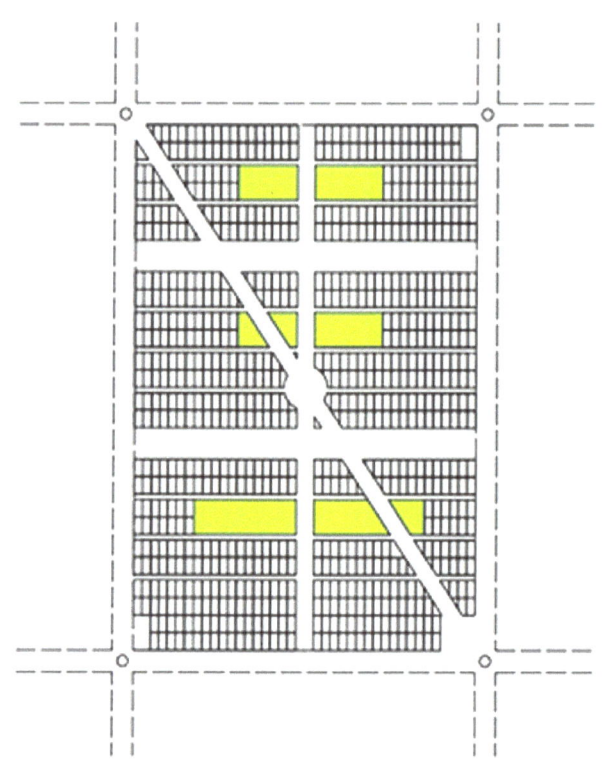

Figure 5.16 Sector re-structuring – Plots with open spaces and diagonal

Highly dense development, however, on a suburban scale can be an alternative with open spaces along its central area.
The diagonal is used to connect the nodes of the sectors and shorten the distance between the sectors.
The diagonal is the shortest distance across the sector.

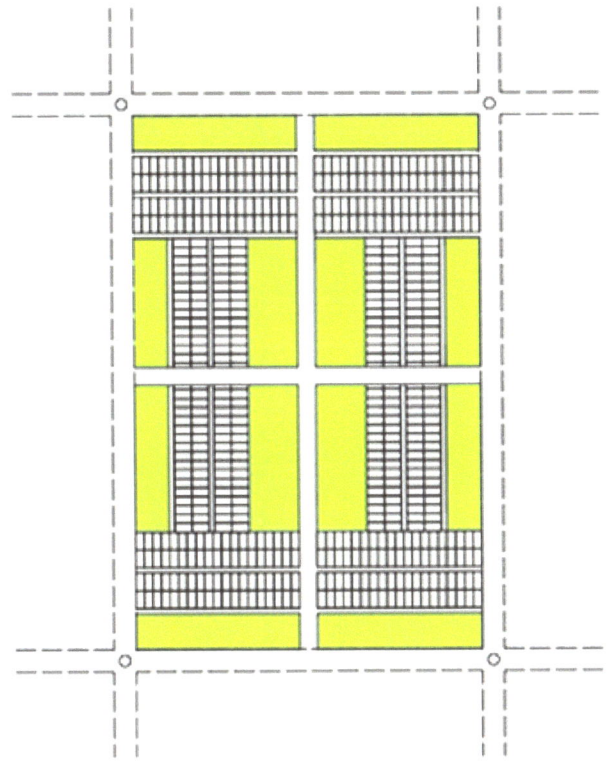

Figure 5.17 Sector re-structuring – Plots with open spaces

Moderately dense plots with more open spaces can be another alternative, wherein the residents can enjoy the suburban character. The aesthetic expression of the buildings can be controlled by an urban design principle or code.

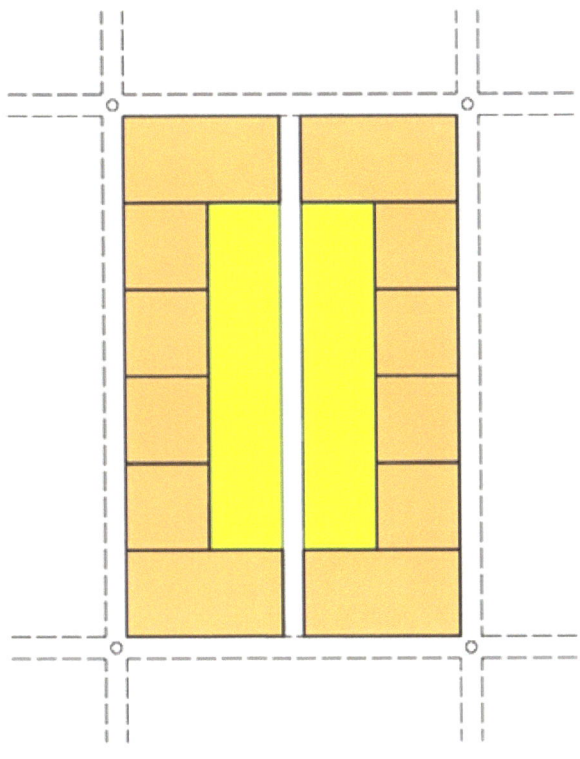

Figure 5.18 Sector re-structuring – Mixed-use perimeter block with communal spaces

Mixed-use perimeter block with apartments with communal spaces at the heart of the sector, utilizes effective land use, accommodates higher densities and contributes to good urbanism as the activities are round the clock.

When compared to New York and Boston (Fig. 5.19), the urban grain of Chandigarh and Gandhinagar are very coarse. The urban grains of rest of the cities reveal their relative compactness. The urban grain of Chandigarh and Gandhinagar result into a uniform street pattern which caters to movement and vast amount of open spaces in each sector. These open spaces tend to be a financial burden in terms of maintenance and moreover act as ambiguous spaces.

76 Master Planning Indian Cities: Achieving Urban Renaissance

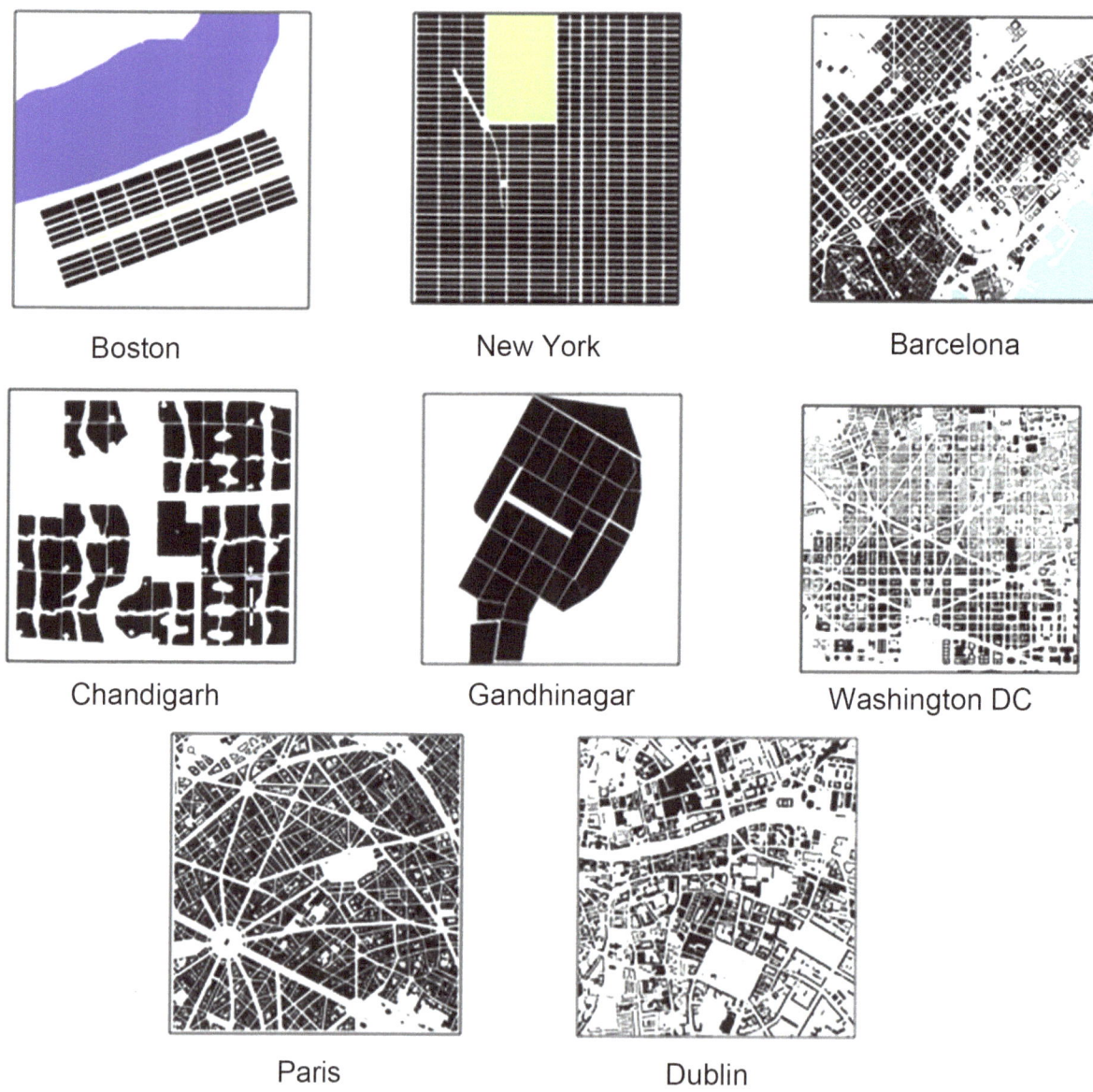

Figure 5.19 Comparison of block grain of Chandigarh and Gandhinagar with New York, Boston, Barcelona, Washington DC, San Francisco and Chicago

Further the sizes of sectors in Gandhinagar and Chandigarh are equivalent of early British new towns which contained a work place.[5]

5.8 Movement Pattern

The movement in Chandigarh is based on the *motor car*. Le Corbusier hailed the motor car as a vital source of movement from his earliest studies of urbanism.

In Chandigarh the movement is categorized into 7Vs. The 7Vs cater systematically for traffic from main roads to the doors of individual houses. The transportation system is based on the analogy of the blood circulation of the human body. Sunand Prasad points out "The basic sector of Chandigarh grid of the master plan measures 1200 × 800 m, which is that of fast wide roads (V3 and sometimes V2) reserved for motorized traffic – in Le Corbusier's original vision exclusively public transport – which bound the sectors and on to which no houses open."[6] Chandigarh's transport strategy was proposed by Le Corbusier, who termed it *les Sept Voies* (the seven Vs). The roads in Chandigarh were segregated based on different uses and are classified as:

- Cross continents, arrive in town – V1
- To go to essential public services – V2
- Cross at full speed without interruption – V3
- Reach the door of dwelling – V5 and V6
- Green areas, schools sports ground areas – V7

In Gandhinagar, movement is given due importance and the sectors are served by roads which are given letters and numbers as CH and 1, respectively. The intersections are thus named as CH1. The classification of roads based on letters and numbers were adopted from the road system prevalent in the United States. The noteworthy feature of the road system is its orientation which avoids harsh climatic conditions – sunlight. The main objective behind the design of Gandhinagar was to reduce the time taken from work place to the residential area. The sectors in Gandhinagar are smaller (750,000 sq. m) than the sectors of Chandigarh (960,000 sq. m) minimizing travel time and congestion in Gandhinagar (Fig. 5.20).

Given the sector sizes of Chandigarh and Gandhinagar (the sector size being less in case of Gandhinagar), the linear movement of traffic and pedestrians (Fig. 5.21) is the same with uniform edges contributed by the rear of houses. While travelling from one sector to another in a linear pattern, one cannot tell the difference between the two cities.

---

[5] Julian Beinart (2002), Chandigarh 1999: Diagrams and Realties, *Celebrating Chandigarh*, Mapin Publishers Ltd., p.147
[6] Prakash Sunand (1987), *Le Corbusier – Architect of the Century* – Arts Council of Great Britain, Mansell U.K. Limited, p.288

78 Master Planning Indian Cities: Achieving Urban Renaissance

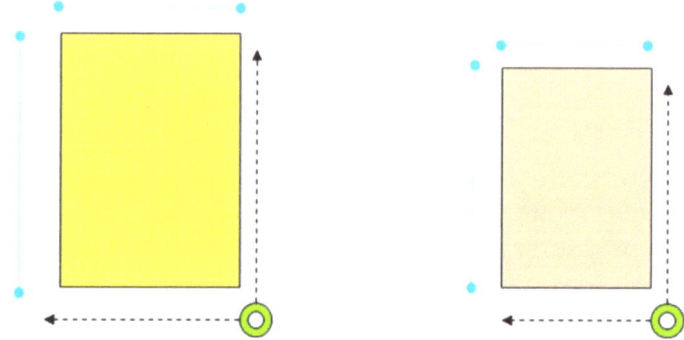

Figure 5.20 Comparison of relative size of sector in Chandigarh and Gandhinagar

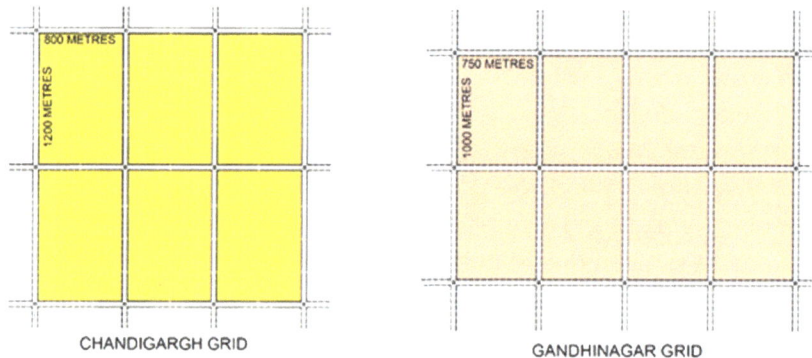

Figure 5.21 Comparison of Chandigarh and Gandhinagar grid

Figure 5.22 Comparison of relative block size of Jaipur and Barcelona

The Jaipur city block measures 800 × 800 m (Fig. 5.22) and in a square format. It is an ideal size to walk along four equal sides equally especially during summer season. Further the blocks are closely placed next to each other shielding the harsh Sun. In comparison, the Barcelona superblock measures 400 × 400 m (Fig. 5.22) inhabiting a population of 5,000 to 6,000 people. It is therefore a city within a city with each superblock having a diverse architectural character. The remarkable character of both Jaipur and Barcelona is the human scale and the ease of comfort while walking around as a pedestrian. Active frontages are one of the major highlights, giving a street life and maintaining commerce along the roads.

5.9 Built Form

5.9.1 Government buildings

The Capitol Complex in Chandigarh with government buildings has vast amount of open space. The proposals by Chilean Architect Perez D Arce (Fig. 5.23) show the Capitol Complex as an urbanized centre providing provisions for residences. In many ways the isolation of Capitol Complex is negated further creating an urban scenario generated by close proximity of the built forms.

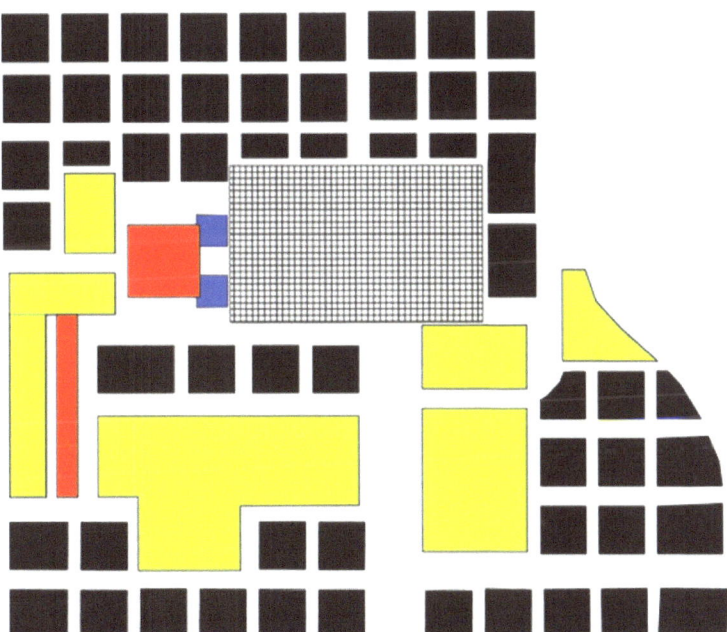

Figure 5.23 Sector 1, the urban blocks, central plaza and open spaces are arranged in a compact formation; building fronting the plaza is the Assembly Hall and behind it is the Secretariat [Interpreted from a proposal by Architect Perez D Arce]

The urbanization is achieved through walls and gardens and series of open space which could be the lost spirit of Chandigarh. The proposal by Chilean architect demonstrates an urban scenario which is the case of many Indian towns which were often densely packed. In Gandhinagar the Capitol Complex acts as a landmark building which is placed in front of an axis and creates a grandeur which is associated with Lutyens' Delhi. However, the prominence of public space is marked by ornamental gardens.

5.9.2 Housing

The dwelling types in Chandigarh (i.e. government housing) denote a specific position in a hierarchy (from Type 1 to Type 13) of income levels. There are flats, row houses and bungalows. In Gandhinagar the residential quarters are categorized (as K, KH, G, G1, GH, CH, CHH and J) based on the income level. The built forms adopted for Gandhinagar are bungalows and row houses. There were no material specifications, but strict buildings bylaws were adopted.

5.9.3 The Commercial Centre

The commercial centre in case of Chandigarh is a centralized district for the entire city with built form along a plaza. The Sector 17 is the commercial centre which has shops with open corridors lined with concrete pillars. It is in stark contrast to the traditional Indian bazaar which connects the buyer to the seller with no physical barriers or enclosed space. The commercial centre is an attractive area with provision of public art and public seating with rigid control on the display of shop banners. In Gandhinagar the commercial centre is reserved only in the city centre. The vertical mixed use gives an opportunity for commercial and office activity to thrive along the street. The vertical mixed use is now a contemporary feature of high-rise buildings in Indian cities which offer retail activity on the lower floors and housing on the upper floors.

5.10 Streets and the Built Form

The widest street in Chandigarh is the Jan Marg. The built forms along the widest street throughout the world offer opportunities to diverse functions such as acting as commercial or retail precinct with offices as observed in Princes Street in Edinburgh, Scotland. Raj Path in New Delhi is an area demarked for government offices and has the President's residence similarly to the Constitution Avenue in Washington D.C. According to *the Case Studies by Zhan Guo and Alex-Ricardo Jimenez of MIT,* "Commonwealth Avenue is a testimony to a bygone Victorian era in which public open space was conceived as a decorative boulevard that enhanced the townhouses of the gentry, and served as a promenade for fine ladies and gentlemen. Formal in design, Commonwealth Avenue today serves as a protected area to enjoy a canopy of trees in the city, or walk your dog. Strollers can be inspired by inscriptions emblazoned on the statues that adorn the mall, commemorating the famous, and reminding us of important events in the history of the city. A paved sidewalk runs the entire length of the mall, bordered by London plane trees spaced evenly to define the park's edges."[7] Fifth Avenue in New York is known for iconic buildings and a successful commercial hub. Jan Marg in Chandigarh offers no such activity as observed in the case of avenues in the United States and Europe, apart from being one of the widest roads in Chandigarh. A proposal of Jan Marg as illustrated (Fig 5.24) if it is to be adopted on the lines of avenues as seen in Europe and the United States seeks to create a micro urban environment which would benefit the city and its inhabitants. The second widest street in Chandigarh is the V2 followed by V3.

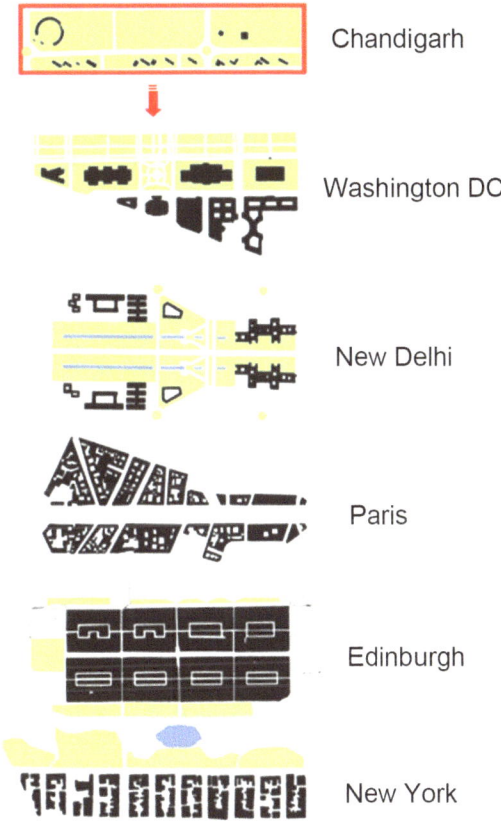

Figure 5.24 Comparison of Jan Marg with Avenues from Europe and America (Top to bottom)

---

[7] http://www.boston.com/beyond_bigdig/cases/comm_ave.htm

82 Master Planning Indian Cities: Achieving Urban Renaissance

If all the V2 and V3 are to be connected with a smart tunnel system, it will enhance the streetscape of Chandigarh rather than elevated transport system. The smart tunnel is a three-tier system, which would carry storm water, additional automobile and accommodate a metro system stopping at the roundabouts or the nodes of Chandigarh.

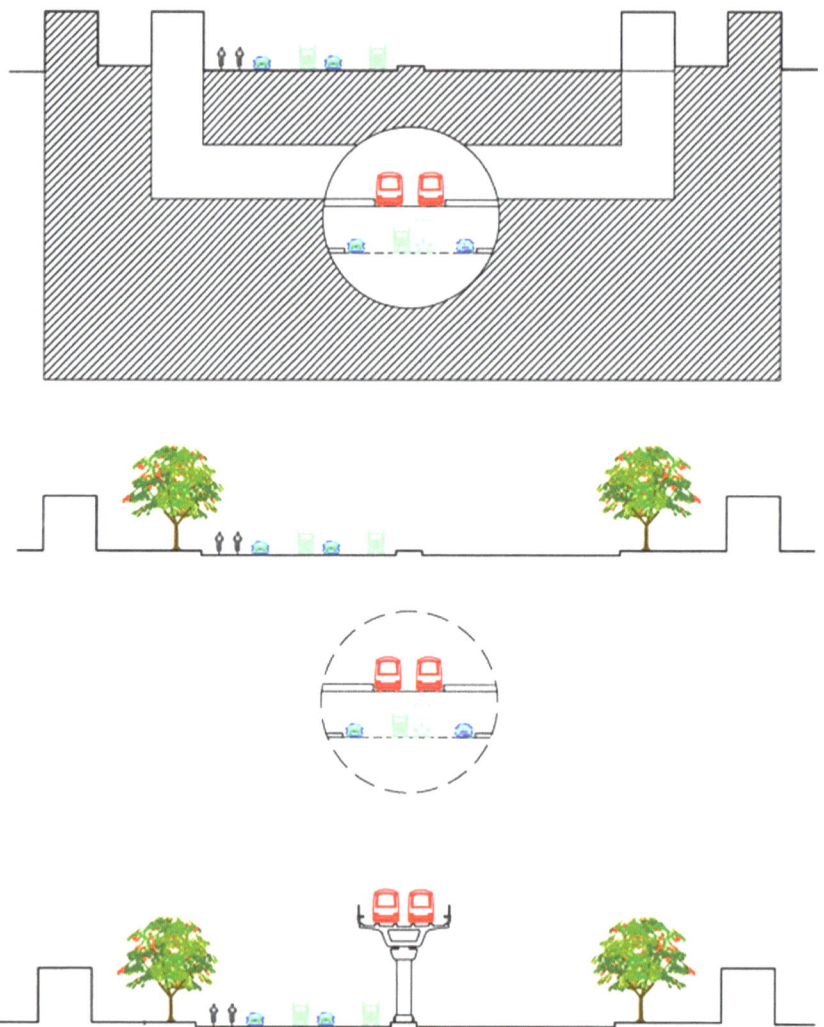

Figure 5.25 Restructuring of V roads of Chandigarh by incorporating a smart tunnel system and discouraging overhead transport system on pillars

The smart tunnel system (Fig. 5.25) could pave way for the futuristic Hyperloop System linking Chandigarh to capital city New Delhi. The smart tunnel system if incorporated in all the major cities will save precious rain water and reclaim the street space, which is currently blighted by the concrete flyovers and Metro transport line. The street space should be given due importance and any infringement in terms of such transport development should be barred.

Gandhinagar on the other hand seems to consider the potential of mixed use although located primarily in the city centre. The town planning development has encouraged high densities along the city centre which is a commercial precinct by mixed use in high-rise developments. These high-rise buildings cater to the demand of the commercial activity on the floors below and office spaces on rest of the above floors (Fig. 5.26).

Figure 5.26 Street section of Gandhinagar [*Source*: Author]

5.11 Availability of Plots

The plots in Chandigarh were sold by the Chandigarh administration. These plots were initially auctioned, fetching high prices. The sale of plots at a high price was attributed to the success of Chandigarh as a city and the validity of the principle of good urbanism as proposed by Le Corbusier. The land policy and sale of plots were later reviewed by the administration; as a result, only a few plots were released on an annual basis. Plots were also made available to people from low-income groups.

The development cost of land in Chandigarh is nearly one-and-a-half times higher than those in the planned city of Gandhinagar. The high cost of land in Chandigarh can be attributed to the wide area of roads covering the entire city.

Strict zoning regulations and strong architectural control over the development of land can be a major drawback, as it does not allow any retail and commercial activity along certain streets. The busiest road in Chandigarh is the Jan Marg which is devoid of any shopping or retail activity.

In Gandhinagar the sale of plots was through the town planning department. The plot sizes were varied and the main objective of the town planning department of Gandhinagar was to mix the occupations of residents through the sale of plots to achieve a healthy social balance. In Gandhinagar the commercial zone is located along the road side, especially beneficial to the retail activity.

5.12　Open Spaces

In Gandhinagar the biggest park is located in Sector 28 designated as a children's park, and covering an area of 10 acres; it is a major tourist spot attracting the residents of Gandhinagar and Ahmedabad. The sectors in Gandhinagar have well-defined gardens covered with woodlands, maintaining the eco-diversity on a small scale.

The Gandhinagar Master plan has provisions for a large playing field in Sector 21, and a sports complex in Sector 15, mainly used for sporting activities such as cricket, football and archery. The sports venue is ideal for hosting inter-district and state-level games.

In Chandigarh vertical bands of green strips run from the north of the city to the south. These green strips cuts through all the sectors becoming individual parks for each sector, often used by the residents of the sectors.

Chandigarh has an artificial lake which was a part of the Master plan, achieved by creating a dam on the river Sukma. The lake and dam also serve the purpose of distributing water to the residents of Chandigarh. Trees along the road were planted as 'green' walls. The trees were specifically chosen for their foliage colour and shape, which vary from sector to sector, giving each individual sector its own identity. The roundabouts are treated differently in terms of landscape, maintaining variety throughout the city. Another contribution of Chandigarh is the Rock Garden, created by Nek Chand Saini, which is the only organically laid out park in the city and draws huge number of visitors.

5.13　Summary

The evaluation of Chandigarh and Gandhinagar reflects the political, planning and the various urban design issues involved in the city building. The site selection for Chandigarh was free from any historic influences. It was designed to be a modern new town in a modern country. The site was chosen next to two rivers which form natural boundaries, whereas the site chosen for Gandhinagar was based on regional linkages.

The Master plan of Chandigarh was designed by Western designers, with modern town planning elements found in major cities of Europe and the United States. The Mayer master plan for Chandigarh had American planning elements such as the green belt and the neighbourhood concept. Le Corbusier later executed the Master plan of Chandigarh on modern town planning principles.

The Master plan for Gandhinagar was designed by Indian architects and town planners. The planning of Gandhinagar in some ways is similar to that of Chandigarh, and the city of Gandhinagar shows the relevance of regional context in a modern new town. Master planning of Gandhinagar was influenced by climatic conditions, evident from its roads layout and the location of prominent buildings. Both cities prioritize efficient traffic movement. Industry is seen as a vital tool to boost the economy of the city, and hence is given a prominent location in the master plan.

The new town of Chandigarh and Gandhinagar were based on distinct unilateral zones. These zones carried out the various functions of the city. For instance, the market zone would carry out all retail activities of the city. Capitol complexes and government buildings served the administrative needs of the state. Both Chandigarh and Gandhinagar were funded on the basis of self-finance. The plot subdivision in Chandigarh was done through auction whereas the assignation of the plots in Gandhinagar was based on mixing the occupation. Both Chandigarh and Gandhinagar have generous open spaces. Parks form the basis of new towns, proving beneficial in terms of maintaining ecological balance and fulfilling the recreational needs of the inhabitants.

6
The Urban Synthesis

"Towns have sometimes been described as the physical expression of nation's civilization. The physical form of a town does in many ways reflect fairly accurately the social condition of the people who live in it, their mode of life, their cultural achievement, their economic status, the kind of government they possess."[1]

Chandigarh and Gandhinagar were designed primarily to perform the administrative functions of the state and to provide housing for its employees. Gandhinagar is close to big cities like Ahmedabad and Mehsana. Due to its proximity to big cities like Ahmedabad, Gandhinagar acts like a satellite town. As Gandhinagar was role modelled on Chandigarh, it followed the dominant character of an administrative capital. The capital city, in spite of good planning, fails to attract people as a place to live; factors such as its purely administrative nature and lack of historical influences could be major factors.

Nowicki proposed the Master plan of Chandigarh which can be termed "organic", due to its leafy form bares a close resemblance to some Indian cities. The buildings can be seen as plant cells, closely accommodating different classes of people. Diversity has always been part of Indian culture, characterized by people from different religious backgrounds and classes. The master plan was further strengthened by the presence of trees. Indian cities in natural settings such as Bangalore and Mysore were designed on the lines of Letchworth Garden city in England, pioneered by Ebenezer Howard. The Moghul planning in 14th century saw the emergence of garden as an integral part of important buildings. Nowicki's organic master plan would certainly have suited the Indian context, as traditional Indian cities developed organically. The built forms in these traditional settlements were of a compact nature, which united the city. The city had gateways and sometimes a moat for defence against its enemies.

The morphology of Chandigarh went through various changes due to many designers involved in it. Looking at the morphology of the city as proposed by Albert Mayer, the city was designed on an irregular fashion. On the whole the city blocks were spaced very closer, tightly bound in a compact fashion. The morphology of the city as proposed by Le Corbusier: Le Corbusier disregarded some features of Mayer's plan, especially the superblocks, which he replaced with sectors which were uniform in size. The sectors gave rise to linear roads for the movement of automobiles; they were beneficial for the inhabitants as they were self-contained, providing basic amenities to their inhabitants. With the inception of Chandigarh the idea of unilateral zoning came into

---
[1] Sharp Thomas (1940), *Town Planning*, Harmondsworth, Penguin Books Ltd, p.16

existence. Gandhinagar the second city built after Chandigarh was designed on the basis of sectors which were the integral part of master plan. Both the cities have zones which acted as distinct districts.

The various functions of the city thus get segregated into distinct zones. For instance, Sector 17 is the commercial centre of Chandigarh located at the heart of the city. Being the only commercial core of the city, it caters to the city and nearby areas. The evaluation of Chandigarh (see Section 5.8 in Chapter 5) shows that the widest and busiest street of Chandigarh is the Jan Marg which is devoid of any shopping and retail activity. Gandhinagar on the other hand realized the potential of market dynamics and thus created a leisurely shopping experience which is a characteristic of Indian city, although restricted only near the city centre. The vast amount of open spaces in Chandigarh tends to be underutilized. The proposals by various architects (see Section 5.11 in Chapter 5) is a response which enhances the urban domain especially with the help of mixed-use development along the streets of Chandigarh.

Functionalist cities were previously non-existent in India. Early cities in India, apart from accommodating their inhabitants, carried out multiple functions from accommodating skilled craftsmen to the administration of the cities. The societies of early cities were based on division of labour, which is reflected in the built form especially in Madurai and Mohenjo-Daro. Modern planning was preferred over the compactness of the built form found in traditional Indian cities, which offered shade in the narrow streets and promoted interaction between the inhabitants.

Chandigarh and Gandhinagar have big wide roads convenient for vehicles, but neglect the social aspects of streets which are vital in terms of social interaction in any Indian city.

The evaluation of Chandigarh and Gandhinagar in Chapter 5 further revels that the urban grain (sector) is introvert in nature. The "sectors" are comparatively enormous when compared to the urban grain of cities in Europe and America. In Chandigarh and Gandhinagar, the sectors were designed as self-contained units, providing all the basic amenities for its inhabitants. All the residential layouts are located in the interior of sector. The outer periphery of the sector does not open out to the roads which could have been used for retail activity. Moreover, both the cities have a universal appeal. The cities of Chandigarh and Gandhinagar are easily identifiable with cities such as Milton Keynes in England.

The major drawback of Chandigarh and Gandhinagar is the sense of place which is contributed by the rear of built form and big wide roads leading to a monotonous townscape. The residential pattern in Chandigarh is based on income groups creating a distinct class which does not allow mixing of people from various income groups. Overall Chandigarh reflects the Western planning approach and does not consider the local context and climatology. Le Corbusier's master plan of Chandigarh bares a close resemblance to European and American cities characterized by fast-moving vehicles and do not resemble any Indian city where the arrangement of the built form promoted social interaction.

On the other hand, the relevance of the past is highlighted in the master plan of Gandhinagar in its internal layout. The architects of Gandhinagar designed the housing layouts with elements of traditional Gujarati towns.

These traditional towns were dense in nature and characterized by '*pols*'. The '*pols*' acted as civic spaces for the residents and slowed down fast-moving vehicles. The wide straight roads in Chandigarh and Gandhinagar are broad monotonous and generate high frequency of traffic in particular zone as these zones act as distinct districts. The main routes in Gandhinagar were based on the American model, which was less hierarchical than that of Chandigarh. Due to their relative sizes, one often confuses with Chandigarh to Gandhinagar and vice versa due to the linear movement around the sectors.

In contrast to Chandigarh, Gandhinagar and towns like New Bagalkot and Aranya are Indian examples, which have open to sky spaces and streets which generate multi-activity space, tailored to way of life, not dominated by car.

The recent developments in planning Indian cities are based on critical regionalism which relies heavily on a contextual manifestation of a place. It recognizes that the inhabitant's behaviour and their social interaction shape the place and consequently the built form. It is not the place or an ideology imposed makes a city but the inhabitant's cultural and social aspiration. The description and the evaluation of Chandigarh suggest that the city reflects the CIAM's ideology with built form as the solution, which embodies the functional aspects of the city. The relevance of context was completely forgotten in the design of Chandigarh, especially in its urban grain – the "sectors". It was designed for a modern living in a modern country which was further exacerbated by the land policy adopted by Chandigarh and offered a quality of life perhaps non-existent in any of the Indian cities at that time.

Gandhinagar on the other hand shows few attempts towards the idea of contextual application in a planned city. The internal layout of sectors in Gandhinagar recognizes the importance of traditional settlement pattern. The residential layout based on traditional Gujarati settlements in conjunction with the modern planning highlights the social aspiration of Indian society.

No doubt the grid was the generator of the city form in Chandigarh and Gandhinagar which provided legibility and easy movement of vehicles but failed to incorporate the social and cultural aspirations of the inhabitants. It is a manifestation of stratified living which was against the ethos of any Indian city.

The planned cities of Chandigarh and Gandhinagar benefited immensely from the idea of self-finance. Self-finance helped the city to develop its infrastructure in order to maintain an industrial base. Due to a well-developed infrastructure, Chandigarh and Gandhinagar are home to major software and pharmaceutical firms. The landscaping in Chandigarh, especially the trees which are different in each sector, gave a distinct identity to the city. The lake and the organically laid Rock Garden are amongst the most visited spots in Chandigarh. Government buildings are the major landmarks in both the capital cities.

The evaluation further reveals that Chandigarh and Gandhinagar have a close resemblance in terms of planning, housing the inhabitants and more importantly the physical form. Gandhinagar is a modification of Chandigarh and attempts to address certain urban design issues in the Indian context but does not incorporate on a city level. Overall the cities tend to be similar and do not appear distinct in any way. In case of Gandhinagar the application of context seems to be valid in certain parts of the city and not on the entire city.

Cities in Europe and America show that a successful place has a strong relationship between the built form and the street triggered by the idea of mixed use. Old settlements and temple towns in India show that the idea of mixed use was prevalent and added vitality to the streets. Due to the physical form of Chandigarh and Gandhinagar, planning methods fail to address the importance of the relationship between the built form and streets.

Chandigarh, in spite of its shortcomings, has much to offer in terms of city infrastructure, organized living and more importantly a city with 'green lungs'. Gandhinagar, on the other hand, embraces both modernity and traditional planning approaches. The many changes made in Gandhinagar in terms of zoning, retailing and innovative housing layout to suit their lifestyle are overshadowed by Chandigarh's modern planning which maintains its identity as the *'Modern City of India'*. In terms of urban design, the functions of the planned cities are isolated and not well-connected owing to their location separated by huge distances.

Although Gandhinagar shows some relevance to the context overall, it is a modification of Chandigarh's master plan which does not function in terms of urban design. Due to their planning ideologies and their design in early 19th century period, Chandigarh and Gandhinagar tend to be similar and do not appear distinct.

7
Achieving Urban Renaissance: Indian History and Culture

7.1 Indus Valley Civilization: The Beginning

The origin of Indian civilization is dated back to the Indus Valley Civilization (IVC), or Harappan Civilization, which was a Bronze Age Civilization (3300–1300 BCE; mature period 2600–1900 BCE). The main characteristic of its cities was a highly organized social structure, which is reflected in its city planning and layout. The grid iron plan was the basis of the city form, and most importantly the city did not have any landmarks. Absence of buildings with extreme heights, as their characteristic, implied that the social structure was considered equal and not hierarchical.

7.2 The Moghul Era (16–18th Century)

The Islamic invasion of Indian subcontinent gave the power to the Moghul rulers. The cities during the Moghul period saw a contrasting and to some extent the imposition of Islamic architecture styles in the prevalent Hindu architecture and planning systems. The city builders had to comply with the Islamic directives to deliver a "Moghul identity" in the Indian subcontinent. This era from early 16th century to mid-18th century saw the coming up of numerous mosques, gardens and palaces and the Taj Mahal, being the epitome of Moghul architecture.

7.3 The British Rule (1858–1947)

The British in the form of East India Company seized the control of entire Indian subcontinent by invading many kingdoms and by imposing heavy taxes on the kingdoms which they could not conquer. Whole of the Indian subcontinent came under the rule of the British monarchy, de facto rulers of England.

The British military heads were given powers to control civic as well as administrative functions of provenances. In subsequent years, governors and viceroys were sent to preside over the provinces. Amidst the Hindu and Islamic population, the British settlement grew to accommodate its military soldiers and appointed governors by the rulers. Cantonments and new stately buildings were erected resembling the architecture found in English cities. The then capital of British Empire Calcutta saw Victoria Memorial Hall as a landmark and Curzon quoted as "Let us, therefore, have a building stately, spacious, monumental and grand, to which every newcomer in Calcutta will turn, to which all the resident population, European and Native, will flock, where all classes will learn the lessons of history, and see revived before their eyes the marvels of the past."[1] During the latter part of 19th century, British architects during the era of (1858–1947) used the Indo-Saracenic style of architecture towards the creation of public and government buildings. Indo-Saracenic style was essentially a mix of Hindu, Islamic and Gothic architectural elements often monumental and huge in scale. During this era, Indian cities saw the addition of town halls, palaces, administrative buildings and government buildings. Cities were planned and designed with cities in England as their role models, with it came the byelaws (a set of rule book for the buildings, which is outdated in England), but still prevalent in 21st century India (Grid iron dates back to settlement of military camps). Bombay, Delhi, Madras and Calcutta were major cities planned during the British Rule. The cities were designed as a major centre and became a magnet attracting population in an agrarian country, where city population was extremely low and villages to a relatively high number. At the beginning of 20th century, Mahatma Gandhi quoted "The soul of India lives in its villages; however, the provinces and new cities saw new landmarks against rural self-sustaining villages. In the new city settlements, there were three distinctive contrasting planning settlements: the Hindu quarter, the compounded British settlement and the Muslim quarter.

In terms of urban design, one could see three distinct contrasting districts: the Hindu settlement with temple at its centre; the Islamic quarter, with mosque as its feature; the British with their bungalows, clubs and cantonments. During the British colonization of India, the apartheid was very clear and distinct towards city building quarters, thus the compound wall came into existence.

Native people were forgotten during the subsequent rise of Moghul and British Empire. Against the wishes of the native population, both the Moghuls and British forgot about India's traditional culture dating back to 35000 years of Indus Valley and Vedic era. One could also see a strong contrasting approach to city design in Indian cities as a result. Notably, a great Scotsman Patrick Geddes remembered till date advocated for "the diagnosis before treatment" preserving the cultural and civic spaces of Indian villages and towns in contrast to Lutyens' monumental city buildings, using a potpourri of various styles (Indo-Saracenic style) for designing the imperial capital of British India. The imperial Delhi, capital of the Empire, was to be designed such that it would rival Paris and be the icon of British Empire much to the displeasure of Indian subjects.

7.3.1 Layering of Indian cities

The role of compound wall during the British settlements was very profound to separate the native population of India. The compound walls of the British bungalows and key buildings were fortified in order to demarcate the territory and to keep away the native population. Since then, compound wall has been regarded as a demarcation or a boundary in plot and housing developments. In the 21st century, private land owners, townships, gated

---
[1] https;//en.m.wikipedia.org/wiki/Victoria Memorial, Kolkata

communities, industrial and government buildings too are compounded to keep away non-employees and non-wanted people away from premises. The compound wall contributes to an urban edge contributing many negative factors such as policing, crime and slum development. As a result, many mini districts are created insular in nature and disjoined to the main city.

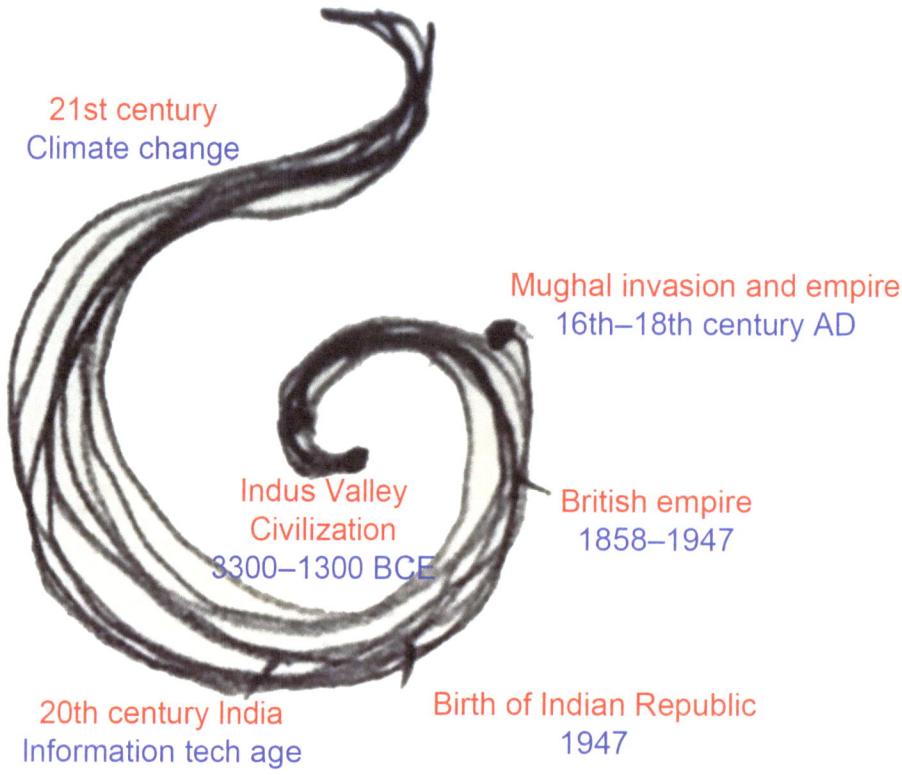

Figure 7.1 Historical layering of India cities [*Source:* Author]

7.4 The Age of Democracies (1947–2000)

What do we do with the past? No matter how atrocious the past, all buildings built by non-native rulers should be preserved as "history fact" and assign a building function, so that it becomes part of the civic society we live in. It should be classified as having distinct architectural character areas and be part of a conservation zone. Being an age-old civilization, India has many urban patterns ranging from various eras. Celebrating the diverse cultures, buildings of previous historical eras due to their varying scales and proportion, with adaptive reuse, can be integrated into the urban fabric of the city without altering its architectural character.

7.5 City Building and Place-Making Principles: Evolution of Indian Cities

7.5.1 Cities defined by its central core

A successful city is defined by a legible historic core. Centre of the city or the centrum is a place of importance where important city functions take place that can be travelled and accessed by all the citizens. The strategic placement at the centre further shields it from the reach of its invaders. Throughout history city centre has always existed but its functions changed through the evolution of time.

7.5.2 Fort/palace as centre – walls as boundaries – housing inside

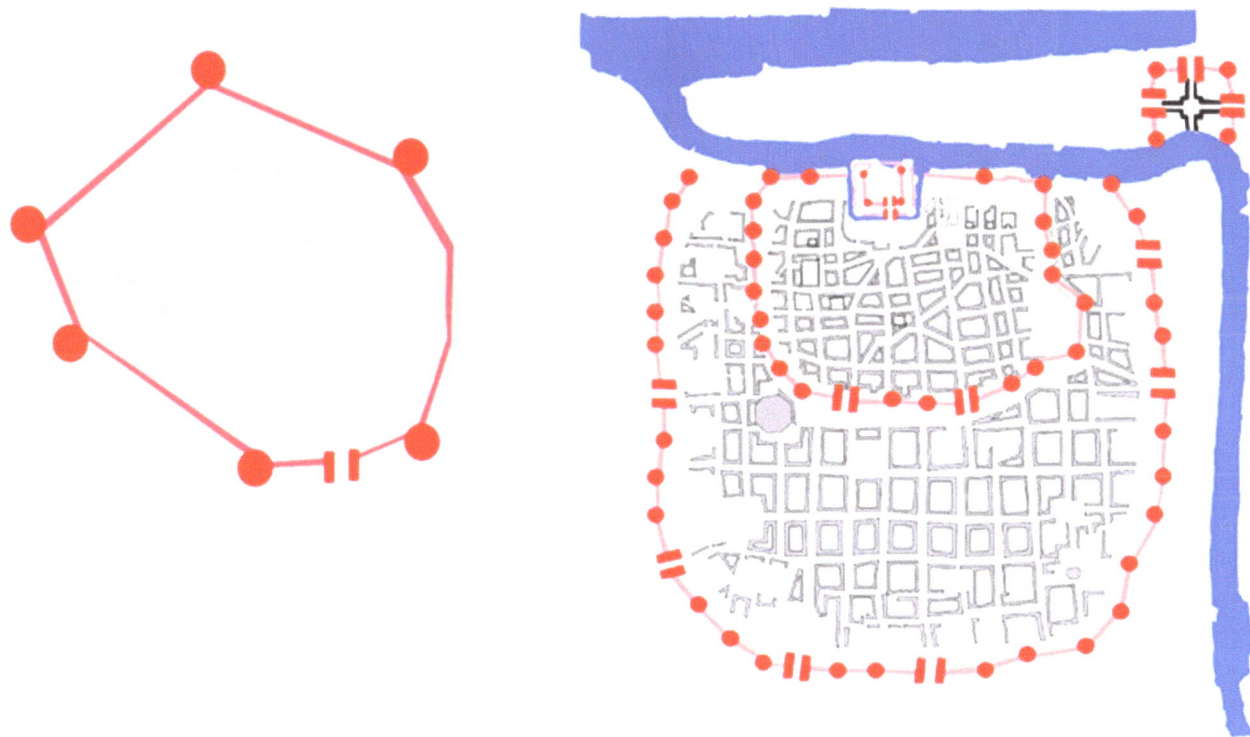

Figure 7.2 Spatial pattern of Madikeri Fort

Figure 7.3 Spatial patterns of Surat Fort and Medieval city

94 Master Planning Indian Cities: Achieving Urban Renaissance

Figure 7.4 Early map of Surat Fort [*Courtesy:* Maharaja Sawai Man Singh II Museum Trust, The City Palace, Jaipur]

7.5.3 Temples and mosques as center housing around a new population

Indian cities grew around temples in a concentric fashion. The temples of India serve as spiritual and prevalent landmarks.

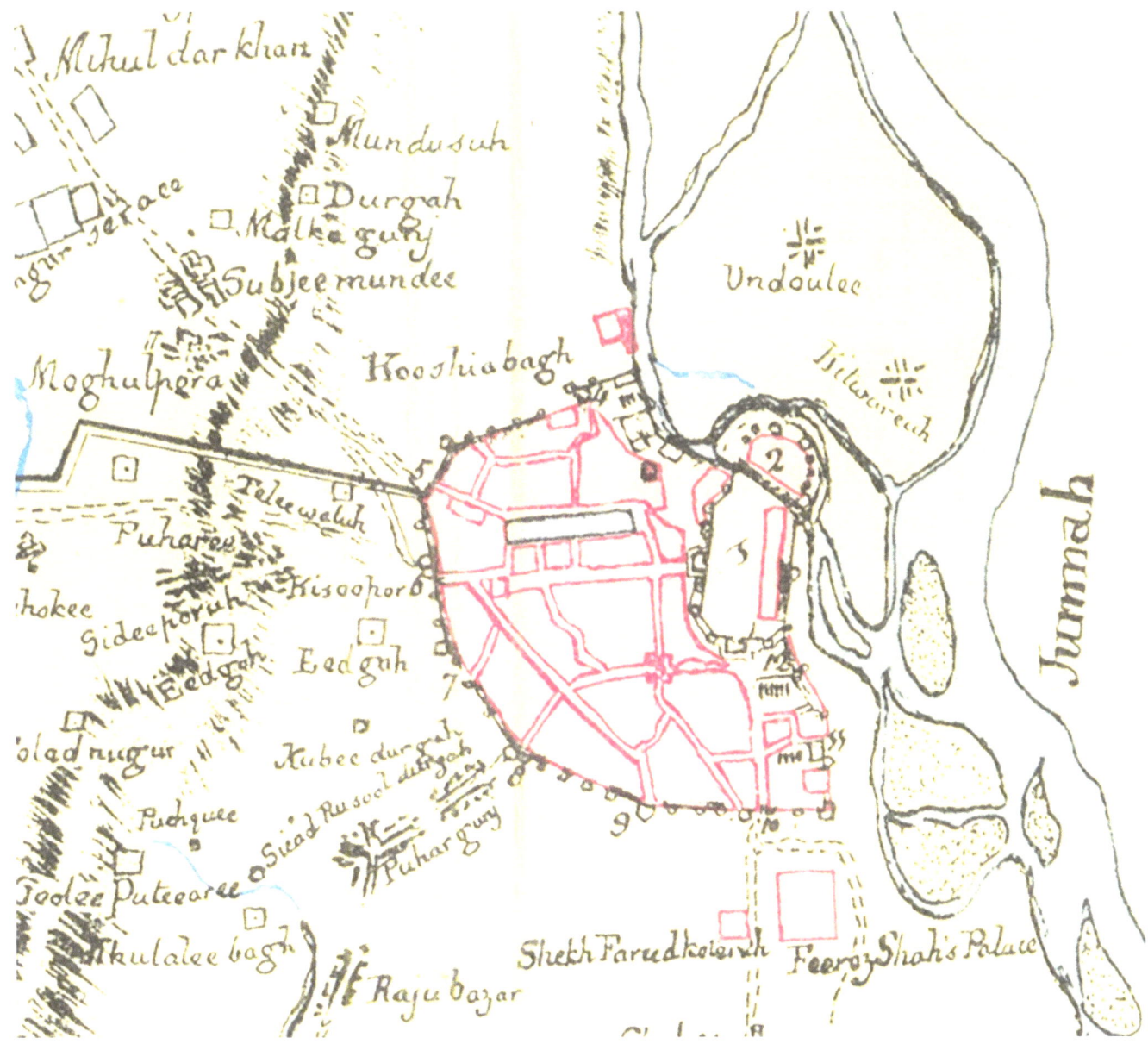

Figure 7.5 Extract from the Antique Map, sketch of the environs of Delhi [*Source:* Survey of India]

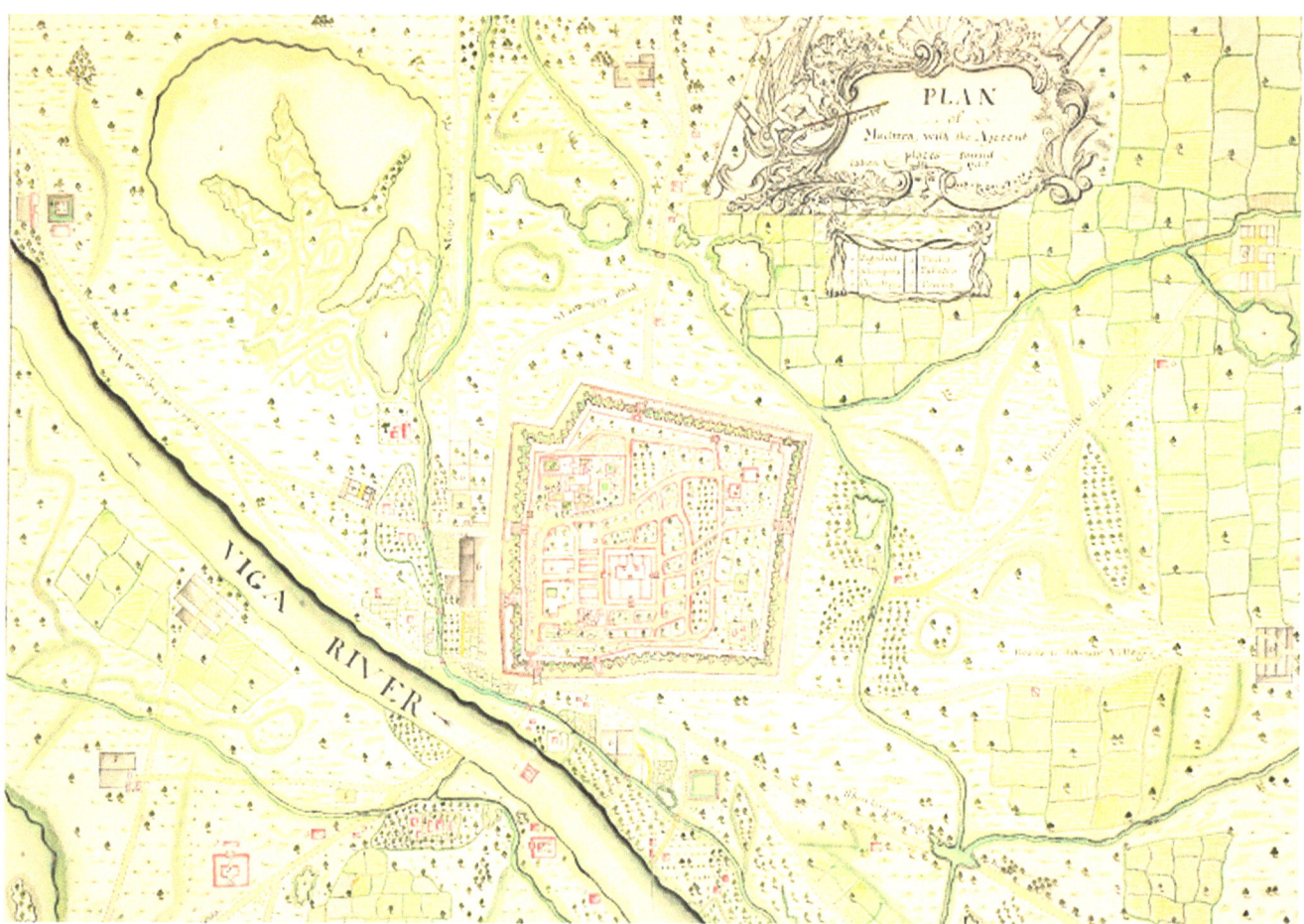

Figure 7.6 Map of Madurai by William Jenings, 1755 [[Credit: ©The British Library Board K. Top.115.87. Digital file 074098]

7.5.4 Colonial British forts and settlement

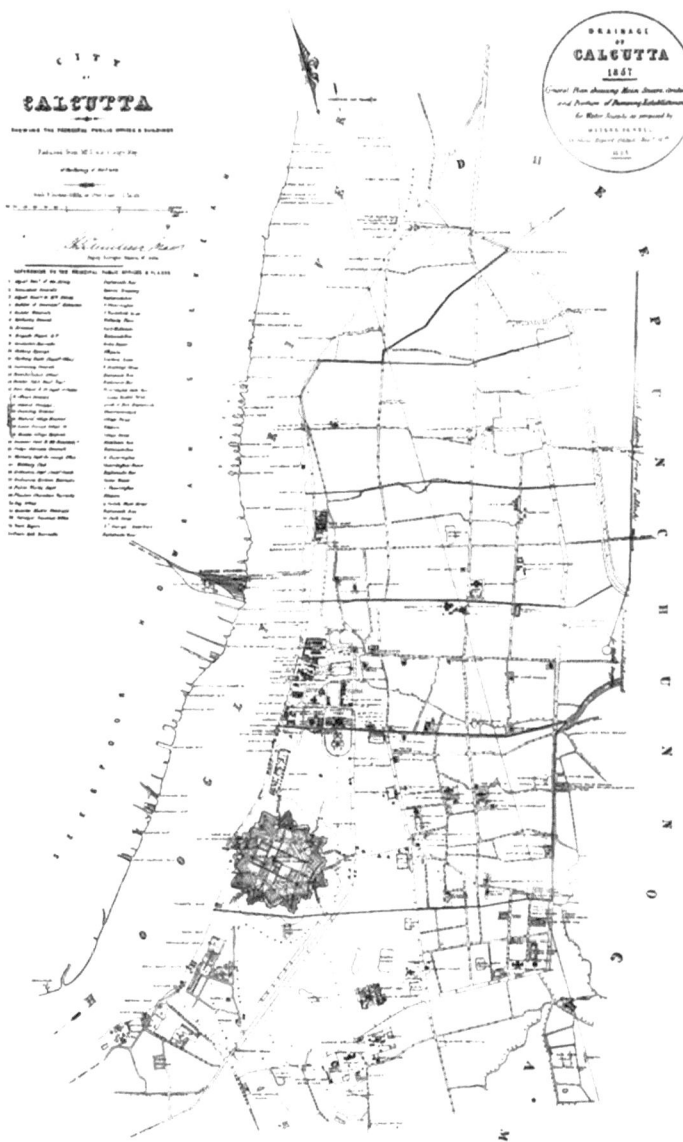

Figure 7.7 Calcutta and its environs [Source: The Survey of India, Dehradun, Republic of India]

7.5.5 Central Business District (CBD) – legislative buildings – govt. offices – various housings – satellite cities – green belt

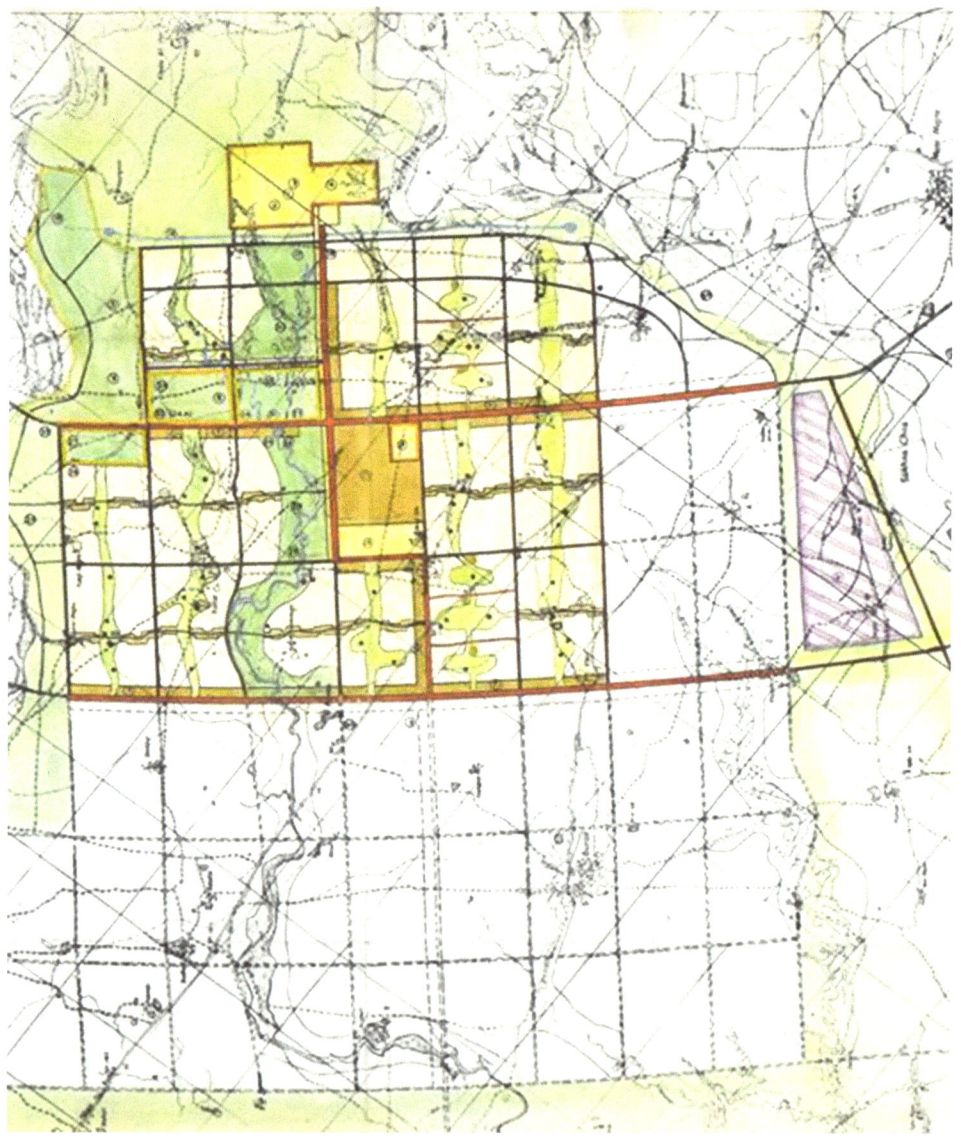

Figure 7.8 Chandigarh city grid extension [*Source:* Survey of India; © FLC/ADAGP]

7.6 Indian Cities: Population, Tradition and Culture

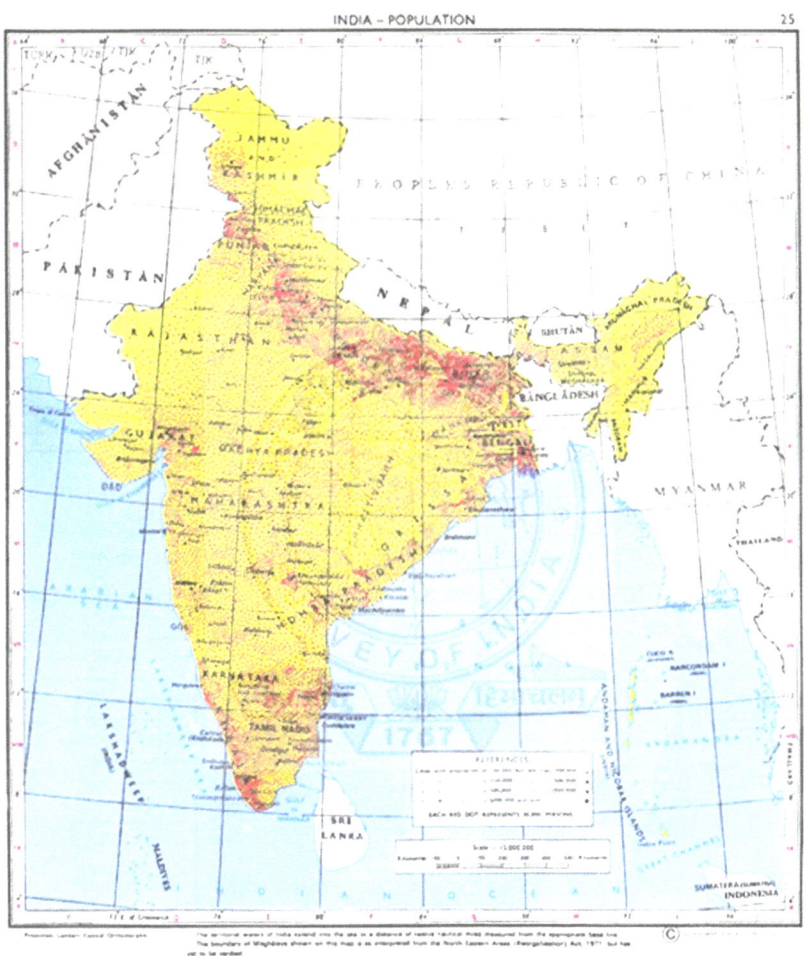

Figure 7.9 Population Map of India [*Source:* Survey of India]

Classification of Indian cities in terms of population:
   Tier 1: 100,000 and above
   Tier 2: 50,000 to 100,000
   Tier 3: 20,000 to 50,000
   Tier 4: 10,000 to 19,999

According to NITI Aayog, 68% of India's total population lives in rural areas (2013–14). By 2030, almost 60% of the world's population will live in urban areas. By 2030, India is expected to be a home to six megacities with populations above 10 million. Currently 17% of India's urban population lives in slums. The Census of India states that India accounts for a meagre 2.4 percent of world surface area of 135.79 million sq. km. On the other hand, it supports 17.5 percent of the world's total population. The population density in Mumbai follows with 31,700 people per square kilometre.

Indian culture and tradition vary from Kashmir to Kanyakumari, with the diversity of languages spoken. India is comprised of 29 states, 7 union territories and 712 districts. According to People's Linguistic Survey of India (PLSI), there are 750 languages spoken in India. The study culture is thus of foremost important determining factor for master planning as it considers the resident citizens' aspiration. For e.g. Ganesh Chaturthi is celebrated all over India, but in Mumbai Ganesh Chaturthi is celebrated with fervour, thus the civic spaces should be designed such that it caters to the aspirations of Mumbaikars. Yakshagana is a traditional theatre performed in the coastal state of Karnataka; the civic areas should be designed where an outdoor theatre can be performed. Likewise, all religious cultures in India should be studied in order to design the civic spaces of India.

7.7 Classification of Indian Cities Based on Geography

Coastal cities: The cities in coastal area where settlements are based on needs of fishing and later on to cater to port development. It is always in close proximity to the sea and expansion is restricted towards sea side.

Mainland cities: Cities in mainland do not have any restriction, and they continue to grow on all sides (with the restriction of hills).

Hill cities: Hill cities were strategically placed on top of a hill to keep the enemy away. The heights can be strategically used to overpower the enemy and usually surrounded by moat or a fort wall.

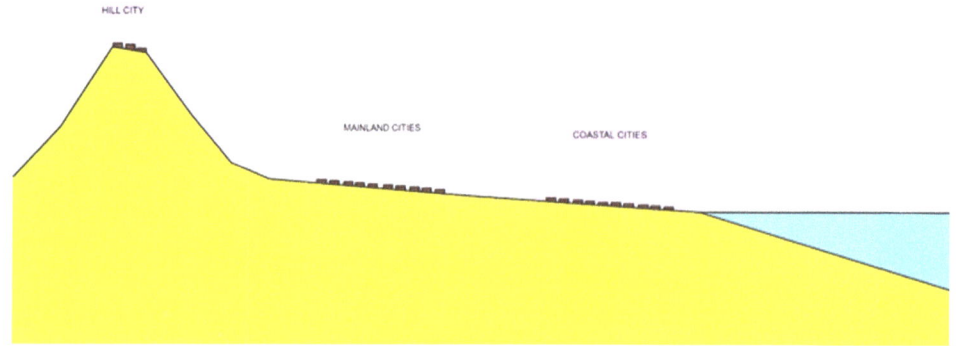

Figure 7.10 Topographical section

7.8 The Urban Morphology

Urban morphology is the makeup[2] of the blocks, movement networks such as the streets, and open spaces are arranged constituting to the city or the place, the interrelationship between the constituent parts and the measure of efficiency expresses a successful place.

The figure ground plan for Mumbai reveals the underlying urban morphology of the CBD district.

Figure 7.11 Figure ground plan of Mumbai

Why is urban structure so important? What do we derive from the urban structure?

The underlying principle of urban structure is the blocks and their arrangement. There are many ways one can compose the blocks, such as the grid arrangement, radial arrangement, circular or composite. Only when a relationship is established with factors such as the open area, the relationship becomes defined.

---
[2] The way in which something is put together: composition; construction

Figure 7.12 Chandigarh: River edge and block formation

Figure 7.13 Chandigarh: River edge, block formation, and open spaces

For identifying movement network and its efficiency for infrastructure and connectivity, urban structure is the underlying blue print. Bigger the block size, more the density and more load on the transport network. Thus, the street and the blocks have a very direct relationship. The arrangement of blocks is done vis-à-vis to the movement network. The movement network, i.e. the figure ground diagram of the urban structure reveals the block patterns, street patterns and further defines the legibility of the area.

Achieving Urban Renaissance: Indian History and Culture **103**

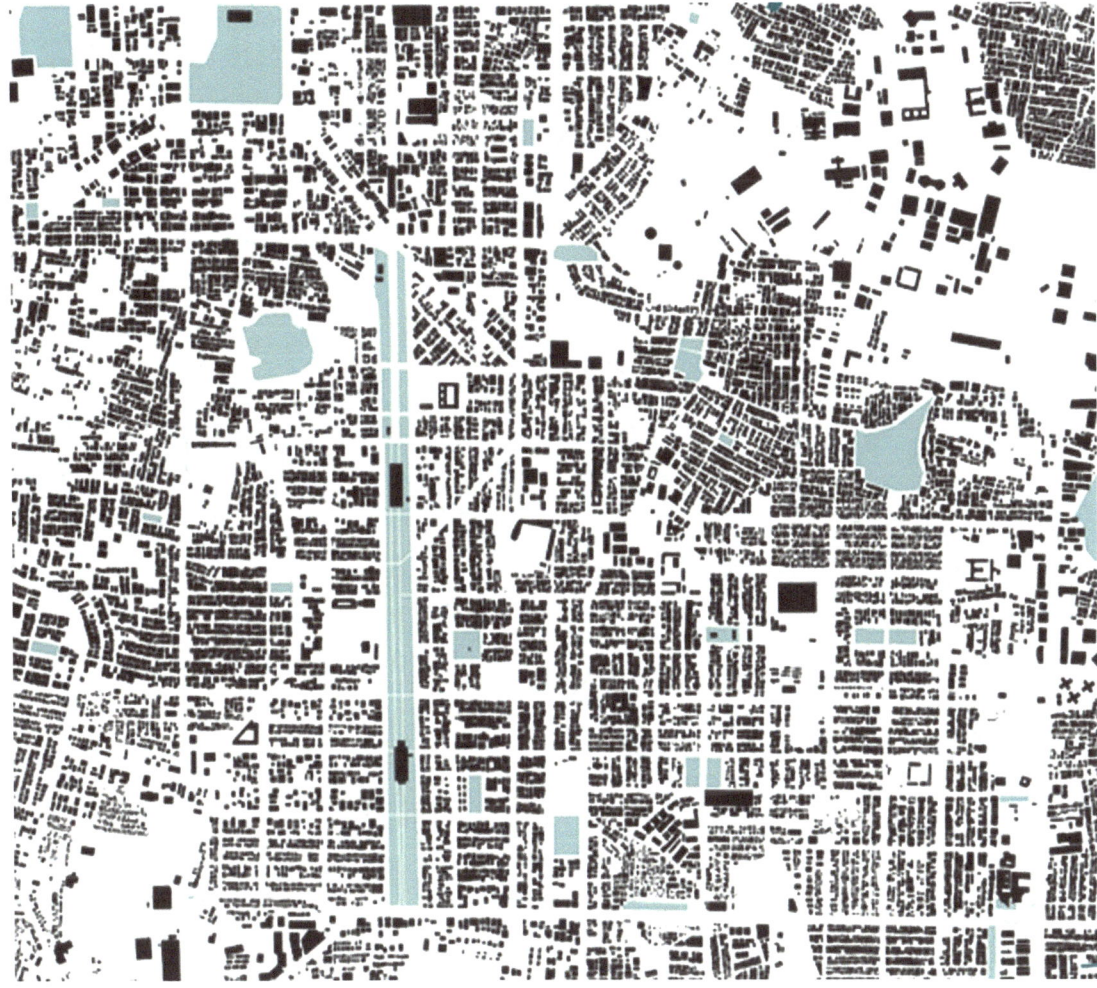

Figure 7.14 Figure ground plan of Jayanagar, Bangalore

It also reveals a relationship in terms of proximities and the nature of open spaces which defines them. Are the blocks well integrated to the open spaces?

The various relationships such as density vs. the open spaces, open spaces vs. street width, study of block sizes, study of block arrangements and most importantly the movement network vs. the urban structure pattern will give forth to certain parameters, a frame or an image is thus created. These images and characteristics form the underlying study for analysis based upon which design decisions and policies are made.

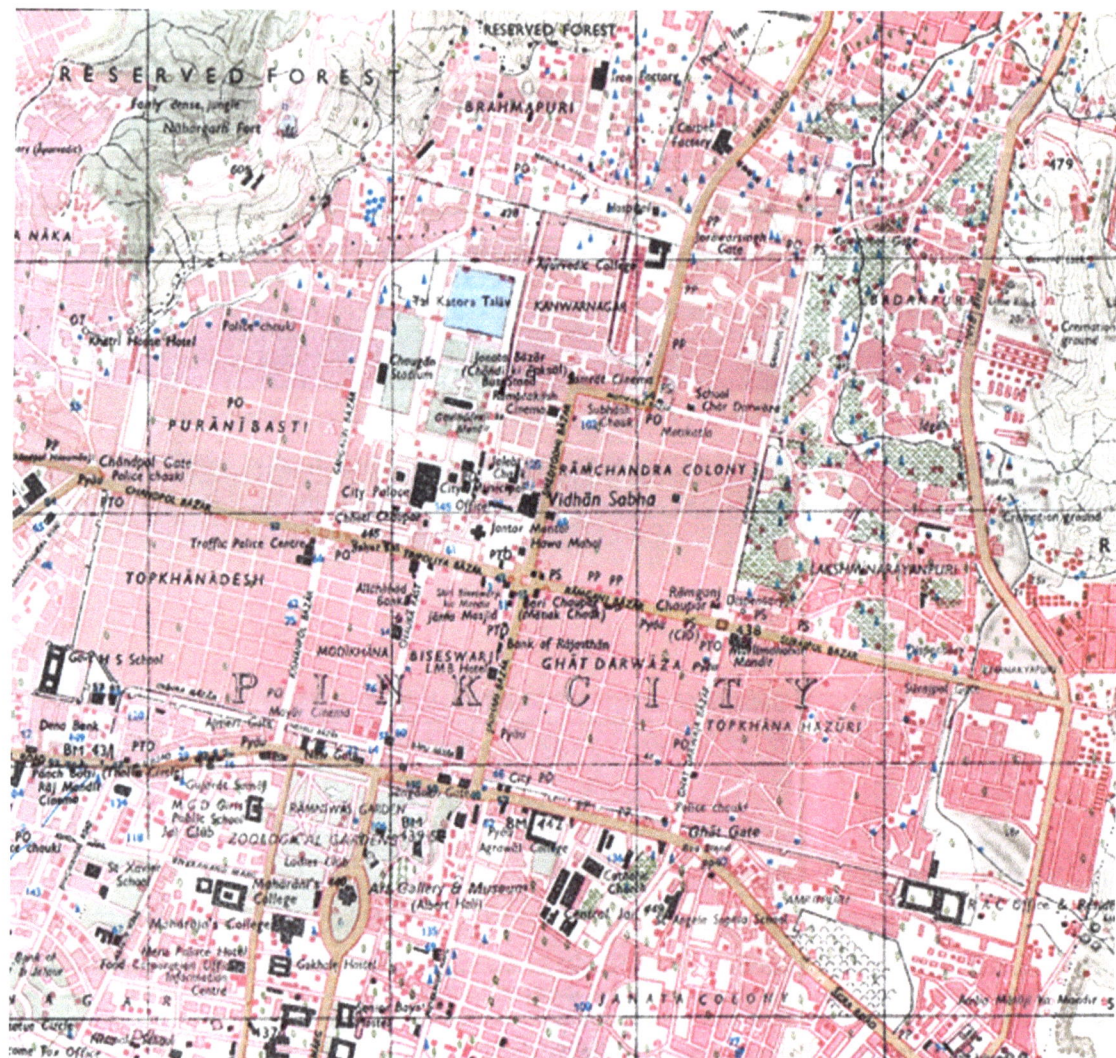

Figure 7.15 Figure ground plan of Jaipur [*Source:* Survey of India]

Relative sizes of the blocks and their relationship to other blocks defines compact nature of the urban structure. For a good grid size, urban blocks play an important role. It can be divided into two parts: size less than 100 × 100 m, suitable for walking and more than 100 × 100 m suitable for factories and warehouses. More compact the urban structure, the better is its legibility.

Achieving Urban Renaissance: Indian History and Culture   **105**

7.9 Movement and Connections: Walking

The 400 m or 800 m walking radius centred on a transport hub gives choices to people to walk, take the urban transport, or cycle, depending upon their suitability. A good movement provides maximum number of options, holistic and legible. In case, the grid offers a seamless thoroughfare around the entire city. The grid-based movement fits in the overall movement network of Chandigarh. Walking should be promoted as a measure of successful place. In case of Chandigarh, the school is kept at the centre of the sector which can be reached from all sides of the sector.

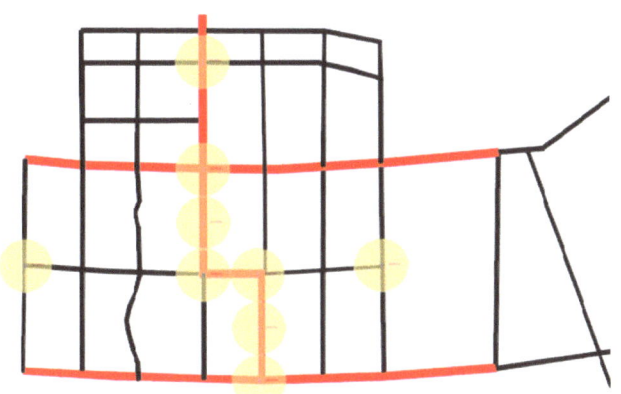

Figure 7.16 Movement network within 400-mile radius in Chandigarh

Figure 7.17 Sector profile

7.10 Walkability Radius

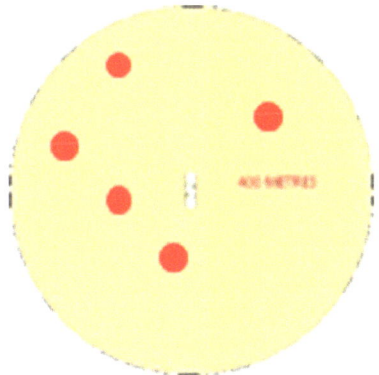

Figure 7.18 400-m walkable radius

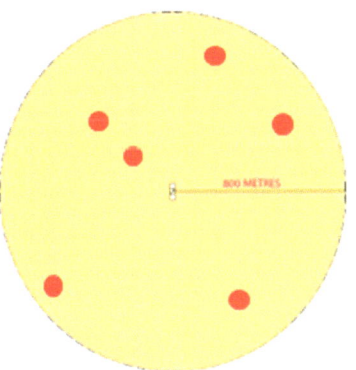

Figure 7.19 800-m walkable radius

The walkability radius is a measure of distance from the centre of the circle in a residential area to the various amenities. The most convenient way to reach a place is walk.

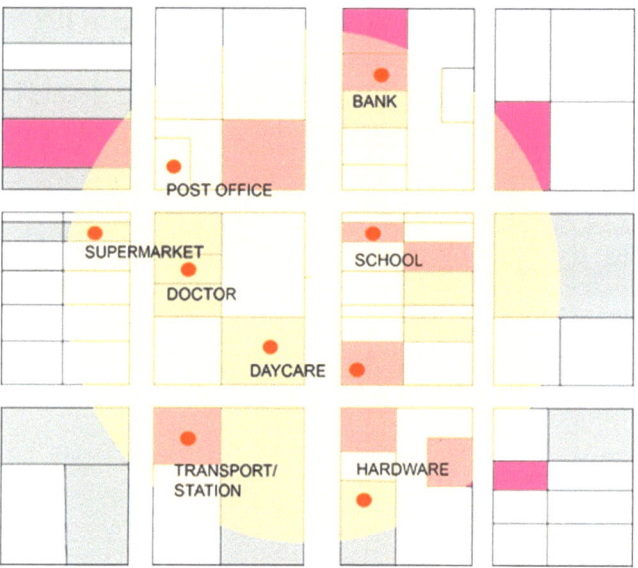

Figure 7.20 800-m walkable radius on a block

Figure 7.21 Walking and cycling lanes on the pedestrian level

Achieving Urban Renaissance: Indian History and Culture 107

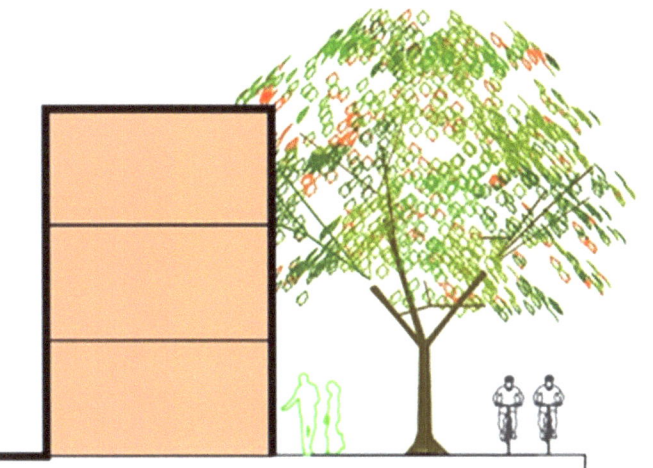

Figure 7.22 The Boulevard

Make walking route through the blocks; the walking route enables greater connectivity to the overall development framework.

Walking route through the open spaces ensures greater interactions and a successful place.

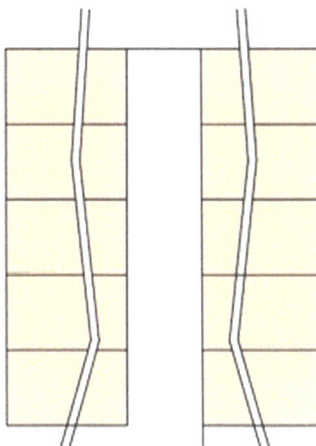

Figure 7.23 Pedestrian walking through apartments

108 Master Planning Indian Cities: Achieving Urban Renaissance

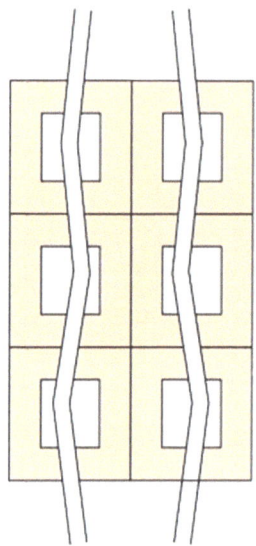

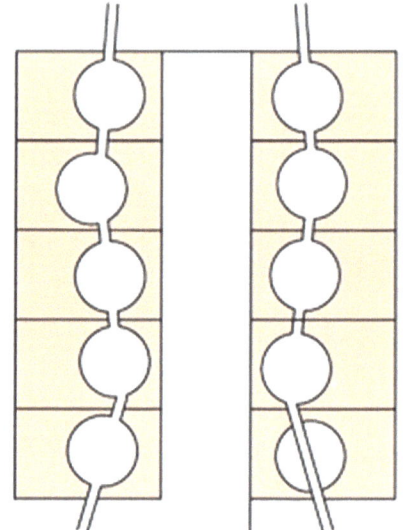

Figure 7.24 Pedestrian walking through perimeter blocks

Figure 7.25 Pedestrian walking through activity generators

Walking route and creating interactive spaces make the place all the more successful. It allows people to communicate and perform various activities throughout the year ensuing community bonds.

7.11   The Urban Girth Effect

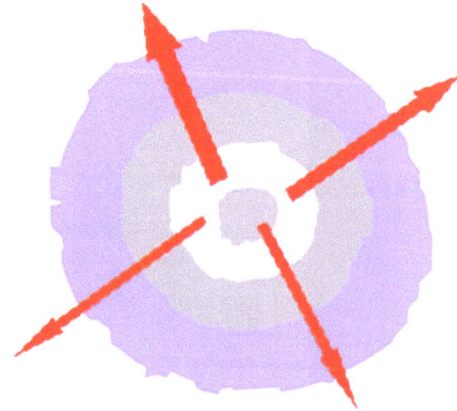

Figure 7.26 Section of a tree showing the tree rings

Figure 7.27 Diagram of urban girth pattern

Cities have often been evolved around a central core. In medieval historical Indian cities, they were fortified forts belonging to the rulers and in the late 20th century it is the CBD. The concentric pattern however gets distorted due to geography or topographical constraints. It comprises of a landmark or a CBD in its core.

Bangalore due to its geographical location, near the centre of peninsular south India, is growing in all direction with the urban girth effect.

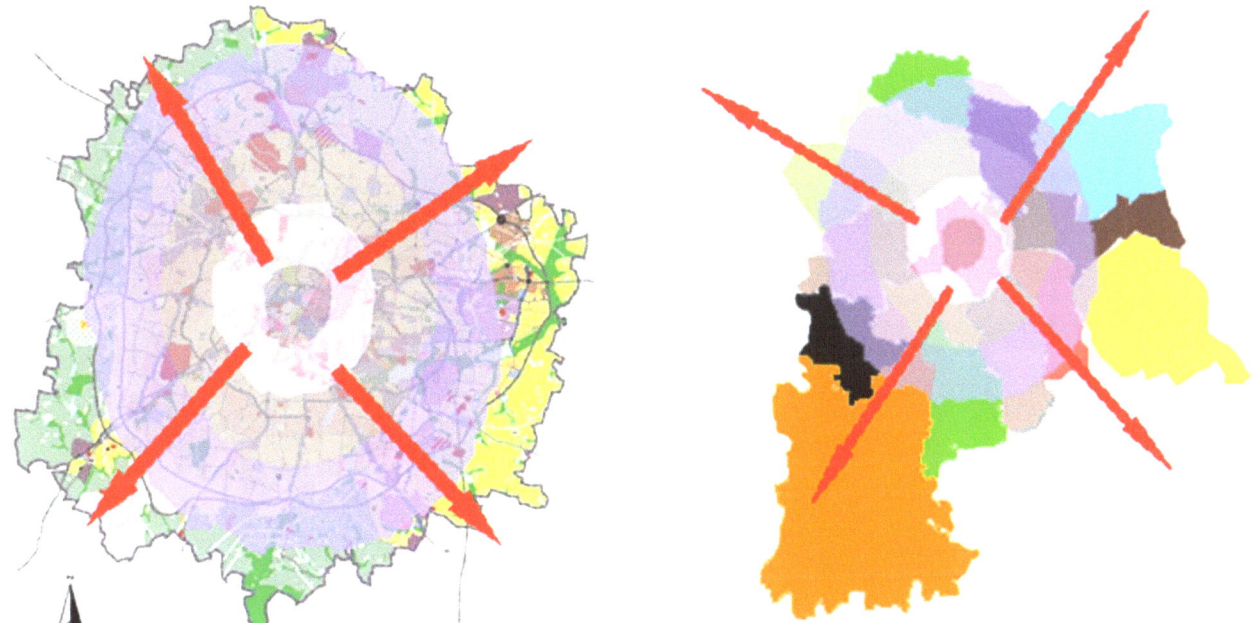

Figure 7.28 Urban girth pattern of Bangalore　　　　**Figure 7.29** Urban girth pattern of New Delhi

New Delhi due to absence of any topographical constraints is growing with 19 districts around it. The urban growth effect is of high order.

Mumbai peninsula region and urban push in the linear direction and creating New Bombay/Mumbai like 21st century Indian cities are characterized by an urban sprawl thus giving rise to 'placeless'. Non-geographic locations are mushroomed throughout the city robing the city of its identity. Development is characterized by wealth generation and the quality of city life is further overlooked. This issue of *placelessness concentrates on an alternate vision for organizing community building: the edge of the city to the city centre transect for future place making and community building*. With the advent of democracy and birth of Indian republic, city planning became more stratified in terms of zoning, still prevalent in some master planning documents. FAR (floor area ratio) become the developmental parameter. How do we design buildings and master plan in such a context is the critical question?

Figure 7.30 Urban girth pattern of Mumbai

7.11.1 The urban strand

The various areas on the outskirts of the city tend to make a suburban characteristic on the city edge. The scale at the core is higher than at the edges and diminishes at the edges. The entire characteristic can be mapped on to a stand, which is a two-dimensional imaginary plane.

7.11.2 Urban strand of Mysore

Mysore is a city known for many historic landmarks. In the context of 21st century, the city is fast losing its urban morphology and more importantly an urban character. Buildings are mushrooming in the city context and eroding its urban characteristics. Urbanization and building development are some of the major triggers, although the population sees no exponential curve in Mysore as witnessed in the metro cities of India such as Bangalore, New Delhi and Mumbai. Application of urban girth to the city of Mysore shall be one of the approaches towards master planning various parts of the city. Plots and sites shall be chosen along the frame and certain design codes shall be applied depending on the various areas of the city, based upon its location and proximity to the historic core.

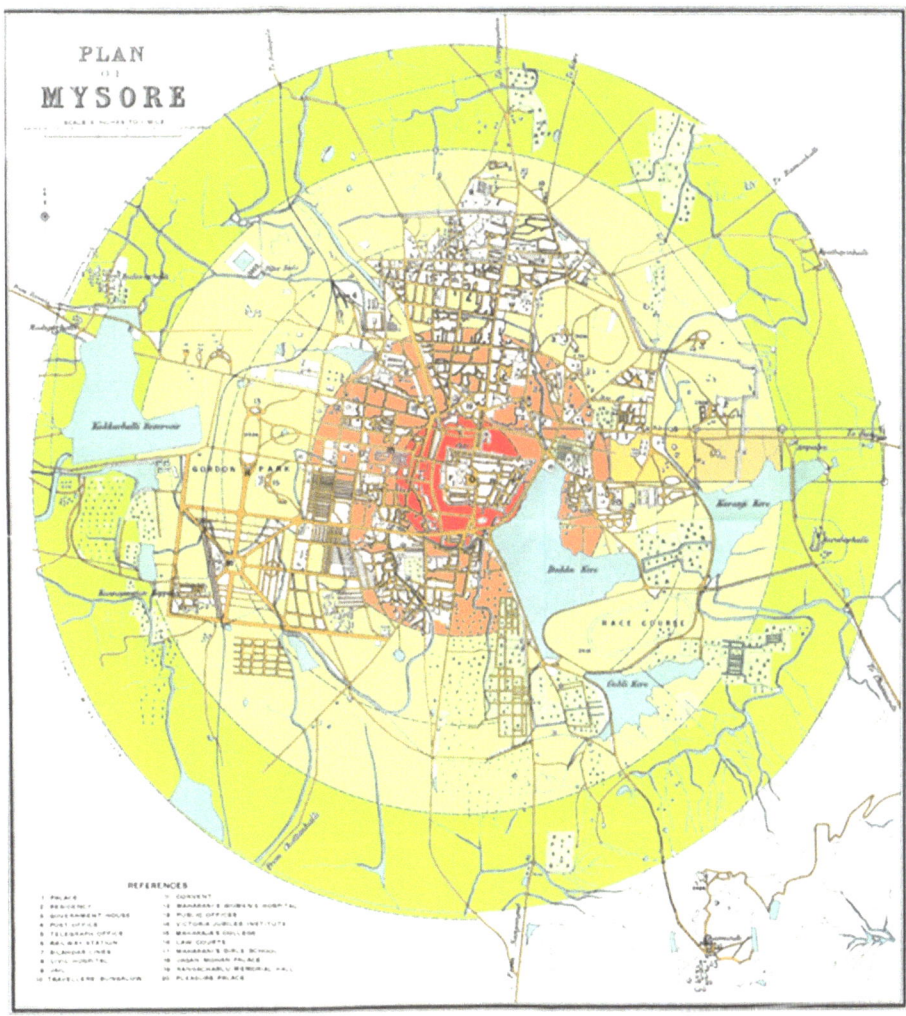

Figure 7.31 Urban girth pattern of Mysore

The zoning plan however is two dimensional, often made on a sheet of paper without the study of geographical or topographical constraints. It works best as a mathematical SET theory, often putting uses in one class and neglecting the much-required interphase, i.e. the inter-relationship. If one were to study the city's urban girth and more so a relevant *urban strand*, the inter-relationship between each *strand* can be identified, strengthening the relationship and contributing to successful city.

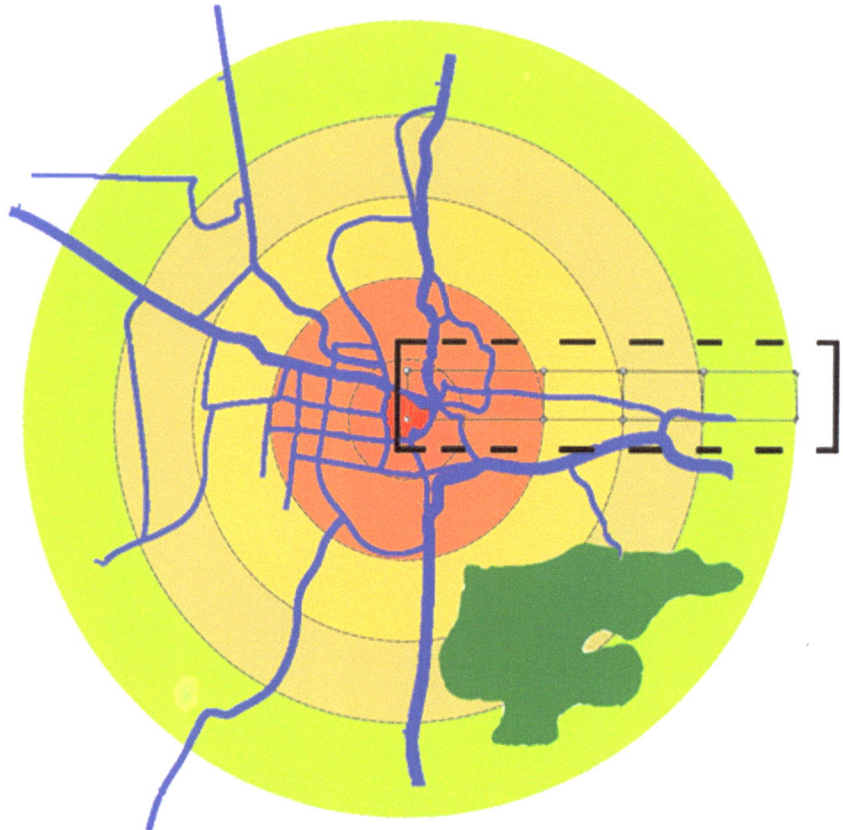

Figure 7.32 Urban girth and urban strand mapped on to present-day Mysore

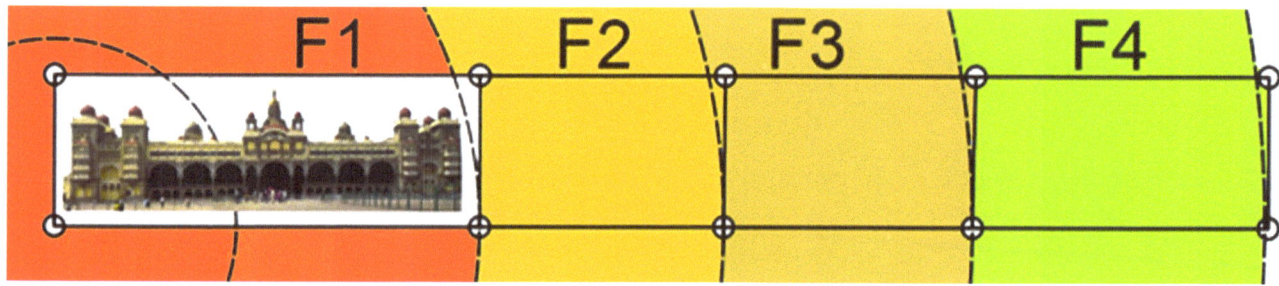

Figure 7.33 Urban strand of present-day Mysore

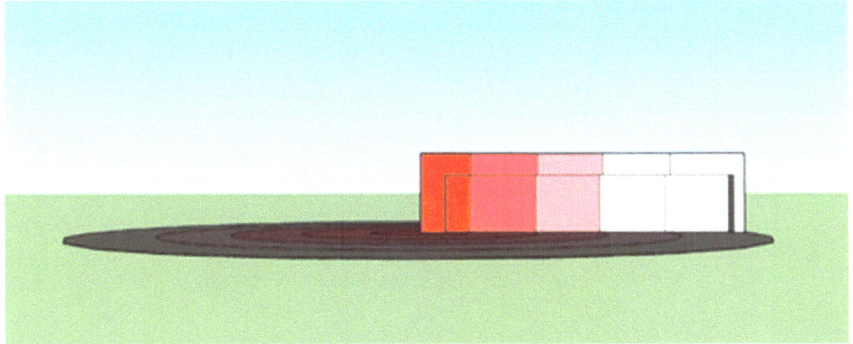

Figure 7.34 Urban strand model of a city

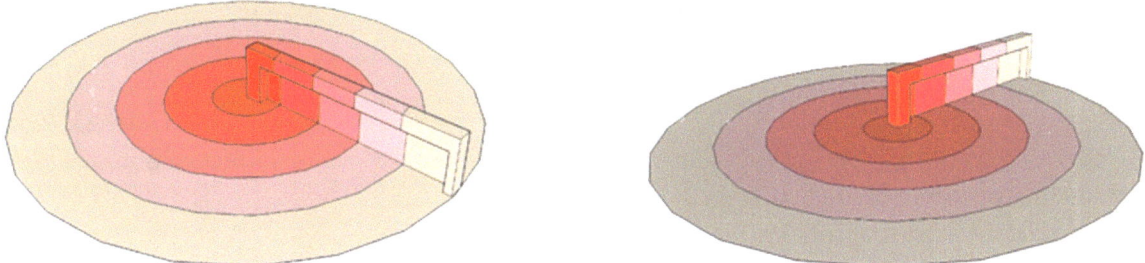

Figure 7.35 Urban strand model of a city at various areas across the city

7.11.3 Critiquing the FAR

The FAR does not consider the relationship at a larger scale. It deals with individual plots with respect to heights and number of stories that can be accommodated. It is a mathematical concept which does not consider the architectural character. Furthermore, it does not consider how the architectural character should be with regards to its surroundings. In a given place there is a streetscape and townscape, the FAR merely suggests the height by an empirical formula and disregards how the most important part of the architectural character can be assimilated with the townscape.

7.11.4 Unifunctional Zoning Model

The unifunctional zoning has a very rigid core often found in North American cities which comprises of the CBD, comprised of office spaces. Around the CBD is the housing area.

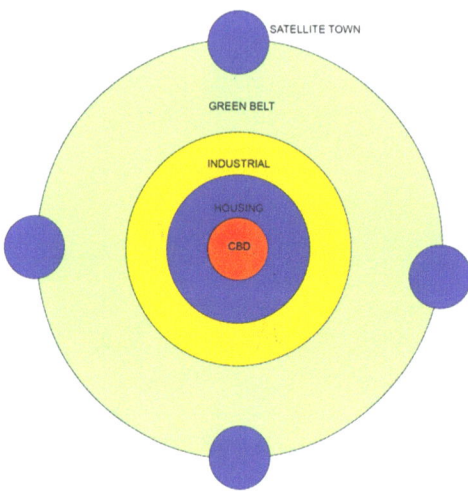

Figure 7.36 Model of unifunctional zoning

People commute to the centralized offices from their respective houses, putting a burden on the arterial roads of the city. On the outskirts of the city lies the industrial area. The industrial area is kept near to the green belt which balances the pollution of the industries. The greenbelt in terms of forest reserves is a place of biodiversity resulting into variation in animal species. Beyond the greenbelt lies the satellite town or new towns to cater to the new population. Satellite towns exist in isolation away from any historical context. They are often made subsidiary to the main city.

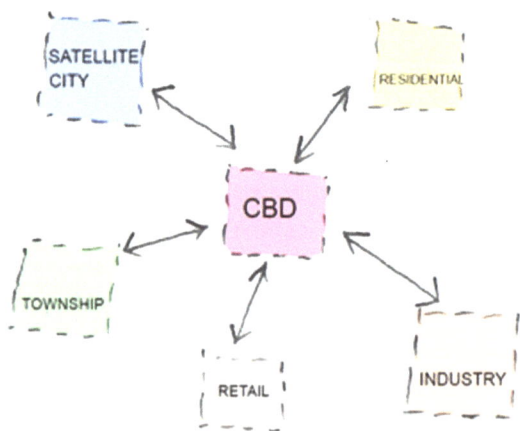

The historic core or the CBD (Central Business District)

Figure 7.37 Sketch of unifunctional zoning pattern

Achieving Urban Renaissance: Indian History and Culture   **115**

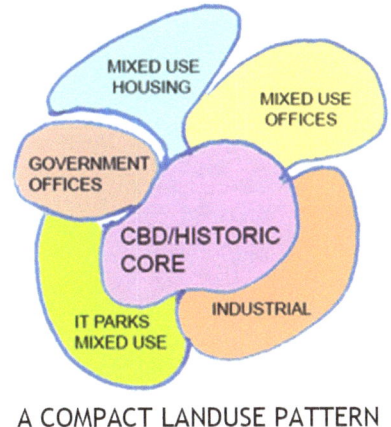

A COMPACT LANDUSE PATTERN

Figure 7.38 Sketch of CBD zoning pattern

> A compact land use pattern offers basic amenities within the reach of its citizens. The travel time is however reduced, cutting down pollution and greenhouse emissions. The historic core or the CBD becomes integrated with the different districts forming the heart of the city.

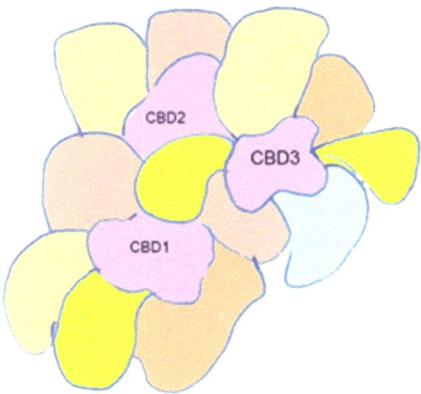

MULTI-NUCLEATED LANDUSE PATTERN

Figure 7.39 Sketch of multi-CBD zoning pattern

> A multi-nucleated land use pattern has multiple central business districts, with various districts around it. The districts offer flexibility to form associations with each other and can grow organically suiting the needs of its citizens.

7.12 Relationship Between the Density and Blocks

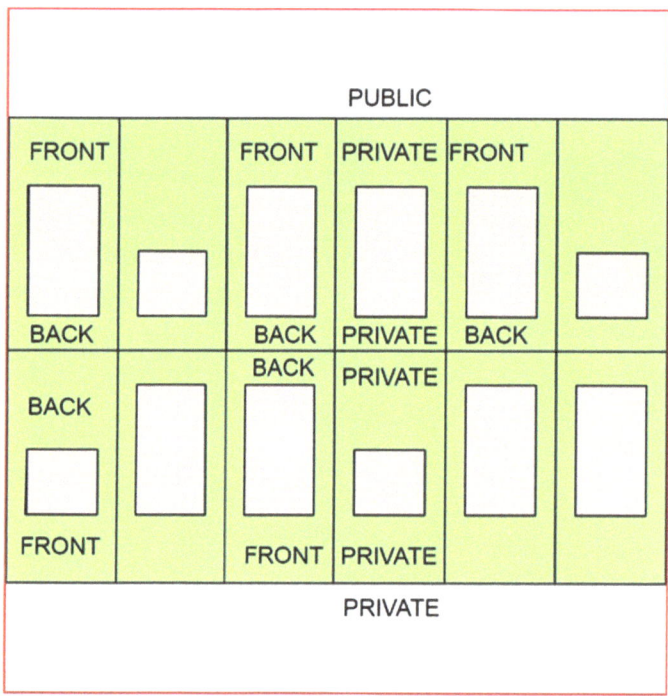

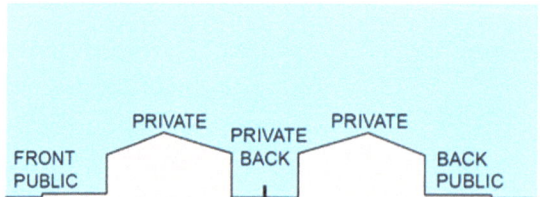

Figure 7.40 Plan of house/villa arrangement and section

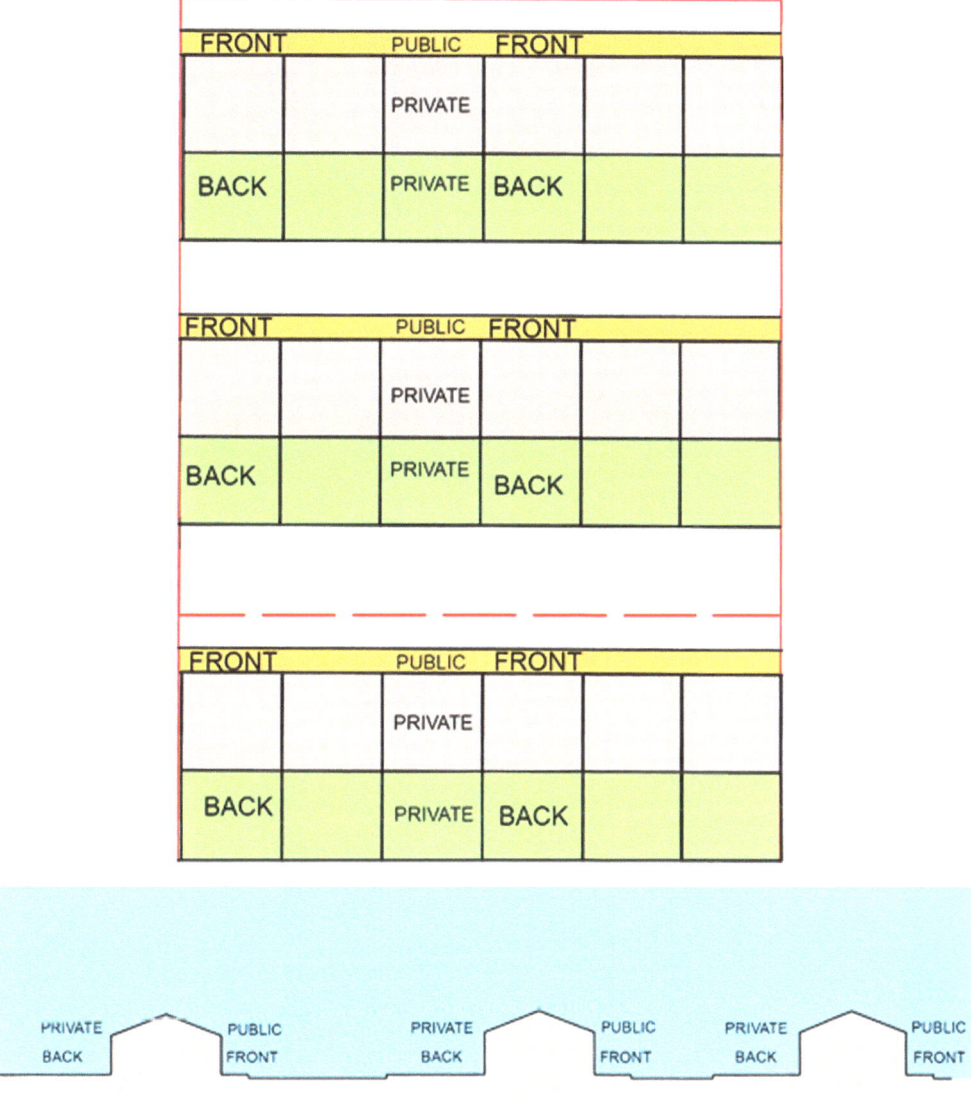

Figure 7.41 Plan of terraces arrangement and section

118 Master Planning Indian Cities: Achieving Urban Renaissance

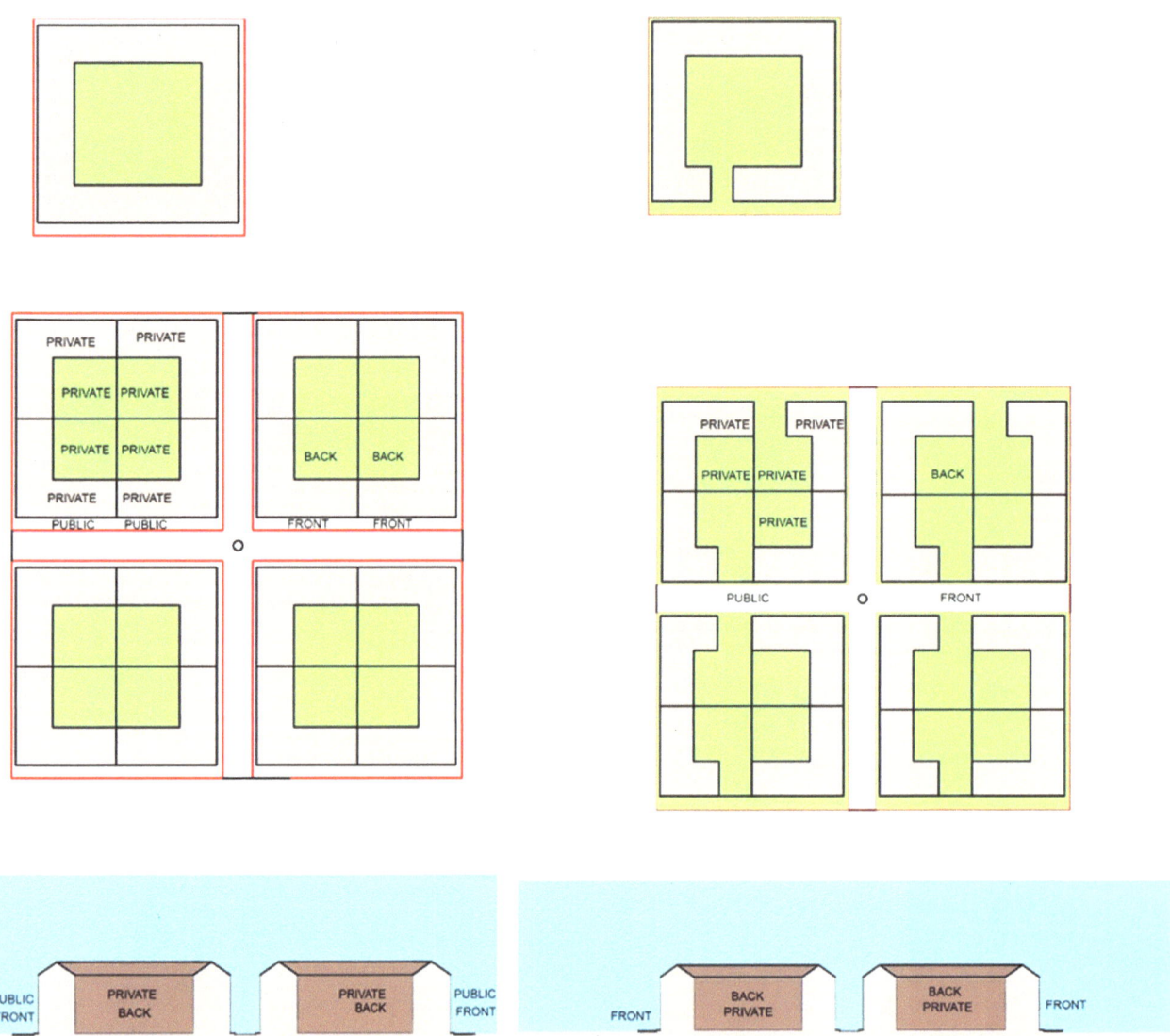

Figure 7.42 Plans of perimeter block apartments' arrangement and section

Figure 7.43 Plan of perimeter block apartments with communal spaces arrangement and section

Achieving Urban Renaissance: Indian History and Culture   **119**

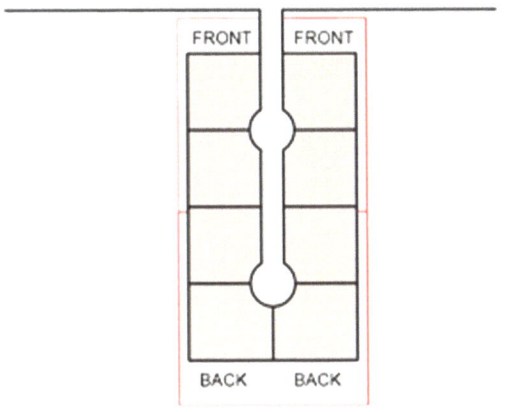

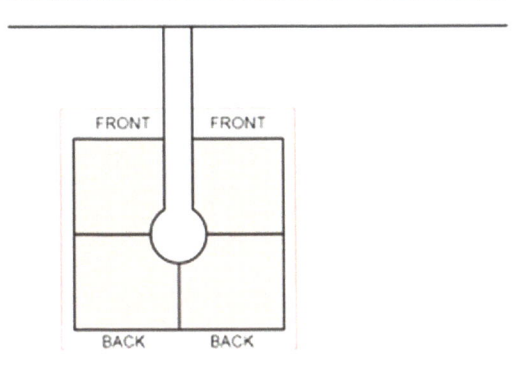

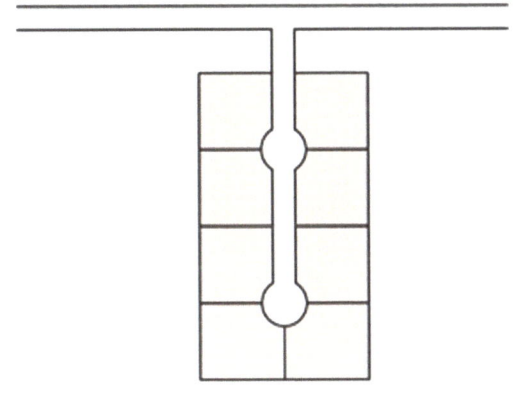

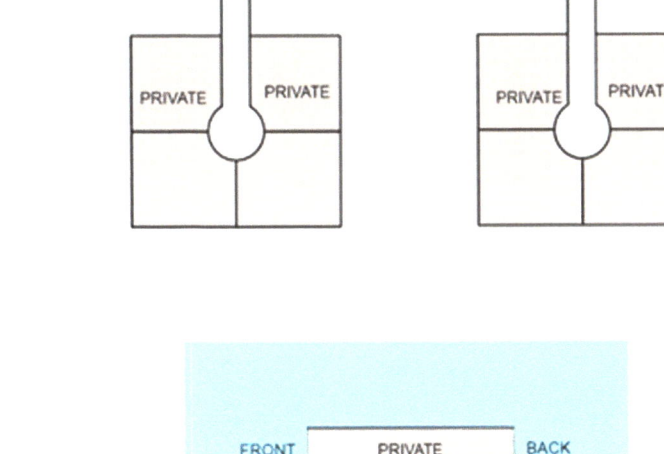

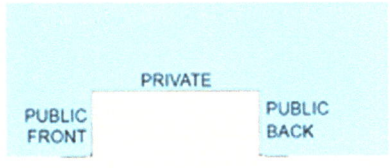

Figure 7.44 Plan of apartments and section

Figure 7.45 Plan of apartments' sections

120 Master Planning Indian Cities: Achieving Urban Renaissance

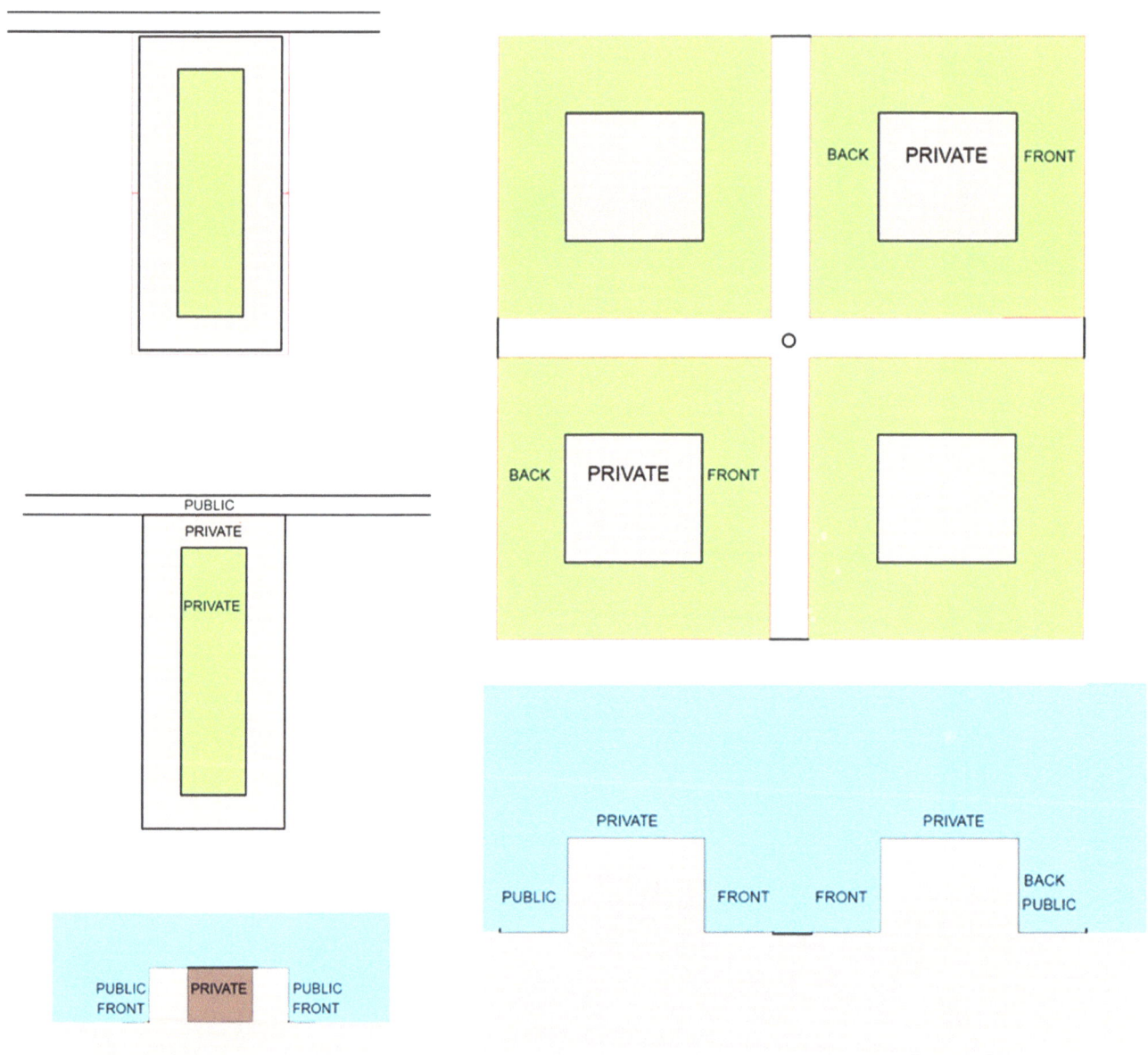

Figure 7.46 Plan of apartment block and section

Figure 7.47 Plan of apartment block and section

Table 7.1–7.3 Urban design attributes to the scale and quality of a place of villa, terrace house, perimeter block apartments

	A Villa or a House	
S. no	Urban Design Attributes	Scale and Quality
1	Communal Spaces	Yes
2	Height	Low
3	Public Space	Yes
4	Private Space	Yes
5	Ground Coverage	Large
6	Geometric Profile	Point
7	Continuity of Street Frontage	Yes

	Terrace Houses	
S. no.	Urban Design Attributes	Scale and Quality
1	Communal Spaces	Yes
2	Height	Low
3	Public Space	Yes
4	Private Space	Yes
5	Ground Coverage	Large
6	Geometric Profile	Line
7	Street Definition	Yes

	Perimeter Block Apartments with Court-I	
S. no	Urban Design Attributes	Scale and Quality
1	Communal Spaces	Yes
2	Height	Moderate
3	Public Space	Yes
4	Private Space	Yes
5	Ground Coverage	Large
6	Geometric Profile	Enclosure
7	Street Definition	Yes

Table 7.4–7.6 Urban design attributes to the scale and quality of a place of perimeter apartments with court and isolated apartments

	Perimeter Block Apartments with Court-II
S. no.	Urban Design Attributes	Scale and Quality
1	Communal Spaces	Minimal
2	Height	Moderate
3	Public Spaces	Yes
4	Private Spaces	Yes
5	Ground Coverage	Large
6	Geometric Profile	Enclosure
7	Street Definition	Yes

	Perimeter Block Apartments with Court-III
S. no.	Urban Design Attributes	Scale and Quality
1	Communal Spaces	Minimal
2	Height	Moderate
3	Public Spaces	Yes
4	Private Spaces	Yes
5	Ground Coverage	Large
6	Geometric Profile	Enclosure
7	Street Definition	Yes

	Apartments-I
S. no.	Urban Design Attributes	Scale and Quality
1	Communal Spaces	Minimal
2	Height	High
3	Public Spaces	Yes
4	Private Spaces	Yes
5	Ground Coverage	Large
6	Geometric Profile	Point
7	Street Definition	No

Table 7.7–7.8 Urban design attributes to the scale and quality of a place of isolated apartments

	Apartments-II	
S. no.	Urban Design Attributes	Scale and Quality
1	Communal Spaces	Minimal
2	Heights	High
3	Public Spaces	Yes
4	Private Spaces	Yes
5	Ground Coverage	Large
6	Geometric Profile	Slab
7	Street Definition	No

	Apartments-III	
S. no.	Urban Design Attributes	Scale and Quality
1	Communal Spaces	Minimal
2	Heights	High
3	Public Spaces	Yes
4	Private Spaces	Yes
5	Ground Coverage	Large
6	Geometric Profile	Enclosure
7	Street Definition	No

7.13   Sustainability and Climate Change

Planet Earth is warming at an alarming stage. According to the UN on Climate Change, "The human influence on the climate system is clear and is evident from the increasing greenhouse gas concentrations in the atmosphere, positive radiative forcing, observed warming, and understanding of the climate system".

Due to the rise of cities in the 21st century, the population density is highest, which is a drain on natural resources due to its confined area or city size. Today's cities are polluted due to the usage of automobiles and other means of transport. Green cover is vanishing in the name of development and infrastructure corridors. Moreover, the city land is maximised to accommodate physical and built structures. Urban heat island effect is one such phenomenon occurring in today's cities which drives the cities temperature hotter than its surrounding villages.

7.13.1 Ecopolis not metropolis or megalopolis

21st Century cities should be designed on the basis of ecology. As the building footprint expands the open spaces, greenbelt and reserve forests are encroached resulting in a conflict between the human activity and natural forces. Landscape should be the determining factor of master planning and buildings. Energy efficient buildings and green buildings help cutting down carbon emissions. Sixty percent of the plot area should be given to green spaces, tall and slender buildings should occupy the demand for density.

7.13.2 Impact of wind currents

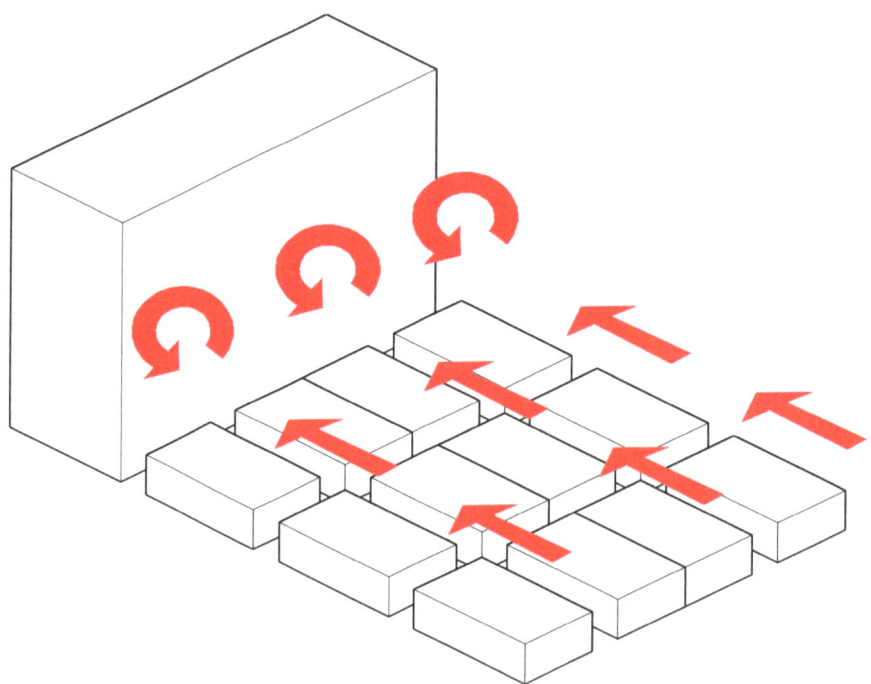

Figure 7.48 Slab block with a sub-urban setting and wind movement pattern

In urban areas wind flow pattern breaks and can cause eddy current much to the uneasiness of the human comfort. Building sizes such as the slab block against a sub-urban scale blocks is subjected to wind currents and creates wind eddies and vortexes. The computer simulation model further shows that the façade of the building, in front and back, creates positive and negative wind loads.

Figure 7.49 Computer wind simulation model of slab block

7.13.2.1 Aerodynamic modelling of the buildings

The slab blocks and the rectangular tower blocks are in no means suitable for an urban environment. Tall buildings due to their height and profile have a negative tendency to stop the wind currents; it is a giant vertical wall which obstructs the winds. Ideally the design of tall buildings should be such that it allows the wind flow due to the nature of an aerodynamic design and yet fulfil the criterion of accommodating high densities. A hybrid geometric typology of tall buildings can be one such example. Natural forms such as animals and plants can serve as an inspiration while designing the tall buildings. All natural forms such as the plant life and mammals work in synchronization with the forces such as wind and water currents adapting and evolving, but never disrupting the natural forces such as wind and sunlight.

Figure 7.50 Cedrus Libani seeds: Nature as inspiration [Credit: Ben Grader]

Figure 7.51 Cut section of a shell: Nature as inspiration and various geometrical profiles and the effect of wind movement [Credit: Lisa Yount]

7.13.3 Impact of Sun

Earth is rotating around its own axis as well as orbiting in an elliptical orbit around the Sun. We receive Sun's rays based upon the geographical region, hemispherical location i.e. northern hemisphere, southern hemisphere and earth's rotation around the Sun. Orientation of buildings and city blocks should be such that it mitigates harsh sunlight and using cavity walls to insulate against harsh solar radiation. Where there is harsh sunlight, Brise soleil should be implemented to allow required sunlight in buildings and reflect back the undesired sunlight back to the atmosphere. The proximity of blocks can also be used to shade the street with landscaping features such as evergreen trees.

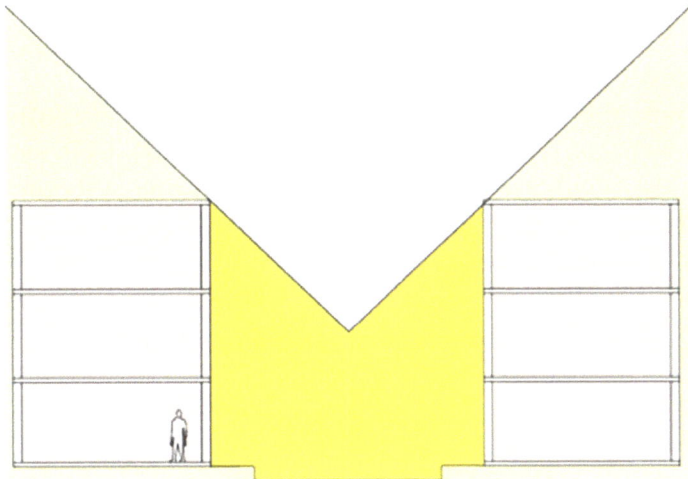

Figure 7.52 Proximity of the blocks and effect of sunlight on the street

Figure 7.53 Blocks with boulevards and effect of sunlight on the street

7.13.4 Importance of topography

Earth's surface is a dynamic entity. Earth has evolved over centuries and presently we are living in Meghalayan Age. There are many geological features of dynamic earth which includes the mountains, hills, rivers and seas. The earth surface should be studied in the wider context of topography. The study of land features on a wider extent gives us an understanding of how the terrain profile is shaped due to its geological features and any development should integrate with the natural forces and not cause any hindrance. For e.g., do not build on low lying lands as it is a catchment area during monsoon season. Always work with the earth and avoid cut and fill to make it a levelled surface.

Figure 7.54 Blocks aligned with the contours

Maps play an important role in understanding the topography of the place. It contains information pertaining to the contours, mean sea level, benchmarks and other geographical features. Master plans should be designed keeping in mind the natural attributes and should be prepared to a suitable scale.

7.14 Relationship Between Landmarks and Frontages

Figure 7.55 Mysore Palace with fortified wall

Historically, landmarks in India have a very close relationship with frontages. The landmark building is used as an object for which an open area is set out which is usually 1.5 times greater than the width of the building, due to their symmetrical layout. Axis plays a very important role as the route is usually on the prevailing axis with the frontages. The frontages are then treated for landscaping for aesthetical and building viewing purposes. Landmarks such as Rashtrapati Bhavan, Taj Mahal exhibit similar characteristics. The frontage 1.6 times the width of the building is the open space in Mysore. The building sits at the end of prevailing axis, and the frontage is used as gardens.

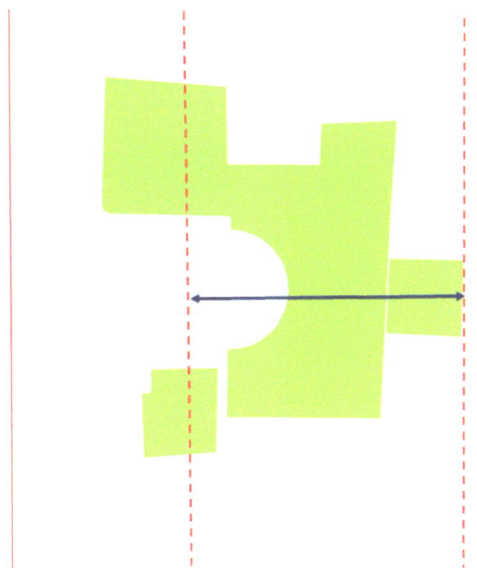

Figure 7.56 Mysore Palace with landscaped frontage ratio

Figure 7.57 Mysore Palace as the landmark

7.15 Mixed-Use Development

Figure 7.58 Street of the walled city of Jaipur

7.15.1 Learning form Jaipur streetscape

Traditional Indian streets, such as the walled city of Jaipur, are well known for mixed use. A mixed use offers retail/commerce at the street level and living on the upper stories. Due to the adoption of the functional ideology of the modernistic zoning plan, mixed use was shunned as pastiche but in reality, mixed use brings vitality to the street level and offers high degree of interactions. In terms of urbanism people encounter is highest.

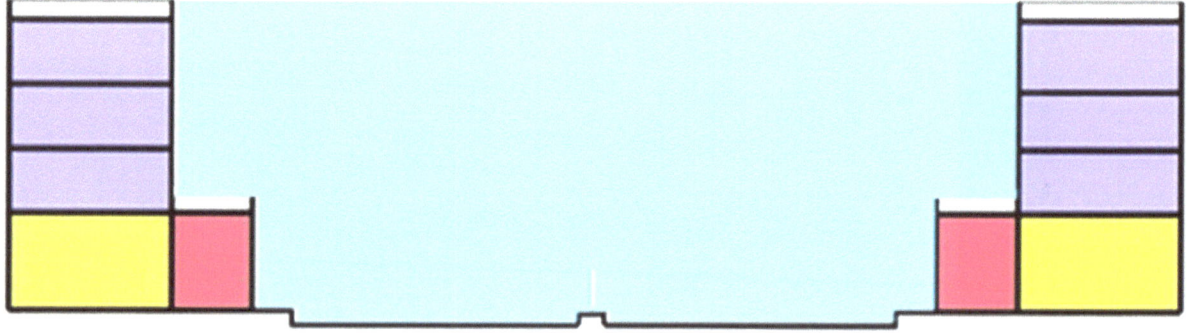

Figure 7.59 Mixed-use development of walled city of Jaipur

- Maintain height uniformity of buildings in terms of scale
- Maintain uniform colours
- Maintain uniform massing of the building blocks
- Maintain a uniform signage proportion
- Maintain a uniform height
- Maintain a uniform tree line
- Active frontages
- Emphasize the nodes of the buildings and the streets in form of squares/chowks

Figure 7.60 Aerial street view of walled city of Jaipur

> Indian streets are known for its vitality; the vitality is in terms of the usage of street. The street usage is through the day and thereby does not require stringent policing. Indian street displays a wide variety of cultural activity during religious festivals and holidays; it is therefore termed as the "Living Street".

7.15.2 Indian streets: Relationship between the street and buildings

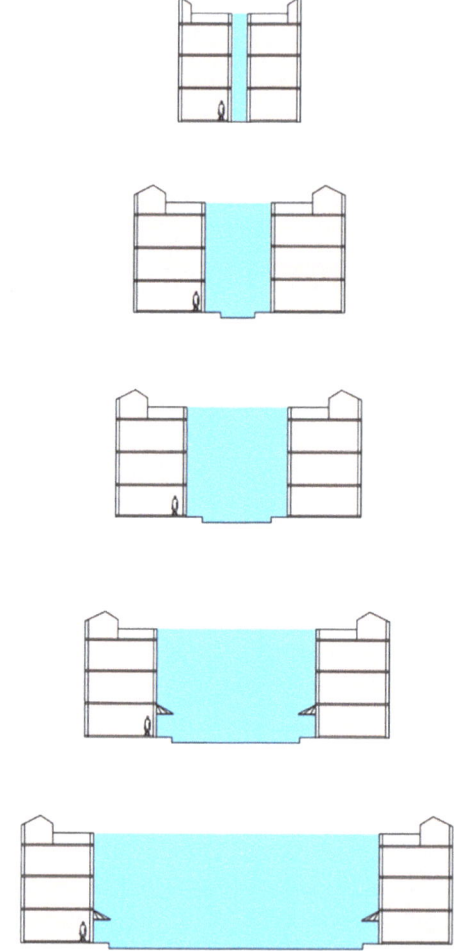

Figure 7.61 Relationship of varying block section widths to the street space

7.15.3 Street space

The area defined by two blocks is termed as street space. Based upon the enclosed space, streets can be termed as positive and negative street spaces.

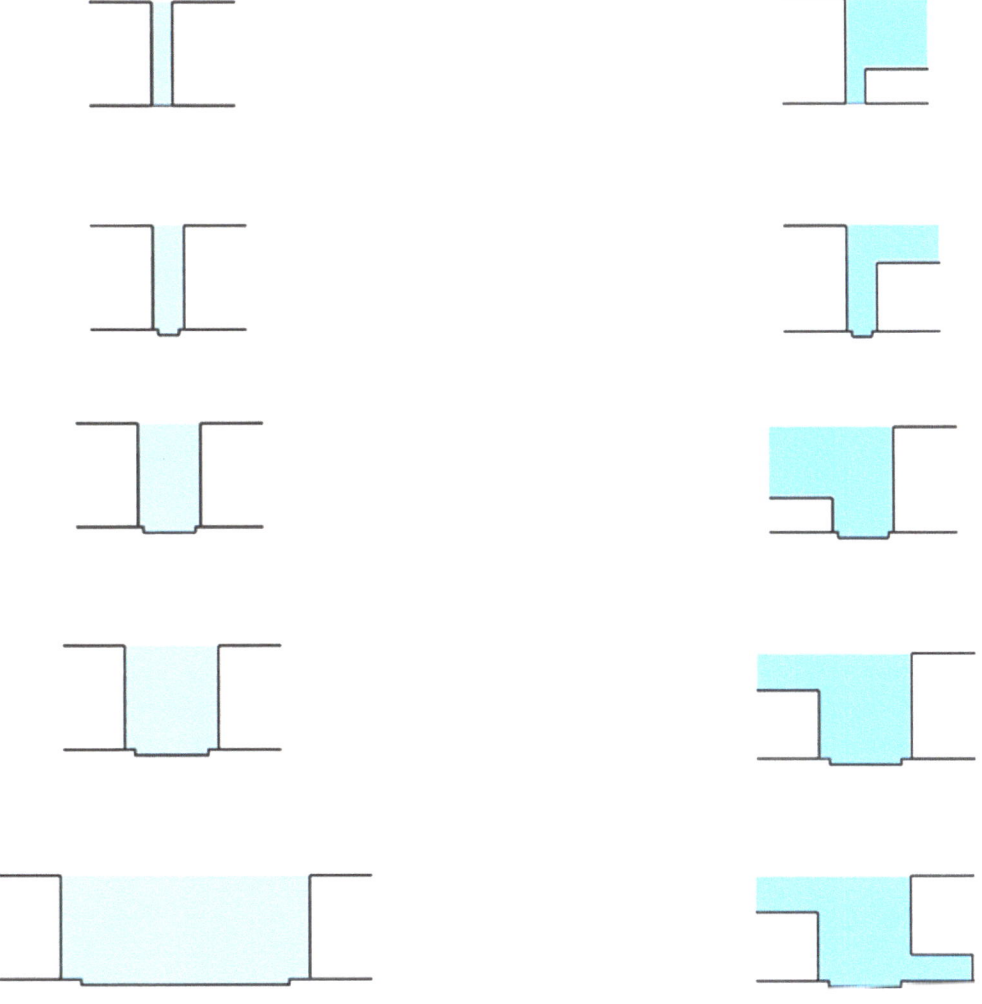

`Figure 7.62 Positive street enclosure   Figure 7.63 Negative street enclosure

7.15.4   Relationship between density and movement

Density of the built form is directly related to the street size. Higher the scale and mass of the building, the width should be bigger for allowing vehicles, people movement and access.

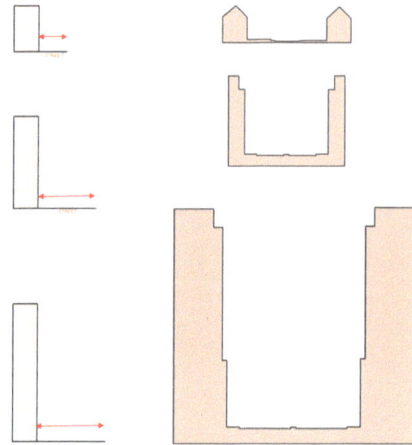

Figure 7.64 Various scales of the buildings and street relationship

7.16 Failure of Tall Buildings and Tower Blocks

7.16.1 Slab blocks

Slab blocks are oblong blocks with a horizontal emphasis and are often characterized by extreme mass and extensive overshadowing. Because of their horizontal emphasis they are strongly directional in appearance. They have a dominant impact and can readily detract from the established character of an area. However, they are the least expensive form of high building and generally provide a greater amount of space per floor.

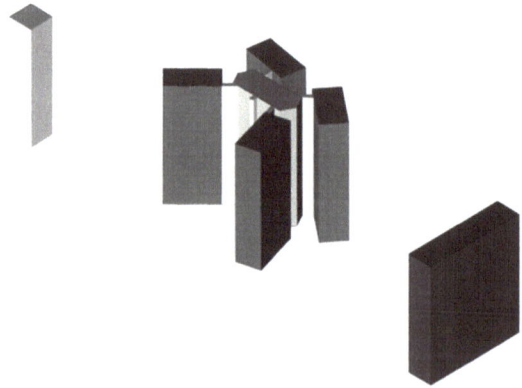

Figure 7.65 Tower block, complex shapes and slab blocks profiles

7.16.2 Tower blocks

They are non-directional in appearance and as regard to usable floor space are more expensive than slab blocks. Slender tower blocks create the least amount of overshadowing; and environmental difficulties associated with those are experienced to a lesser degree.

7.16.3 Complex shapes of buildings

Such high buildings may combine any of the advantages or disadvantages associated with both slab and tower blocks, depending on their design, and because of this usually require more skilfully handling.

7.17 Aftermath of World War II: Post-war Period

Tall buildings tended to accommodate high densities of building. The vertical nature of cities tended to be the dominant character of the city. It tended to accommodate high densities in form of tall buildings and affected the streetscape. Tall buildings tended to create an impact on the human scale; one common feature of tall building is that it stands as a point block, monolithic in appearance and in not to human in scale.

7.18 Single Point/Tower Block

- No private gardens or amenities directly available to the inhabitants
- No direct relationship between the building and the surrounding streets
- Large open space demands significant levels of investment to manage and maintain it at acceptable standards
- A tower block with all the setbacks and FAR and setbacks doses not account for street enclosure

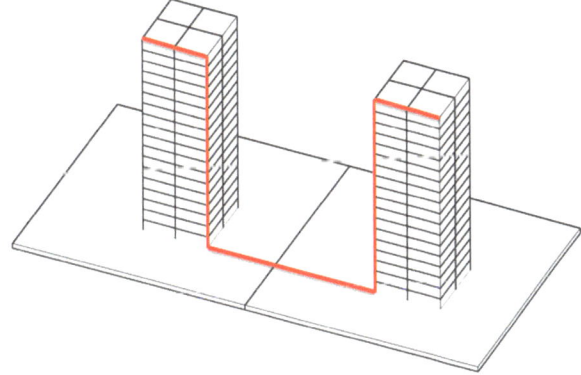

Figure 7.66 Tower blocks in isolation with no street enclosure

Le Corbusier's Plan Voisin for Paris to accommodate higher densities of office and housing model is a failure in terms of urban design and place-making principles. The tower blocks are isolated and there appears to be a zoning order and a clear distinction between housing work and transport. Human beings are socially and culturally driven species. Any imposition of such order on the creative aspirations of its inhabitants limits the human development and progress. The Plan Voisin became an empirical model of development and accommodating people all over the cities of the world regardless of the context and cultural sensitivities; it is therefore a prototype.

Figure 7.67 Model of Plan Voisin for Paris, by Le Corbusier [© FLC/ADAGP]

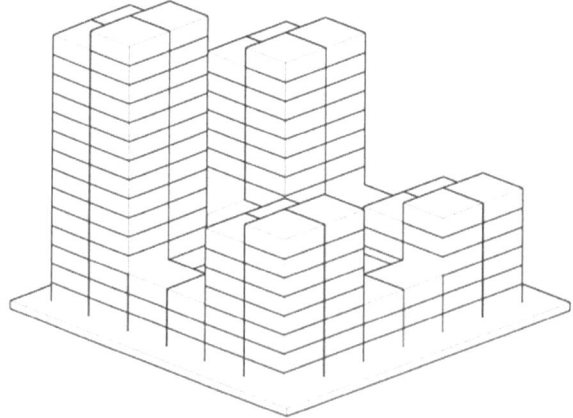

Figure 7.68 Tall buildings grouped with perimeter development

Density and tall buildings have a very strong co-relation. However, the density of the urban form can be accommodated in different ways and means as shown in the illustration. The same density 72 units per hectare can be accommodated by varying building height and depth. The three-storey perimeter block building has the same density of a tower block with lesser footprint and no active frontages.

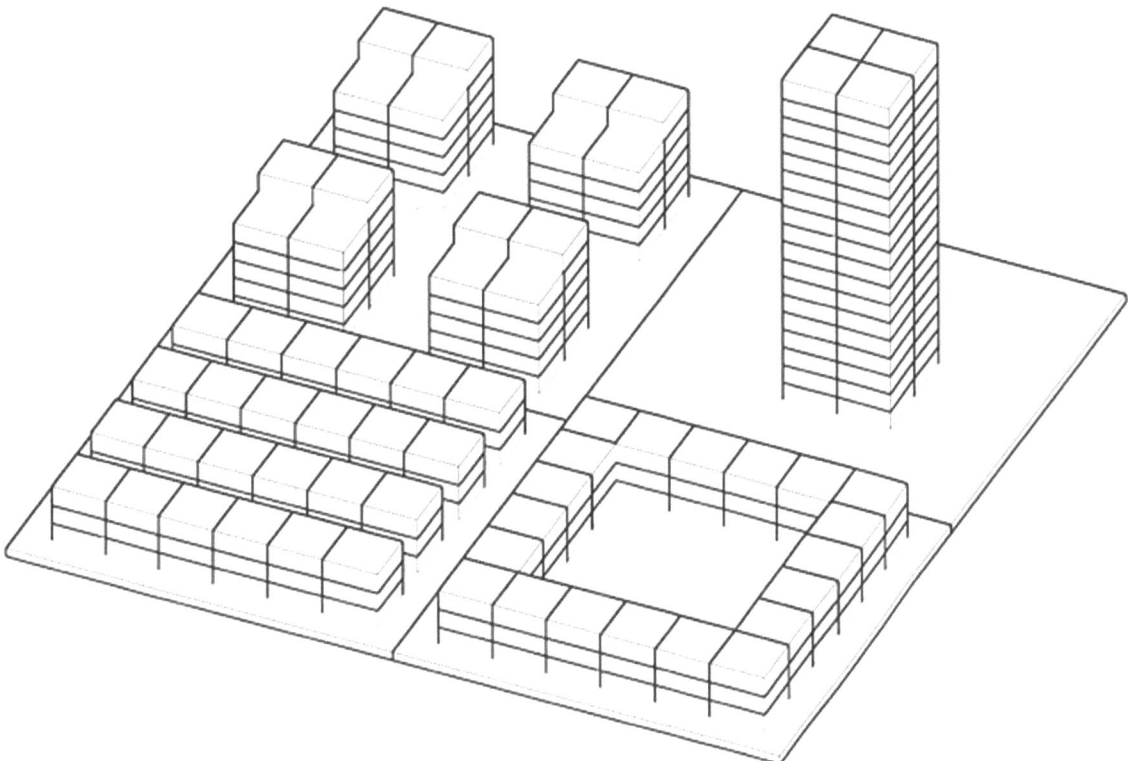

Figure 7.69 Density of 72 units per hectare can be arranged in plots in the form of tower blocks, group of towers, terraces and perimeter blocks

7.19   Terrace Development

- 2–3 storey traditional back-to-back terraces
- Public space is well defined by continuous street frontages
- Clear definition of public and private realms, with all dwellings having access to private back gardens
- Commercial and public activities located at ground floor level, provide an active street frontage

7.20 Perimeter Development

- More space is available for rear private gardens, communal areas or a park
- Street frontages are defined and uniform
- Active frontages to the streets with a mix of shops/retail and housing
- The court or inside open space can be used for play area/ communal spaces and can be defined in terms of ownership.
- Mixed use can be achieved, with commerce at ground floor and housing on upper floors.

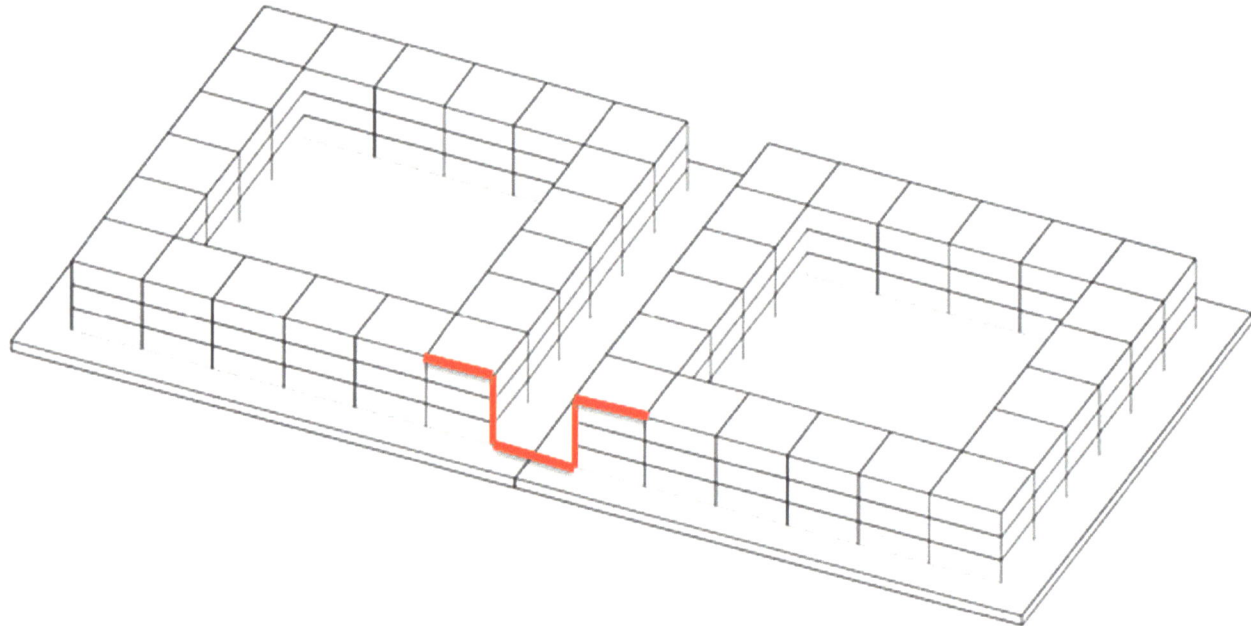

Figure 7.70 Active frontages and formation of street with the perimeter development

7.21 Tall Buildings: The Way Forward

Proposals for tall buildings must be considered on a citywide basis. This will require assessment and design criteria and impact that may result upon the city centre as a whole, as well as individual site conditions.

Additional tall buildings must be introduced selectively. This will maximize opportunities to create new landmark structures and make a positive contribution to the city's urban form and image.

The advantages of tall buildings, such as concentrating activity within the specific area, need to be considered against broader developmental objectives for the city. Refurbishing and reusing the existing vacant space could enable the positive flow-on effects of development to be spread more evenly throughout the city centre.

- Detailed urban design analysis must be undertaken for each proposal or development site, which is under consideration for a tall building. This must include a thorough analysis of the site, its surroundings and design of the building, its potential impacts in both the immediate and broader contexts. Architectural models and three-dimensional drawings should be used to gain an accurate understanding of:
- How the building will appear in the streetscape.
- How it will relate to other structures and landmarks.
- How the building will shape the city's skyline.
- Weather it will impede any important views from, to or within the city centre.

The appropriate height and location of tall buildings in the city will ultimately depend upon how each proposal satisfies overall the design standards and land-use planning considerations, as set out below.

7.22 Analysis of the Location

The detailed urban design analysis of the tall buildings vis-à-vis site should be carried out as well as identified on the city maps for:
- Define gateway sites
- Mark an area or site of civic importance
- Mark a principal activity node within the city centre
- Form the focal points of the vistas

This map also identifies important local landmarks, heritage, conservation areas and the areas surrounding them, which are considered to be more sensitive to proposals for tall buildings. Within these areas, tall buildings should possibly be avoided. These should not impinge on the setting of important views of listed buildings or conservation areas. In general, tall buildings should relate well to the urban grain, visual axes, general context, sense of place and topography of surrounding conservation areas; and this should be tested through detailed character and impact assessment.

7.23 Tall Building as Landmark and Its Relationship with Routes

Tall buildings can play a positive part in the design of the city centre by marking places of civic, commercial or cultural importance, or focal points of activity such as major gateways in city centre. The city skyline could be redefined by a number of landmark tall buildings, over 15-storey in height but grouped along with other densities such as the perimeter development with varying height and scale (see illustration). Skylines are generated due to the height of the buildings. A silhouette is created against the backdrop of the sky. Such buildings must be striking in their form, design, appearance and serve to distinguish the skyline, so as to create a unique image of the city. Tall buildings will fail to perform as a landmark function if their use is indiscriminate or too widespread or cluttered. For instance, a religious landmark of a Coventry has been chosen for study purposes. The cathedral or spire has been the landmark since medieval times, radial routes emanating from and towards the spires should be studied with respect to one another, key nodes must be identified where the spires can be seen; thus any future tall development should be studied and designed keeping in mind this fundamental relationship (landmark–routes). Landmark and routes have a very strong relationship; the further one goes away from the landmark a distinct silhouette is generated, and the closer one stands, its massive scale overwhelms us. To disregard these existing visual features by allowing development, which by its location, height or scale masks or dominates the prevailing landmark would disturb the essential character of the area. Buildings especially tall buildings should demonstrate the relationship of the landmark on the routes. The visual effect of the landmarks is gained not only by their height but also by their spiky outline or profile and further their spatial relationship. The use of material could impart a sense of history to an otherwise modern city centre.

Figure 7.71 Relationship between landmark and radial routes

Landmarks aid in legibility, serving as visual references within a city or from external vantage points. Landmarks may act as focal points, terminating significant vistas or punctuating a sequence of spaces or movement

corridors. Usually they will signify an important building, space or focus of activity. Key landmarks in the city should be identified on the map. These landmarks must be retained and enhanced. Careful attention must be paid to the sitting and design of new development, particularly tall or large-scale structures in close proximity to these landmarks, so that these important visual and spatial references are preserved. New buildings should be sited and scaled so that they do not impede views to landmarks nor detract from the visual prominence of landmarks. The visibility of landmarks on the skyline and as viewed from within the city must be taken into consideration. Tall or large-scale buildings must be carefully sited in relation to other landmarks to create a stimulating urban composition. New landmarks can be created in strategic locations throughout the city centre to signify:
- Gateway sites
- Focal points such as road junctions
- Activity nodes, such as the proposed tower in new retail quarter
- Important buildings or spaces

New landmarks can take many forms:
- Tall buildings
- A highly contemporary or striking piece of architecture
- A spire or tower
- A major public artwork
- An important building or space, which is a focus of civic community or commercial activity

7.24 The Wider Context

The impact of a tall building upon the skyline, and the overall composition of built form within the city, should be analysed and assessed through the use of architectural montages. Given the flattening effect that tall buildings have on the city skyline, these should be clustered in higher parts of the city.

Tall buildings should only be permitted at a limited number of strategic sites. Tall buildings should be located so that internal vistas to important focal points or views out to the surrounding countryside are not impeded. The location and design of tall or larger scale buildings will potentially have important focal points or views out to the surrounding towns. The location and design of tall or larger scale buildings will potentially have an impact upon the visibility of landmarks. Within areas in close proximity to landmarks, as identified on the maps, the effect that a tall building may have upon the prominence or visibility of a landmark will be a consideration. Tall buildings have the potential to irrevocably change the urban grain of a part of the city.

7.25 The Local Environment

A tall building must make a positive contribution to the appearance and activity of the streetscape and not detract from the pedestrian experience at their base.

At ground level, the detailed design and function of a tall building must be in scale with its immediate environment and contribute to the 'sense of place'. It is important that the ground floor use of tall buildings is compatible with the activity of the street and the locale. Tall buildings should aid in the permeability of their context by allowing through-block pedestrian connections. Tall buildings can better integrate with their surrounds by providing internal or external spaces for public access such as parks, cafés, shops, thoroughfares, etc. Particular attention must be paid to the impact a tall building may have upon adjacent heritage sites or areas of special urban character. Additionally, the impact that a tall building may have upon natural features, such as waterways or landscapes, or public spaces is also an important consideration. Microclimate impacts such as the creation of negative wind currents or overshadowing must also be considered.

7.26   Architectural Quality

Of importance in the design of tall buildings is the form, profile and massing of the building, particularly in the roofline, as these elements will create its silhouette on the city's skyline. The design of tall buildings should be striking and distinctive so that they become identifiable landmarks on the skyline. It is recommended that tall buildings are slender in form and proportion having a vertical emphasis to its overall mass. Tall buildings that are slab like in form and proportion should be discouraged. Also important are the treatment of facades and the colour and reflectivity of building materials.

7.27   Existing Tall Buildings

A tall building, which is to be removed, can be replaced with a building, which is more responsive to the immediate and wider context. The recommendations for tall buildings will indicate whether replacement with a building of a similar height is appropriate, or whether a smaller scale structure would be a more appropriate response. Buildings can be given a new lease of life through remodelling and relatively simple measures such as:
- Recladding with a material of a more contemporary appearance, a different colour of reflectivity
- Addition of upper floors to change the profile of a building
- Removal of obscuring of unsightly services
- Introducing active uses at the ground floor to create a connection with the streetscape. Landscaping of the grounds to improve streetscape appearance
- Internal conversion to allow a change of use, for example from office to residential

7.28   Views and Viewing Corridors

Significant views of the tall buildings need to be protected in the city. Any proposed development over four-storey in height located in proximity to landmark buildings or structures, or along major view corridors, should undergo a contextual urban design analysis. This should demonstrate that they will not: detract from important focal points, disrupt viewing corridors within the city centre and inhibit views to the surrounding hills and green spaces.

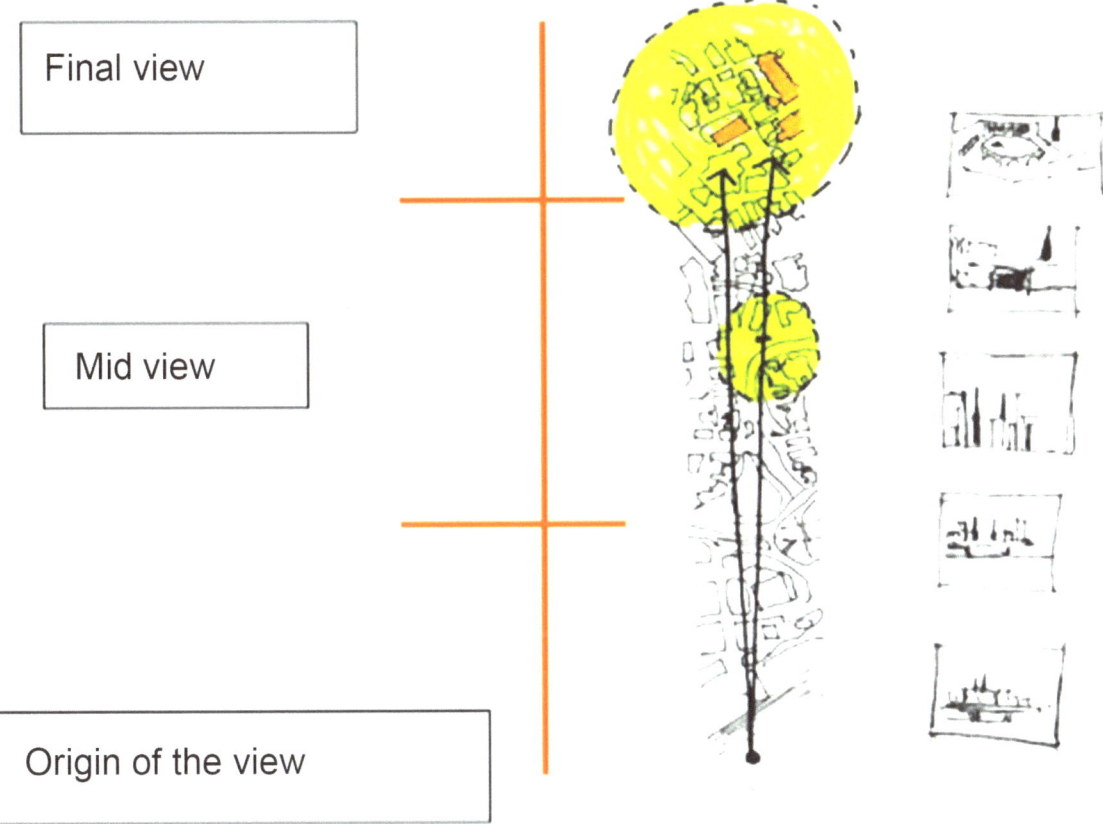

Figure 7.72 View cones or viewing corridors with landmark at its focal point

7.29   Tall Buildings: Impact on Street, Height Mass and Transitions Criteria

The design of high-rise buildings should respect potential negative impacts on adjacent properties, including overshadowing, overlooking and wind tunnel effects. Therefore, building height and mass should be appropriate to the type and nature of adjoining development. Proposed development should also disregard the "Canyon Effect".

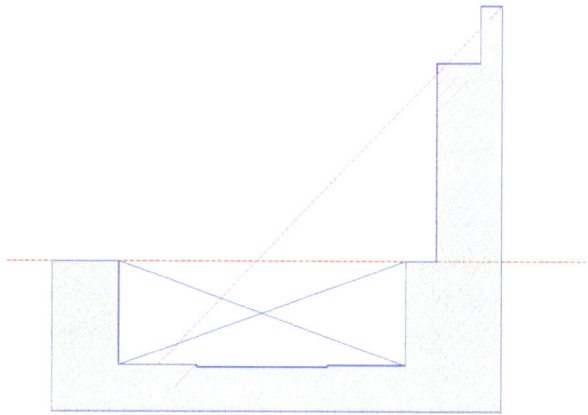

Figure 7.73 Tall buildings and setbacks

Nodes and major intersections are the appropriate locations for the design of tall buildings. Step backs of upper storey should be provided so that building bulk is minimally perceived from the vantage of a pedestrian on the street. Step backs should be considered for buildings above 3 storey. A step back of the building wall should occur above the building base. The step back distance should be minimum of 2.0 m. Setbacks should be used to determine appropriate building envelopes. A visual angle is typically measured from pedestrian areas located opposite the proposed development or from the boundary of an adjacent property.

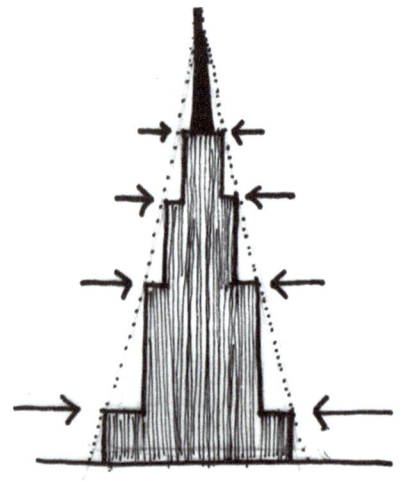

Figure 7.74 Tall buildings with multiple setbacks

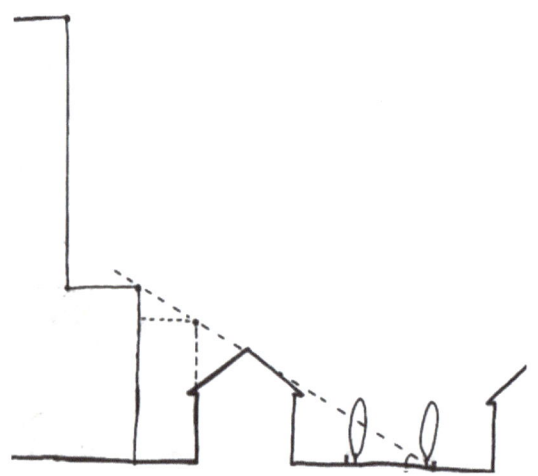

Figure 7.75 Design of tall buildings with setbacks in a rural setting

7.30 Design Criteria of Tall Buildings in an Urban Context

7.30.1 Visual impact analysis

360-degree evaluations of the development and its surrounding context with potential visual impact of the proposal on the city's urban domain should be conducted. These may be illustrated through the computer visualizations and photomontage techniques that consider, but are not limited to, the following:

- The built and the natural environment
- Key strategic views and approaches
- Conservation settings and listed buildings
- Special importance should be given to the developments near conservation areas and city centre.
- A detailed urban design analysis of surrounding areas that details the positive and negative contributions that the proposed tall building makes to the visual quality of the area; the taller the building the more extensive the area of analysis.

Tall buildings should be sited in areas of the city that have a minimal visual impact on sensitive historic environments. Retaining and enhancing key strategic views through the careful siting of tall buildings is a key objective.

Drawing such building plans, sections and computer views, supported by illustrating the design strategy, will successfully integrate the building(s) into its surroundings. Drawings will clearly indicate existing and proposed building context, showing zoning envelopes, setbacks, and property lines, street widths, building heights, angular planes and sun/shadow impact.

For developments on prominent sites, it should be provided with an evaluation of the potential visual impact of the proposed development on to the surrounding urban context, illustrated through computer visualization from a pedestrian point of view, photomontage techniques, aerial photographs, and/or physical model.

7.30.2 Site settings, tall buildings

Demonstrate, by means of a townscape/landscape impact assessment, how the proposal sits within the existing townscape and landform.

Describe the extent to which the proposal contributes to the creation of an attractive cluster of tall buildings or creates an individual landmark.

Wherever a building is situated amidst a cluster of tall buildings or in close proximity, the scale of the building would then become an important factor for the proposed development. The construction of a scale model will be often useful in addition to the computer generated 3D model.

7.30.3 Massing and views of tall buildings

Massing of the proposed tall building and its surroundings show how it is integrated with the surrounding buildings; helps in showing that how the proposed building contributes to the imagery on the human scale (pedestrian scale) and from a distance; describe its views on local vistas, views and landmarks; demonstrates the visual and aesthetic qualities of the tall building which are very important in terms of urban legibility and aids navigation.

7.30.4 Form of the building

Provide a design statement that describes in detail the rationale for the form of the proposal. In case of a landmark building, the building should translate into account the following key points:
- Iconic building justification
- Silhouette
- Cultural and climatic references
- Articulation
- Context applications/references
- Skyline studies

7.30.5 Tall buildings and transportation

Tall buildings due to their higher densities have a dire consequence on the transport corridor. It should therefore be integrated with a transport system such as metro or subway system.

7.30.6 Tall buildings and microclimate

Tall buildings due to their height will evidently affect the wind movement and the microclimate balance of the place.

It is therefore suggested to study the following:
- Tall buildings subjected to wind tunnel tests
- Tall buildings studied under the computer fluid diagrams
- Tall buildings studied under the computer simulation of wind environmental conditions

Development throughout much of the city has the potential to impact adversely on potential views and more important the skyline. Oversimplified building forms and unattractive roof structures can have a similar harmful effect on views generated by the radial routes of the city. Careful consideration should be given to the integration of all new developments with the surroundings in order to protect city-wide and local views outside the city centre and towards the city. Tall buildings due to their height are going to create an impact on the skyline and the city imagery; however, if urban design considerations and tall building design criteria are implemented, it can contribute positively and bring towards the urban renaissance of Indian cities.

7.31   Role of Art in Cities

Art is stated as a pastime, creative activity; also is a visual medium. Since Indus Valley Civilization, sculptures of humans and animals were depicted and were an expression of the civilizational culture. During the various Hindu kingdoms, art is depicted in form of sculptures and paintings representing the glory of God in the entire temple complexes.

The caves of Ajanta and Ellora can be attributed as the first ancient art gallery in the Indian subcontinent. The rock cut caves depict sculptures and paintings of Buddhism in 30 different caves.

Art has been an indispensable part of Indian culture but is now completely lacking its part in today's Indian cities. As on date, there is a pseudo art activity, which is merely painting the unwanted, dimly lit flyover walls for beautification. True art can reconcile the aesthetical vacuum of today's Indian cities. There are many avenues wherein art can play a true role such as, the civic spaces, traffic islands, walls of public places and as murals on the front walls of government buildings. True art forms a relationship with the surroundings, environment, buildings and the citizens of the republic. Chandigarh is well known for Le Corbusier's modern paintings, murals, sculptures which are displayed in its civic spaces and depicted on the walls of the public buildings. More bodies/agencies need to be formed, such as the Art Council India, which can support, fund and form art policies funded by the Government of India. An art policy is a must for every ward, every district and the entire city covering the private bodies, non-governmental bodies and trusts.

Art can transform the city's experience, its civic space and can impart a unique identity; thus, creating a visual culture. In a city, citizens have a varied role and day-to-day activities. When it comes to leisure time activities, art can be that escape from a mundane living and further elevating them to a much higher perceptions and visual delight. Aesthetic experience can transform a citizen's life; it can bring closer a group of people, individuals and create a sense of belonging.

Expression of art is the highest level of expressing one's creativity and should be the fundamental right of Indian citizens. A charter should be thus prescribed and placed in every city and every area how one can express himself through a medium called art.

7.32   Urban Design: Is It a Cosmetic Product in the Name of City Beautification?

If you go to a physician, worried about some disfiguring ailment and seem apologetic about your concern over something that may seem to be merely "cosmetic," you will probably find that the physician doesn't regard personal self-esteem as trivial. The physician has no problem with providing "cosmetic" improvement.

That's what urban design is about: civic self-esteem. A city that is no more than an urban jungle of self-serving competitors, each clawing to get ahead of the other, is not civilized. Civilization means being civil, which means sharing some common values of mutual respect and group solidarity. Civilization requires recognition that only by working together can everyone's condition be improved.

Civilizations produce cultures. Evidence of a culture is its ability to create and sustain a desired environment for living. A great culture produces civilized cities, and the greatest cities result from the arts, particularly architecture and urban design.

There is no difference between architecture and urban design, in terms of mission. Both are concerned with the making of places. The scale of the place may vary, as may the type of clients for the projects. But otherwise urban design is merely one facet of architecture, just as residential design is another facet, at another scale.

The great cities of the world – those that we regard as the most civilized, evidencing the richest cultures – are enriched by ambitious urban design projects – Haussmann's transformation of Paris, Nash's London projects, L'Enfant's Washington. But urban design is not merely a matter of grand public works. Urban design consciousness may have larger effect on the quality of the environment at a more modest scale, when the level of community taste requires new projects to defer to a larger sense of context – being good neighbours rather than boorish intruders into an existing milieu. It's for this reason that urban design consciousness needs to be integrated into architectural education.

First of all, one should be made aware about how urban design may improve the quality of urban life and then how urban design has to be accomplished. In short, however, some indication of the first issue may be preference of people for particular cities. Why do many of us yearn to visit Paris, and when there why do we prefer to stay in the old city rather than in the newer sectors? The second general problem suggests a historical review of how successful urban design was achieved. Frequently, the communal benefit require a communal will, resulting in governmental regulation of buildings so that they would conform to some larger purpose – as the Parisian requirement for a uniform cornice line on the grand boulevards. In other instances, coherent urban neighbourhoods evolved from mutual consensus, a common taste for what was appropriate, such as the Georgian towns of England and Scotland which are all of a piece, so that all the parts add up to a collective whole that is greater than the sum of the parts.

If you regard a city as merely an aggregation of people, all trying to survive and advance competitively, then you may have little appreciation not merely for urban design as a function of architecture, but of urbanism as a cultural achievement. If we architects regard each project merely as an opportunity to assert our clients' (or our own) self-serving interests, even though we may produce distinctive individual buildings, but we may fail to contribute to the larger coherence of the city. Architects, alas – even respected, world-class architects succumb and do violence to a city because the project at hand seems rewarding.

If architecture is to advance globally, it won't be because designers come up with new novelties. The bizarre soon becomes familiar; what seemed wonderful because it was strange becomes merely aberrant once it is recognized as familiar. Architecture will really advance when architects (and of course their clients) will cease to think merely in terms of individual projects that glorify the builders, but start thinking more about enhancing the collective quality of the city[3]. That's urban design.

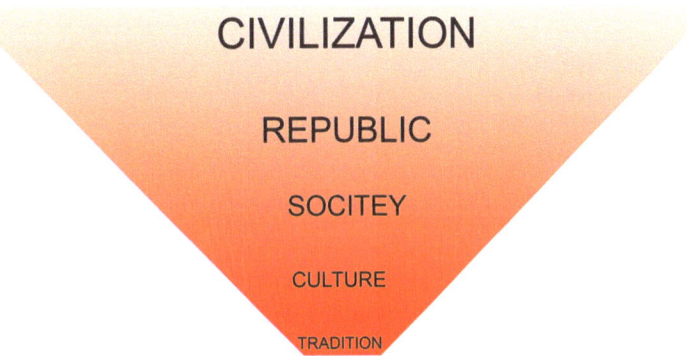

Figure 7.76 From 'tradition' to a 'republic'

7.33 Master Planning: What Is It?

Master planning started as a military necessity. Each kingdom wanted to seize maximum territory of a finite land available on the planet. Lands were surveyed in order to quantify and eventually conquer. Military units needed to be mobile and their bases need to be fortified and, in some cases, well-guarded against its enemies. Till date military planners regard grid discipline as sacrosanct for troop station. The grid offers flexibility and is highly legible in terms of movement. Master planning involves study aspects of all three disciplines: architecture, planning and landscape. It is a scientific study with an outcome in artistic manner involving city building. A master plan contains visual and written description of a geographical area to be inhabited into a city. It contains and highlights policies detrimental to the built form, movement strategies and open spaces. It is a doctrine in the form of strategic interventions and implementation mechanism in illustration and written form for achieving a vision.

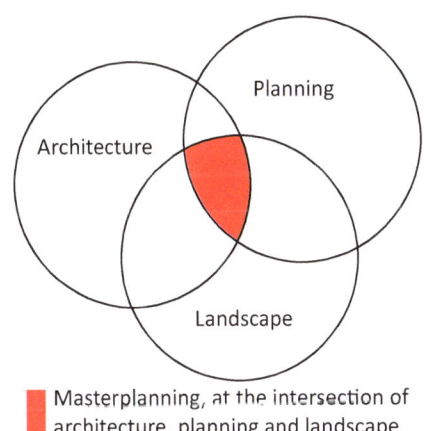

Masterplanning, at the intersection of architecture, planning and landscape

---

[3] Late Mr. Paul Malo taught architectural design and history in the Syracuse University of Architecture for over 30 years until his retirement as professor emeritus in 1992.

7.33.1 The development plan

The development plan should start with a vision "what kind of a city is envisaged" – techno city, e-city, heritage city, etc. How shall we imagine this city to be in years to come. What are the underlying strengths of the city? And what are the citizens' aspirations? It should contain development-related policies and urban design principles; additionally it should be area specific keeping in mind culture of the particular area.

7.33.2 Planning guidance

Planning guidance should detail out policies in order to enable developers/architects/designers to carry out the proposed development. The guidance should be area specific, highlighting clearly development principles and urban parameters such as:

- Scale
- Density
- Architectural character
- Massing
- Sustainable design policies for buildings and development

The document shall be the basis of judging any planning application for submission. The government and the judiciary should consider the planning guidance document central to any decision making.

7.33.3 Urban design guidance

It should be specific to a particular district, area or ward. It should comprise of urban design framework and development brief. Urban design guidance should aid and define urban parameters in a document such as the following:

- Streetscape
- Streets
- Landscaping
- Signages
- Lighting exterior
- Tall buildings
- Landscaping and tree planting

7.33.4 The master plan

The master plan is a document which contains overall vision, design principles, framework timeline and details how these have to be achieved. City wide master plan and area /local wide master plan can be produced. Master plans are prepared by or on behalf of site owners or a development body. It does not contain any design detail but contains development-related guidelines and principles. Master plan is a statutory document, also a planning document, which should be prepared with the help of citizens' participation and contains information with regards to the following:

- Design brief
- Planning rules, development control, master planning context (statutory) rules applicable
- Site context
- Site location and surroundings
- Site considerations
- Holistic context
- Landscaping context
- The Master plan
- Vision
- Methodologies
- Phasing
- Site areas
- Design principles
- Landscaping framework
- Master planning layout
- Design guidance
- Design consideration

7.33.5 Design codes

A design code is a document describing in detail the various urban parameters which is deemed necessary to adhere for a building or proposed development in heritage areas, conservation zones and areas marked for special future development. The design code can be a set of architectural controls determining exactly what is being sought, how the proposed development should be in a detailed manner. The urban parameters are defined clearly in the form of urban design guidance or development brief such as colours and texture to be use, window sizes, materials, scale, massing, etc.; the objective being to define the project as clearly as possible to design, delivery and execution.

7.33.6 Development brief

Development brief should be area specific and should not contain any detailed design or policies; it should be flexible and give direction, give forth a vision of the development. Writing a development brief is an individual task and can only be considered a success if the design is as per the design brief. However, what if some designers/architects opt out or go against the design brief. This is the dilemma of the results of design brief and possible outcomes. Architectural designs have multiple connotations. What is right and what is wrong only depends on the eye of the beholder.

7.33.7 Urban design framework

It consists of illustrations and describes the master plan in detail: How the objectives of the master plan are to be achieved such as defining the routes, connections and integration of districts to name a few urban characteristics. It is also a broad spatial analysis which defines the main master plan goals in a visual format. It also highlights the strategies which need to be incorporated while making of the master plan. The urban design framework can also be defined in a computer generated 3D modelling of the urban area to be master planned. The aim is to give an insight into the relationships of the buildings to open spaces, height of buildings to the streets, how the street, squares and the streets are related.

7.33.8 Design statements

They are used to explain the proposals when the design is in preliminary stage and contains no details. It gives an insight to the proposed structure about how the development is being proposed and how the primary issues are addressed regarding the development. It sets out the intention for the development of site, although not in any detail or depth.

Vision is referred to as the ability to see things, imagine, visualize pertaining to a city or any aspect of it in the form of visual medium such as sketches, drawings, photomontages. It may me sketchy and surreal; however, it should have an ability to convey the image of the desired city to be transformed.

The urban renaissance for Indian cities lies in its study of culture, the geographical settings, living streets, the compact arrangement of blocks and integration of communal spaces such as the *chowks* or the square in its urban morphology.

India has the infinite capacity to synthesize all the cultures of the world but it will never give up its age-old traditions, culture and principles; yet it evolves, reinvents, reimagines and reinterprets itself in the years to come.

A world without borders is not a distant dream…

7.34 The Master Planning Process: Stages

	Masterplanning stages
Stage 1	Indian cultural and traditional study Cultural activity generators and mapping Cultural aspirations Language studies Meeting community heads Set forth cultural activity and principles
Stage 2	Urban morphology & movement studies Figure ground analysis Development pattern of blocks Identify diversity and architectural character areas Block typologies Add new growth areas and blocks to the existing area or study area Study urban girth effect Develop 3-dimensional computer visualisation 2-Dimensional model for brainstorming and group discussions Urban strand studies and analysis
Stage 3	Uniting the connections Analyse individual block movement studies Study the overall movement framework Study streetspace Relationship studies of block and street
Stage 4	
Stage 5	The master plan Executive summary Design brief Planning rules, developmental control, master planning context (statutory rules applicable) Site context Site locations and surroundings Holistic context, site and its environs Landscaping context Vision Methodologies Phasing Design principles Landscaping framework The master plan (drawing) Implementation

Figure 7.77 Steps in master planning

8
Urban Design Principles

8.1 Ecopolis and Sustainability

Cities should be built with the natural setting. Buildings and spaces should be such designed that they integrate and respond to the natural systems.

8.2 Legibility

- Ease of understanding a place that has a clear image and is easy to understand
- Landmarks and focal points not obstructed
- Views to historical landmarks, panoramas and viewing corridors to be established
- Clear and easily navigable routes for walking and transportation
- Gateways to particular localities and areas
- Lighting at nights for safety and security of citizens, highlighting prominent landmarks and create qualitative spaces
- Promoting works of art and craft in public spaces and buildings
- Signage and way markers for navigation
- Clear distinction between public and private space
- Avoiding gaps in the line of buildings
- Enclosing streets and other spaces by buildings and trees of a scale that feels comfortable and appropriate to the character of the space

8.3 Self-Sustained Localities

The principle behind designing the cities should be that people can live, work and receive basic services all within their localities. A self-sustained locality with amenities such as school, shopping/market, and primary health care centre should be the main focus.

8.4 Ease of Movement

- Cities should be easy to transverse by walking, and transportation should be made accessible and efficient.

- Reducing car-dependency must be a key objective and imperative. Alternative modes of transportation, namely walking, cycling, and transit, would result in more sustainable urban environments, and thus an improved quality of life.
- Connectivity and permeability should be a focus point to design a place that is easy to get to and move through.
- Public transport should be made the best where density is high.
- Roads, footpaths and public spaces must be connected to well-used routes.
- Easy accessibility will help people to move with ease.
- Direct routes should be focused that could lead to where people want to go.

8.5   Heritage Conservation

A city's history and historic architecture of great value should be preserved, restored and used by its citizens.

8.6   Human Scale

Cities should be built at human scale. Height and massing of the building have a direct relationship on the human scale and psyche. Cities that do not have a human scale are detrimental to nature. Building scale is the only governing factor to control urban sprawl. Uniformity in scale of the buildings contributes to an identity and harmony, and creates a distinctive architectural character and setting.

8.7   Architectural Character

Localities have a unique character that has value, sense of place and history. A place should respond to and reinforce locally distinctive patterns of development and landscape: building materials, values, local culture and traditions, locally distinctive buildings.

8.8   Public Spaces for Indian Culture, Traditions and Customs

Cities are built for people and its citizens. Localities are social and lively with spaces for personal solace, companionship, family and community gathering. Machines such as cars and industrial sites tend to detract from a city. Where they are required, they should be designed to take the background. Natural areas, beaches, parks, public squares and streets that are open to the public have a profound value to a city which showcases city's culture, tradition and customs.

8.9   Quality of Life

Citizen's overall health is directly related to the health of air, water, land, and climate in which one resides. The way we live, choose to move around, develop land, have a direct impact on the city's urban structure and thus a distinctive urban pattern is formed. The health and integrity of wildlife and vegetation are also a priority. Protecting existing biodiversity, indigenous or endangered species, wetlands, the tree canopy, are all a necessary aspect of preserving the ecosystem. Quality as measured by people self-reported happiness is a primary goal of urban design. A high quality of life tends to be a virtuous cycle that attracts greater economic activity and investment leading to improved quality of life.

8.10 Regional Integration

Various localities should be integrated with cities and cities integrated with regions. For example, transportation has little value without regional links. Urban corridors have no meaning and further create conurbation. The street and highway should be studied as an urban strand, one of the many yet an integral part of the city leading to connectivity but not merging into another city.

8.11 Adaptable Design

Cities tend to change slowly and can't be transformed overnight. Urban design is a practical discipline that takes transitional steps towards following goals:
- Flexible uses
- Possibilities for gradual change
- Buildings and areas adaptable to a variety of present and future uses
- Reuse of important historic buildings

8.12 Art Expression

Art expression should be the fundamental right of every district, community, locality and city.

Glossary

Accessibility: The ability to reach or enter a place or building[1]. It is the ease of movement for the convenience of pedestrians from the entrance of the building to the bus stops, Metro stations, normally shown in plan in terms of distances.

Accessibility = Distance from public transport----Travel time (or time taken) ----- Entrance of the building/Population Density

Adaptability: A building mainly historical which can be suited or made to suit the current or present-day requirements/building use. For e.g., a historic building such as palace to be converted into a hotel or a library.

Amenity: Something intended to make life more pleasant or comfortable for people especially in the public realm for e.g. Street furniture and benches.

Appearance: The look or the outward image of the building.

Area appraisal: The systematic study of a place, involving a method to analyze the urban design characteristics.

Apartheid: (especially in the past in South Africa) a political system in which people of different races are separated[2], Segregation of communities based on the skin color of human beings.

Background building: It is a building when viewed against a prominent building, landmark or an urban skyline.

Backland development: The area of the land which is behind the building such as a garden.

Barrier: It is a physical boundary which separates two distinct areas or parts of a place.

Block: A collection of buildings grouped together as well as a plots which are coherently placed together with the road as perimeter.

Border: An imaginary line defined by human beings to demarcate a country, territory, land and city.

Building envelope guidelines: The external or the outward appearance of the building consisting of walls, doors, windows contributing to an architectural character of the building by the selection of an appropriate material. The fenestration arrangements can be used to achieve maximum daylight and ventilation.

---
[1] Cambridge dictionary definition.
[2] Cambridge dictionary definition.

Building line: The edge of the building along the street within the setback or on the setback line. For e.g. Row houses, the building line can be linear or wavy by the arrangement of plots and buildings.

Building shoulder height: The top most part of the buildings.

Bulk/mass: The volume of the building when viewed as a single entity especially in terms of its geometrical profile.

Built form: Human activity in terms of construction or building activity such as houses, offices and government buildings.

Character appraisal: It refers to the appearance of the building in terms of its use of material, form, texture fenestration and details. It is also applicable to the wider area such as a conservation area or central business district.

Character area: It is an area where a building or a group of a buildings have a distinct architectural feature. It can be a conservation area, a modern zone, a sector, or master planned area.

Character assessment: Examination and study of buildings in terms of its visual appearance, unique construction method and any other distinctive features pertaining aesthetic delight.

Conservation area: Buildings of a past era in a group which are preserved for its architectural features. Buildings in the conservation areas are usually listed in terms of Grade I, II, and II*in U.K. The outward appearance of the building is not allowed to alter, however internally the design characteristics may differ. They are legally protected from demolition.

Context: The location of the site or area in geographical setting.

District: A set (mathematical) of buildings when grouped together having mutually exclusive functions. For e.g. a residential district, business districts.

Density: The floor area or the floor plate of the building to that of the site, generally expressed as a ratio.

Design advisory panel: A group of specialist person from the field of design evaluating and suggesting the local government.

Design and build: Design and build is a type of contract undertaken by a contractor from a client to execute a project. The contractor is the sole authority in all matters pertaining to designing, building and execution of the project.

Design champion: A person with sufficient knowledge, experience and design skills who can contribute and conclude the design

Desire line: It is the shortest line or distance taken by human beings to reach a particular destination.

Developmental appraisal: The act of examining or judging a development, critiquing the merits and demerits in order to suggest the viability.

Development brief: A short and concise document highlighting the design or developmental requirement without elaborating in detail the design expressions.

Development plan: A policy document prepared by the local government

Development control: A body with the local authority which controls and regulates the building activity and proposes guidelines pertaining to buildings and growth patterns of the city

Development: Any activity pertaining to building or built environments by human beings.

Elevation: A spot or a point on the ground above the mean sea level or the front side of the building.

Enclosure: The shell of the building used to enclose the floor plates or building functions.

Energy efficiency: Buildings consume electricity and oil. Through passive design methods and using green building rating systems, energy efficiency can be optimized. According the European commission further highlights that "buildings generally need fewer than three to five liters of heating oil per square meter per year, older buildings consume about 25 liters on average".

Enquiry by design: In U.K it is a process facilitated in the planning system which brings in stakeholders of the development to bring forth design requirements required for a community.

Edge: The physical and non-physical i.e. imaginary line created by buildings in a particular layout, infrastructure, landscape or natural features. For.eg. river edge.

The edge contributes towards a boundary, defines limits or a terminus.

Façade: The front part of the building which is often big in scale

Feasibility: The economic viability of a development based on a business model within the economic or the

Fenestration: The arrangement, proportioning, and design of windows and doors in a building.[3]

Figure/ or figure and ground plan: The built-up area (open spaces and courtyards to be shown in white) when blackened completely and viewed against a white backdrop to a suitable scale. It shows the spatial interrelationships between the built and open spaces as well as private and public spaces.

Floorplate: The area of habitable space or building function or activities.

Form: The shape or appearance of the building or a physical entity.

Indicative sketch: A sketch executed to highlight a vision pertaining to development or building. It is sketchy and surreal in its expression.

Landmark: A building which is prominent in its context and scale. Landmarks are known for its form, scale and has grandiose quality.

---

[3] Webster's dictionary definition

Landscape: Natural feature of land which is in pristine condition, containing botanical features such as trees, plants on a geological stratum.

Layout: The arrangement of plots in a particular fashion.

Legibility: The ability to navigate through an urban space without any confusion and having absolute clarity.

Local distinctiveness: Physical and collective imagery of a place contributing to a character for e.g. such as a townscape.

Massing: kindly see bulk

Mixed use: Commercial or office activity/function when combined with the residential function in a building vertically.

Movement: A function defining the kinetics of the space. There are different forms of movement for instance pedestrian movement, vehicular movement, and disabled movement.

Node: Intersection of two or more routes contribute to a node albeit not a junction

Path: It is a route taken from a particular point to another which defines the movement network. Path is dependent on direction and movement.

Permeability: The degree of entry to a place or enclosure.

Permitted development: It is the development which is sanctioned by government and in accordance with the local bye laws.

Place check: Examining a place through a thorough system of urban design principals and policies to determine a successful place.

Municipality: A governmental body constituted by the citizens elected in a democratic manner working towards the governance and development of the city. The developmental body of the municipality lays down the byelaws and masterplan of the city after due consultation with the citizens.

Plot ratio/F.A.R: It is the total floor area pf all the floors of the building to the area of the site. Prevalent in the American planning system it is called as the F.A.R i.e. Floor Area ratio.

Public realm: A space defined and designated for the people for.eg squares of the city. Pedestrian, Roads etc.

Scale: Vertical measurement of the building from ground to the top of the building. It is the height characters tic with relation to the human height.

Section: A slice or cut through or across the building to illustrate/show the inner parts of the building. Sections are technically drawn and to the scale.

Settlement pattern: The arrangement of houses, plots, roads and open spaces in a district or village, when viewed holistically.

Sight line: A line emanating from the eye of the person to the desired object, usually represented by two rays emanating from the top and bottom of the eye towards the subject.

Strategic view: A view which is unobstructed, of high importance and contributing to aesthetic delight while experiencing the city or an urban area.

Street furniture: Furniture meant for the people who are in public realm. They can be artistic or traditional contributing to the pedestrian's ease of movement, often located around a public square, parks and open areas.

Topography: The shape or profile of the terrain, its appearance with the presence of geographical and natural features. It is often represented in a map format to a suitable scale with wavy lines called as contours. Contour lines have elevations (in meters) measured above the mean sea level. Topographical maps have colors in gradation to depict the height differences of the selected area.

Urban cacophony: When the urban design parameters of the city has unharmonious relationship, it contributes to urban cacophony. For.eg. the scale of buildings is highly varied along the street, Improper sizes of signage, landscape which is unmaintained etc. Any imbalance of urban design parameters contributes to urban cacophony.

Urban design: Urban design[4] is the process of shaping the physical setting for life in cities, towns and villages. It is the art of making places. It involves the design of buildings, groups of buildings, spaces and landscapes, and establishing the processes that make successful development possible.

Urban grain: It is the arrangement of the plots roads and open spaces and the interrelationship amongst them. Urban grain can be coarse (the arrangement between plots, roads and open spaces to be wider) or fine grain (the arrangement of plots roads and open spaces highly compact).

Urban structure: It is the pattern in which buildings, plots, roads, blocks and open spaces are interrelated to form a coherent system

Vernacular: a style of building which is of distinct quality devoid of any stylistic influences and constructed by the craftsmen and designers with locally available material. It has a quality and a narrative, distinctive of its locale. For e.g. houses in Dakshina Kannada have Mangalore tiled pitched roofs and built out of laterite stones.

---

[4] http://www.udg.org.uk/careers, As defined by urban design group,U.K

Index

A

Ahmedabad, 2, 28, 32, 39, 40, 49, 50, 58, 64, 84, 86,
architectural character, 79, 92, 93, 113, 150, 153, 155
area, 1, 4
art expression, 147
art, 147, 155, 156
articulation, 146
axis, 21, 32, 36, 44, 60, 80, 127, 129

B

bazaar, 30, 43, 80
blocks, 4, 13, 20, 40, 42, 46, 59, 71–73, 75, 78, 79
boulevard, 21
bronze Age, 90
Build, Operate and Transfer, 49

C

Calcutta, 21, 90, 97
cantonments, 90, 91
canyon effect, 143
capitol, 32, 35, 36, 42, 45, 47
CBD, 91, 108, 109, 113–115
central core, 93, 109
Chandigarh, 1, 2, 3, 5, 7'25, 27–47, 49, 63–85, 86–89, 98, 102, 105, 147

city centre, 53, 55, 58, 61, 65, 66, 80, 83, 87, 93, 109, 138–141, 143, 145, 146
city Green, 27
civic spaces, 88, 91, 1 00, 147
civic square, 57, 71
climate, 30, 51, 123, 142, 146, 155
clustered, 141
coastal cities, 100
community structure, 55, 57, 58
compact, 1, 10, 41, 42, 61, 62, 65, 67, 71, 75, 79, 86, 87, 104, 115, 152
complex, 5, 7, 32, 35, 36, 37, 44, 45, 47
concentric, 13, 94, 109
container, 42
culture, 1, 2, 7, 21, 27, 86, 90–153

D

density, 5, 25, 30, 46, 72, 73, 100, 102, 103, 116, 123, 124, 133, 137, 150, 155
design codes, 110, 151
design statements, 152
development brief, 150–152
development plan, 150
diversity, 40, 66, 84, 86, 100, 114, 156
dwelling, 1, 10, 77, 80, 137

E

ecological, 85
economic, 3, 42, 46, 52, 54, 61, 66, 86, 156
eddy current, 124
edge, 10, 44, 60, 65, 68, 70, 71, 77, 81
experience, 2, 4, 67, 68, 87, 135, 141, 147

F

Fatehpur Sikri, 25
figure ground plan, 101, 103, 104
finance, 4, 5, 27, 49, 62, 64, 85
flanked, 10, 13
fortification, 2
fortified, 14, 20, 91, 109, 128, 149
frontages, 42, 60, 68, 70, 79, 121, 128, 129, 131, 137, 138
functionalist cities, 87

G

Gandhinagar, 5, 7, 25, 50–62, 63–85, 86–89
gardens, 14, 16, 25, 46, 61, 80, 84, 90, 129, 135, 137, 138
green lungs, 89
green spaces, 18, 58, 89, 123, 143
greenbelt, 114, 124
grid, 8, 14, 2058–60, 64, 69, 77, 78, 88, 90, 91, 98, 101 104, 105, 149
grid iron, 2, 8, 14, 20, 90

H

hill cities, 100
hindu, 2, 90, 91, 147
historic core, 93, 110, 114, 115,
human scale, 79, 135, 146, 155

I

Indian subcontinent, 8–25, 90, 147,
Indo-Saracenic, 91,
Indus Valley Civilization, 8, 11, 90, 147
industrial magnets, 21,
industrial Revolution, 21,
infrastructure, 27, 28, 49, 64, 88, 89, 102, 143,
Islamic, 2, 5, 90, 91

J

Jaipur, 12

L

land, 1, 4, 27, 28, 38, 42, 46, 49, 50, 61, 64, 66, 75, 83, 8488, 91, 115, 123, 149, 128, 155
landmark, 10, 13, 20, 27, 60, 80, 88, 90, 91, 94109, 110, 128, 129, 138, 139, 141–146
leaf plan, 40, 64
legibility, 88, 102, 104, 140, 146, 154

M

Madurai, 13, 14, 87, 96
mandala, 12, 20
map, 11, 17, 18, 23, 24, 70, 94–96, 99, 110, 112, 128, 139, 141, 153
master plan, 1–3, 7, 30, 32, 33, 37, 47, 52, 55, 58, 62, 64, 77, 84, 85, 86, 87, 89, 100, 109, 124, 128, 149–153
meandering, 1, 21, 25, 58

military camps, 91
Modern planning, 1, 3, 47, 87–89
modern, 22, 2
Mohenjo-Daro, 2
movement, 13

N

nature, 2, 5, 12, 40–42, 55, 58, 86–88, 92, 103, 104–125, 126, 135, 143
nodes, 21, 131, 140, 141, 144,
New Delhi, 5, 6, 21, 24, 25, 47, 109, 110

O

open spaces, 4, 5, 13, 39, 47, 61, 87, 101–103, 107, 124, 149, 152
organic, 3, 14, 21, 39–41, 86, 88, 115
organisms, 32
organs, 32
orientation, 58, 77, 127
ornamental garden, 60, 61, 80

P

park belts, 43, 44
paths, 44,
Patiali Rao, 28, 63
pattern, 2–4, 13, 14, 20, 32, 42, 44, 56, 58
pedestrian, 5, 30, 36, 37, 44, 46, 52, 58, 59, 61, 66, 72, 77, 79
Plan Voisin, 136
planned, 1–5, 7, 8, 11, 19, 21, 42, 47, 50, 52, 61, 84, 88, 89, 91, 152
planning guidance, 150
planning, 1–3, 5, 11, 12, 21, 25, 27, 30, 41, 44, 46, 47, 62, 64, 71, 83-85
plant cells, 86
plaza, 36, 45, 66, 67, 69, 80
pleasure gardens, 14
park belts, 43, 44
plots, 4, 5, 20, 28, 46, 58, 61, 67, 74, 75, 83, 84, 110, 113, 137
pols, 3, 55–57, 71, 88
precinct, 13, 46, 80, 83
principal, 37, 139
prototype, 3, 137
public spaces, 122, 123, 142

R

recreational, 10, 47, 52, 58, 63, 71, 85
regionalism, 10, 88
relationship, 4, 5, 19, 89, 101–104, 111, 113, 116, 128, 129, 132–135, 139, 140, 147, 152, 153, 155
route, 67, 68, 72, 88, 107, 108, 129, 139, 140, 146, 152, 154, 155

S

Sabarmati River, 50, 63
satellite towns, 114
seals, 9
sector, 2–5, 30, 37, 38, 39, 42–44, 47, 50, 54, 57, 58, 59, 60, 62, 66, 67, 69, 70, 71, 72, 73, 74, 75, 78, 79, 80, , 84, 86, 87, 88, 105, 148
self-contained units, 47, 69, 70, 87
self-esteem, 147, 148
self-financed, 27
self-sustained, 154